NORMAN PERRIN

REDISCOVERING
THE TEACHING OF JESUS

NORMAN PERRIN

REDISCOVERING THE TEACHING OF JESUS

1817

HARPER & ROW, PUBLISHERS

New York, Hagerstown, San Francisco, London

First Harper & Row paperback edition published in 1976.

LIBRARY OF CONGRESS CATALOG CARD NUMBER: 67-11510

ISBN: 0-06-066493-2

76 77 78 79 80 10 9 8 7 6 5 4 3 2 1

To Rosemary

CONTENTS

ABBREVIATIONS AND EXPLANATIONS

Arndt and Gingrich, Lexicon	*A Greek-English Lexicon of the New Testament.* Translated and edited by W. F. Arndt and F. W. Gingrich from W. Bauer's *Griechisch-deutsches Wörterbuch*,[4] 1949–52; Chicago: University of Chicago Press, and Cambridge: University Press, 1957.
ATR	*Anglican Theological Review.*
AV	Authorized Version (King James Bible).
b or B.T.	Babylonian Talmud.
BJRL	*Bulletin of the John Rylands Library.*
Billerbeck, Kommentar	W. L. Strack and P. Billerbeck, *Kommentar zum Neuen Testament aus Talmud und Midrasch*; München: C. H. Beck, 1922–8.
BZ	*Biblische Zeitschrift.*
CBQ	*Catholic Biblical Quarterly.*
ET	English Translation.
EvT	*Evangelische Theologie.*
ExpT	*Expository Times.*
FRLANT	Forschungen zur Religion und Literatur des Alten und Neuen Testaments.
HJ	*Hibbert Journal.*
HTR	*Harvard Theological Review.*
j	Jerusalem Talmud.
JBL	*Journal of Biblical Literature.*
JBR	*Journal of Bible and Religion.*
JR	*Journal of Religion.*
JTS	*Journal of Theological Studies.*
Lauterbach	*Mekilta.* Edited and translated by J. Z. Lauterbach. 3 vols.; Philadelphia: Jewish Publication Society of America, 1949.
LXX	Septuagint.
MT	Massoretic Text.
NEB	New English Bible.
NTS	*New Testament Studies.*

R	Rabbah (i.e. Midrash Rabbah).
RGG	*Religion in Geschichte und Gegenwart.*
RSV	Revised Standard Version.
RV	Revised Version.
TLZ	*Theologische Literaturzeitung.*
TR	*Theologische Rundschau.*
TWNT	*Theologisches Wörterbuch zum Neuen Testament* (founded G. Kittel, edited G. Friedrich).
VC	*Vigiliae Christianae.*
ZNW	*Zeitschrift für die neutestamentliche Wissenschaft.*
ZTK	*Zeitschrift für Theologie und Kirche.*

Qumran materials are abbreviated according to the standard established in the official publication, *Discoveries in the Judaean Desert*, edited by J. T. Milik and D. Barthélemy; Oxford: Clarendon Press, 1955ff.

Tractates in the Mishnah and Talmuds are abbreviated according to the standard established by H. Danby, *The Mishnah*; Oxford: Clarendon Press, 1933.

A raised numeral following the title of a work or preceding a date of publication indicates the number of the edition, e.g. *RGG*[3] or [2]1964.

In the case of works of more than one volume where the volumes were published in different years, the date of publication follows the number of the volume, e.g. III (1959).

Leben-Jesu-Forschung, Life of Jesus Research and Life of Christ Research are used as interchangeable terms.

Sitz im Leben (setting in life) is used as a technical term. It indicates the context of a pericope or saying, but 'context' understood in a most dynamic sense, as influencing form and content. *Sitz im Leben Jesu* indicates context in the ministry of Jesus, *Sitz im Leben der alten Kirche* that in the life and work (proclamation, catechesis, paranesis, liturgy, etc.) of the early Church. No special term has been used for a context in terms of the theology or purpose of an evangelist. This has usually been indicated by some such phraseology as, 'This saying serves a purpose in terms of the theology of the evangelist . . .' Recent Roman Catholic work has tended to use *Sitz im Leben Jesu, Sitz im Leben Ecclesiae, Sitz im Evangelium*, for these three things (see Annotated Bibliography No. 5 for an example).

Preface to the Paperback Edition

THIS BOOK WAS first published in 1967, and it was an attempt to meet a distinct need in life of Jesus research. Virtually our only source for knowledge of the historical Jesus is the synoptic gospels and the tradition they represent, and our understanding of these gospels and their tradition had been dramatically affected by the impact of form criticism. Because of this impact scholars concerned with achieving historical knowledge of the teaching of Jesus had to accept the responsibility of working their way back through the tradition to the earliest form of the material they could determine. Having reached this form they had then to accept, further, the responsibility of attempting to determine its authenticity. The absolute prerequisites of serious life of Jesus research became an ability to write a history of the synoptic tradition and the development of criteria of authenticity for the earliest forms of the material that could be reached.

These needs were first recognized and met in Germany in the period immediately following 1945, when serious theological scholarship became possible again there after the Hitler period and the Second World War. They were recognized and met, above all, by the pupils of the pioneer form critic Rudolf Bultmann, especially Günther Bornkamm, Ernst Käsemann and Hans Conzelmann, and by Joachim Jeremias in his epoch-making work on the parables of Jesus. It had been my privilege to be a pupil of Jeremias, and I had also come to know and to appreciate the work of the Bultmann *Schüler*. It seemed natural for me, therefore, to attempt a systematic presentation of this work in English. But Jeremias and the Bultmann "school" were at opposite ends of a particular theological spectrum, which meant that their work could not simply be presented as a unity. The reader who compares the first section of Bultmann's *Theology of the New Testament* with the first volume of Jeremias's *New Testament Theology* can see that there would be enormous differences between Bultmann's pupils and Jeremias. Yet they belonged together in the sense that they had together made possible a new stage in life of Jesus research. I, therefore, who knew them all, took the bold step of attempting to integrate their insights in a synthesis of my own. The result was this book, an attempt to address particularly the problem of *method* in life of Jesus research in light of the impact of form criticism and then of the work of, on the one hand, the Bultmann "school" and of, on the other, Joachim Jeremias.

I am glad to say that the book has received a measure of acceptance, both in English and in German. It has remained steadily in demand in English, and it has been translated into German as *Was Lehrt Jesu Wirklich?* (Göttingen: Vandenhoeck & Ruprecht, 1974). It is now being reissued in paperback form in the hope that it will continue to meet the need for which it was originally designed. Since it is fundamentally a discussion of method it has not been revised for paperback publication.

Since 1967 I have myself continued to work on aspects of the subject matter of this book. I continued to work on the Son of Man material, and the results of this work can now be found in N. Perrin, *A Modern Pilgrimage in New Testament Christology* (Philadelphia: Fortress Press, 1974). Then I made a further presentation of Jesus, including both his life and his teaching, in *The New Testament: An Introduction* (New York: Harcourt Brace Jovanovich, 1974). Finally I took up again the central aspects of the teaching of Jesus, the Kingdom of God and the parables, in *Jesus and the Language of the Kingdom* (Philadelphia: Fortress Press, 1976). A full discussion of the relevant work of other scholars will be found in those books. I have not returned to the subject of chapter five of this book, "the question of the historical Jesus," although it is my intention to do so shortly. In the meantime I call attention to Van A. Harvey, *The Historian and the Believer* (New York: Macmillan, 1966 [paperback 1969]), a most important discussion of the issues involved.

NORMAN PERRIN

Christmas, 1975

NORMAN PERRIN

REDISCOVERING
THE TEACHING OF JESUS

I

THE RECONSTRUCTION AND INTERPRE-
TATION OF THE TEACHING OF JESUS

THE RECONSTRUCTION OF THE TEACHING OF JESUS

THE FUNDAMENTAL PROBLEM in connection with knowledge of the teaching of Jesus is the problem of reconstructing that teaching from the sources available to us, and the truth of the matter is that the more we learn about those sources the more difficult our task seems to become. The major source, the synoptic gospels (Matthew, Mark and Luke), contains a great deal of teaching material ascribed to Jesus, and it turns out to be precisely that: teaching *ascribed* to Jesus and yet, in fact, stemming from the early Church.

The early Church made no attempt to distinguish between the words the earthly Jesus had spoken and those spoken by the risen Lord through a prophet in the community, nor between the original teaching of Jesus and the new understanding and reformulation of that teaching reached in the catechesis or parenesis of the Church under the guidance of the Lord of the Church. The early Church absolutely and completely identified the risen Lord of her experience with the earthly Jesus of Nazareth and created for her purposes, which she conceived to be his, the literary form of the gospel, in which words and deeds ascribed in her consciousness to both the earthly Jesus and the risen Lord were set down in terms of the former. This is a fact of great theological significance, and this significance will concern us in our last chapter, but it is also the reason for our major problem in reconstructing the teaching of Jesus: we do distinguish between those two figures and when we say 'the teaching of Jesus' we mean the teaching of the earthly Jesus, as the early Church did not.

Further, the gospel form was created to serve the purpose of the early Church, but historical reminiscence was not one of those purposes. So, for example, when we read an account of Jesus giving instruction to his disciples, we are not hearing the voice of the earthly Jesus addressing Galilean disciples in a Palestinian situation but that of the risen Lord addressing Christian missionaries in a Hellenistic world, and if the early Church had not needed instructions for those missionaries in that situation, there would have been no such pericope in our gospels. Of course, there may have been a faint echo of the voice of the earthly Jesus, for example, instructing his disciples to proclaim the Kingdom of God, but if this is the case, it is overlaid and almost drowned out by the voice of the risen Lord, so that fine tuning indeed will be needed to catch it.

Many will say that all this is supposition and the purpose *could* have been historical reminiscence. To this we can only reply that *could* is not the point. The point is that contemporary scholarship, as we shall argue below, has been completely successful in explaining pericope after pericope on the basis of the needs and concerns of the early Church, and that over and over again pericopes which have been hitherto accepted as historical reminiscence have been shown to be something quite different. So far as we can tell today, there is no single pericope anywhere in the gospels, the present purpose of which is to preserve a historical reminiscence of the earthly Jesus, although there may be some which do in fact come near to doing so because a reminiscence, especially of an aspect of teaching such as a parable, could be used to serve the purpose of the Church or the evangelist.

To defend this statement we will now give some of the considerations that have led us to make it, for we began our work on the gospel materials with a different view of their nature, and we would claim that the gospel materials themselves have forced us to change our mind.

We have been particularly influenced by a consideration of Mark 9.1 and its parallels:

> **Mark 9.1.** And he said to them, 'Truly, I say to you, there are some standing here who will not taste death before they see the kingdom of God come with power.'

> **Matt. 16.28.** Truly, I say to you, there are some standing here who will not taste death before they see the Son of man coming in his kingdom.

> **Luke 9.27.** But I tell you truly, there are some standing here who will not taste of death before they see the kingdom of God.

Here it is clear that the Matthaean and Lukan sayings are theologically motivated variations of the Markan. Matthew has a characteristic concern for the expectation of the coming of Jesus as Son of man which he betrays in several ways: he is the only evangelist to use the technical term 'parousia' (24.27, 37, 39); he alone has the parable of the sheep and goats, a kind of *haggada* on the theme 'When the Son of man comes in his glory . . .' (25.31); he introduces a reference to it into a saying from Q (Matt. 19.28; cf. Luke 22.28–30). So here he has understood the coming of the Kingdom 'in power' in Mark to be a reference to the eschaton and has then reformulated the saying to express his own particular conviction with regard to the form of that eschaton. It should be noted that he has also strengthened the reference in the previous verse, changing Mark's '. . . the Son of man . . . when he comes . . .' to '. . . the Son of man is about to come . . .' (Mark 8.38; Matt. 16.27). Matthew leaves his readers in no doubt as to what it is they are to expect!

Luke, on the other hand, completely reformulates the primitive Christian eschatology. It is true that he maintains the traditional form of the expectation (Luke 21.27 = Mark 13.26), but it is no longer for him a point of major concern. His major concern is the ongoing life and work of the Christian community as it settles down to face, so to speak, the long haul of history. So he subtly alters the tone of the whole pericope by a series of omissions and insertions which transform the Markan challenge to preparedness for martyrdom into a Lukan challenge to bear the burden of a continual witnessing.[1] Two of the subtlest but most effective of his changes in the text of his Markan *Vorlage* are the insertion of 'daily' in Luke 9.23 (cf. Mark 8.34) and the omission of 'come with power' in our text. The former changes the concern of the whole to a continual witnessing, and the latter makes the reference to the Kingdom a quite general one which we, following Conzelmann, would interpret as a reference to the Kingdom which becomes visible in the ministry of Jesus, but which will be truly known only at the End. Another possible interpretation is that of Streeter, who refers it to the era of Pentecost and the Christian Church, an interpretation denied by Conzelmann.[2] In either case, the saying in its Lukan form reflects a Lukan conception of the Kingdom and serves a purpose in terms of the Lukan theology; that is the point which concerns us.

[1] E. Haenchen, 'Die Komposition von Mk. 8.27–9.1 und Par.', *Novum Testamentum* 6 (1963), 108f.

[2] H. Conzelmann, *Theology of St Luke* (ET by Geoffrey Buswell of *Die Mitte der Zeit* [²1957]; London: Faber and Faber, and New York: Harper & Bros., 1960), pp. 104f. B. H. Streeter, *The Four Gospels* (London: Macmillan Co., 1936), p. 520.

The Matthaean and Lukan versions of the saying are theologically motivated productions of the evangelists, but how does the matter stand in the case of Mark 9.1 itself? A study of the composition of this pericope as a whole shows that it has been carefully composed by Mark.[1] The first question, 'Who do men say that I am?' (v. 27), answered in terms of a tradition the evangelist had already used in 6.14f., leads to the second, 'But who do you say . . .?' (v. 29), answered by Peter as spokesman for the disciples, and for the Christians for whom Mark was writing, in terms of a post-Easter Christian confession. Then we have the dramatic presentation of the theme that, as the way of the Christ was not without suffering, so also the way of the Christian may involve martyrdom. This is then developed through a group of sayings about discipleship, martyrdom and reward, ending with the warning which the Christian must heed in his hour of trial: those who fail their Lord and reject him will be rejected by him when he comes as Son of man. But they need expect to suffer only a little while, for God is about to act 'in power' and thereafter there will be no more suffering, only glory, no more death, only life.[2]

The pericope moves to its climax, then, with the verses 8.38 and 9.1, and these sayings, in their present form, are essential to the Markan purpose. They form the climactic combination of warning and promise with which the pericope closes. In the case of Mark 8.38, we know that Mark has not composed the saying itself, because it is part of a tradition with a very complex history;[3] rather, he has modified a saying in the tradition to make it suitable for his purpose. In this respect, Mark 8.38 is like Matt. 16.28 and Luke 9.27, where we can see the theologically motivated work of the evangelists because we have the earlier forms of the sayings upon which they worked. But in Mark 9.1 this is no longer the case. We have no other and earlier version of this saying. However, if we examine it carefully, we can see

---

[1] E. Haenchen, 'Die Komposition . . .', *Novum Testamentum* 6 (1963), 81–109, esp. 81–96.

[2] We have expressed the themes in our own words without claiming thereby to be representing Haenchen. But it was his essay that convinced us that the passage is a Markan construction and that the scene is created by Mark rather than representing a Petrine reminiscence. The artistic nature of the scene is clear: the setting of the questions to build up to a climax; the representative role of Peter; the post-Easter confession; the sudden appearance of the crowd when the time comes for general instruction, as so often in Mark; the reflection of the situation of a Church facing the possibility of persecution; and the way in which the whole pericope moves to its climax in the last two verses.

[3] See below, pp. 185–91.

that it is a very complex saying indeed. As we shall point out in detail later in our discussion of sayings which set a time limit to the coming of the End,[1] it is related in form and wording both to Mark 13.30 and 8.38. It shares with 13.30 its overall form, its solemn introduction and its particular negation (double negation with subj.), and with 8.38 its final reference to the eschaton 'coming'. Furthermore, it has a number of features either particularly relevant to its present function in the pericope or apparently characteristic of Mark himself. '. . . some . . . who will not taste death . . .' is an expression from the world of Jewish apocalyptic where it refers to men who have been removed from the earth without dying, especially Enoch and Elijah, and who were expected to return with the Messiah to inaugurate the time of salvation and blessing.[2] Its presence is, therefore, peculiarly appropriate in a saying promising final deliverance from a time of persecution, certainly understood by Mark as the period of the 'messianic woes' immediately preceding the End (cf. Mark 13.30: '. . . this generation will not pass away before all these things take place'). The idea of 'seeing' the parousia is a feature of Mark (9.1; 13.26; 14.62),[3] as is also the use of 'power' and 'glory' in this connection.[4]

We shall argue later that the explanation for these phenomena is that the saying is a Markan construction, modelled on the saying now found in 13.30 and deliberately echoing the last part of 8.38, but with

[1] See below, pp. 199–202.

[2] IV Ezra 6.25f. R. H. Charles, *Apocrypha and Pseudepigrapha of the Old Testament* (Oxford: Clarendon Press, 1913) II, 576 (G. H. Box).

[3] Matthew follows Mark on each occasion. Luke transforms the first into a non-parousia reference and omits the 'seeing' in the third (Luke 22.69). Matthew nowhere has the verb in connection with the parousia except in dependence on Mark, nor has Luke.

[4] This point is important here and will be important also in our discussion of the apocalyptic Son of man sayings, so we must give the evidence. *Mark 8.38:* the Son of man 'comes in the glory of his father with the holy angels'. Both Matthew (16.27) and Luke (9.26) follow this with modifications. *Mark 9.1:* the kingdom will 'come with power'. Matthew (16.28) has the Son of man 'coming in his kingdom'; Luke (9.27) has no parousia reference. *Mark 10.37* has 'in your glory' which Matthew (20.21) modifies to 'in your kingdom'; Luke has no parallel. *Mark 13.26:* The Son of man 'coming in clouds with great power and glory'. Both Matthew (24.30) and Luke (21.27) follow this with modifications.

There is no such use in Luke independent of Mark and only one in Matthew. Matt. 25.31 begins the parable of the sheep and the goats: 'When the Son of man comes in his glory, and all the angels with him, then he will sit on his glorious throne.' In view of Matt. 19.28 ('. . . in the new world, when the Son of man shall sit on his glorious throne' [no parallels]), this looks like a combination of Matthaean and Markan characteristics. Finally, Mark 14.62 has 'power', but then it is used in a quite different way, i.e. as a circumlocution for God.

variations from both of these sayings which can be accounted for in terms of the Markan style and of the specific use Mark intends to make of the saying as a promise to a church facing the possibility of persecution.[1]

The three sayings: Mark 9.1; Matt. 16.28; Luke 9.27, therefore, are, in our view, all products of the evangelists, each creating the particular saying, Matthew and Luke transforming Mark 9.1 and Mark producing a new saying from Mark 13.30 and 8.38. But if this is true of Mark 9.1 and its parallels it can be equally true of any and every saying in the gospels. Any and every saying in the gospels could be the product of an evangelist or transmitter of the tradition. Nor can we assume that the sayings will be based upon genuine sayings of Jesus. Mark 9.1 is not, and both Matthew and Luke simply use the saying before them without concerning themselves as to its origin, and the saying they use is, in fact, a Markan production. The freedom of the evangelists to produce theologically motivated variations, and their lack of concern for the origins of sayings which they find in the tradition, are clearly revealed in Mark 9.1 and its parallels, and they are very significant indeed, so far as our understanding of the nature of the synoptic tradition is concerned.

Let us continue to examine the nature of the synoptic tradition by considering the results of the work of the scholar who has probably done more than any other to make available to contemporary scholarship historical knowledge of the teaching of Jesus, Joachim Jeremias of Göttingen, whom we are proud to acknowledge as our teacher. Jeremias has achieved his most spectacular results in connection with the parables ascribed to Jesus in the tradition, for he has been able to reconstruct a history of the parabolic tradition, working back from the texts as we have them, through the various stages of the

[1] See below, pp. 199–201. We have therefore abandoned our previous views on this saying (*The Kingdom of God in the Teaching of Jesus* [hereinafter, *Kingdom*] [London: SCM Press, and Philadelphia: Westminster Press, 1963], pp. 137ff.) and can no longer follow W. G. Kümmel (most recently in his article 'Die Naherwartung in der Verkündigung Jesu', *Zeit und Geschichte. Dankesgabe an Rudolf Bultmann zum 80. Geburtstag*, ed. E. Dinkler [Tübingen: J. C. B. Mohr (Paul Siebeck), 1964], pp. 39ff. [= W. G. Kümmel, *Heilsgeschehen und Geschichte* (Marburger Theologische Studien 3 [Marburg: N. G. Elwert, 1965]), pp. 464ff.]) in regarding Mark 9.1 as an authentic saying of Jesus. But it should be noted that the difficulties Kümmel sees in fitting this saying into the context of a prophetic word addressed to a community troubled by the delay of the parousia (so, above all, G. Bornkamm, in his article 'Die Verzögerung der Parusie', *In Memoriam Ernst Lohmeyer*, ed. W. Schmauch [Stuttgart: Evangelisches Verlagswerk, 1951], pp. 116–19) are real difficulties.

Church's influence on it, to the tradition as it must have existed at the beginning of the history of its transmission by the Church. At this point he is able to argue that the tradition in this form must be ascribed to Jesus rather than to the early Church, because it now fits the situation of the ministry of the historical Jesus much better than that of the earliest Christian community and because its theology, and in particular its eschatology, is Jesuanic rather than early Christian.[1] The results of this work on the parables have been widely accepted, and most recent works on the teaching of Jesus make extensive use of them. We shall return to Jeremias's work on the parables again and again, for it is epoch-making in several respects, but for the moment we want only to call attention to the consequences of this work so far as a general view of the nature of the synoptic tradition is concerned: the success of Jeremias's work demands that we accept his starting-point, namely, that any parable as it now stands in the gospels represents the teaching of the early Church and the way back from the early Church to the historical Jesus is a long and arduous one.[2]

There are a limited number of instances where the parable in very much its original form made a point of significance to the early Church, even if that was different from the point originally intended by the historical Jesus, and in such cases the gospel form of the parable may approximate to the original, e.g. the Good Samaritan and the Prodigal Son. But these are exceptions, and they are exceptions which prove the rule. They are presented in more or less their original form because in this form they served the purpose of the Church, or the evangelist, and not because there was any historical interest in the original form as such. Most of the parables, however, have been considerably modified in the tradition; they were transformed into allegories, supplied with new conclusions, interpreted and reinterpreted, and always under the pressure of meeting the need of the Church in a changing situation. Certainly, every single parable in the tradition has to be approached with the basic assumption that, as it now stands, it represents the teaching of the early Church: that the

---

[1] J. Jeremias, *Parables of Jesus* (ET by S. H. Hooke of *Die Gleichnisse Jesu* [⁶1962] [London: SCM Press, and New York: Scribner's, 1963], representing a revision of the first English edition of 1954), *passim*.

[2] It should be emphasized that we are now drawing our own conclusions as to the consequences of Jeremias's work for a general view of the nature of the synoptic tradition. Professor Jeremias himself has not discussed the matter in these terms, and in this instance the pupil does not claim to be necessarily representing the mind of his teacher.

voice is the voice of the risen Lord to the evangelist, and of the evangelist to the Church, not that of the historical Jesus to a group gathered by the sea of Galilee.

But the parables represent by all odds the most markedly individualistic characteristic of the teaching of Jesus; both in form and content they were highly original and strongly stamped with the personality of their author. If they could be so readily and completely transformed in the tradition, how much more must not less strongly individualistic forms of teaching have been transformed?

Another point to be considered in this connection is the increasing degree of success attaching to efforts made to analyse forms of teaching present in the gospel tradition as forms known to be characteristic of the early Church. One can mention here, as a good example, Ernst Käsemann's brilliant 'Sätze heiligen Rechtes im Neuen Testament',[1] which clearly shows that there existed in the early Church what we shall call an eschatological judgement pronouncement tradition having its roots in Christian prophecy and its *Sitz im Leben* in the Eucharist. The characteristic form of this tradition is that of a two-part pronouncement with the same verb in each part, in the first part referring to the activity of man and in the second to the eschatological activity of God. We give four examples of this form, two each from the gospels and epistles respectively.

I Cor. 3.17. If anyone destroys God's temple, God will destroy him.

I Cor. 14.38. If anyone does not recognize this, he is not recognized.[2]

Mark 8.38. For whoever is ashamed . . . of him will the Son of man also be ashamed. . . .

Matt. 6.14f. For if you forgive . . . your heavenly Father also will forgive you . . . if you do not forgive . . . neither will your heavenly Father forgive you. . . .

Käsemann's argument that this *form* of pronouncement comes from early Christian prophecy is careful and convincing, with the result that we must accept the fact that in their present form the two gospel sayings come from an early Christian tradition and not from the

---

[1] First published in *NTS* 1 (1954/55), 248–60, and now in Käsemann's collected essays, *Exegetische Versuche und Besinnungen* (Göttingen: Vandenhoeck & Ruprecht II (1964), 69–82.

[2] Understanding the passive as referring to the eschatological activity of God. The passive referring to the activity of God is an Aramaism frequently to be found in the New Testament.

teaching of Jesus. This does not mean that they may not ultimately be based upon a saying of Jesus—Matt. 6.14 is certainly derived ultimately from the central petition of the Lord's Prayer and Mark 8.38 will concern us later—but it does mean that these gospel sayings are a *direct* source for knowledge of early Christian prophecy, not of the teaching of Jesus.

Another instance of the way in which material now in the gospels can be shown to be the product of early Christian tradition may be quoted from Barnabas Lindars, *New Testament Apologetic* (London: SCM Press, and Philadelphia: Westminster Press, 1961). This is a most important book, developing new insights into the nature and formation of earliest Christian tradition from observation of the use of the Old Testament, an observation made possible by information derived from the Qumran *pesharim*. It is evident that the earliest Christians made most significant use of the Old Testament in their theologizing. They developed major aspects of their belief and expectation from Old Testament texts, interpreting the texts in the light of their experience and their experience in the light of the texts. The Christian practice here paralleled that of the Qumran scribes and, like those scribes, the Christians read the Old Testament texts as strictly relating to themselves and their experiences, and they exercised very considerable freedom in regard to the wording of the texts. An example of the development of Christian exegetical traditions as we see the matter, having taken our starting-point from Lindars's work, may be found below in the discussion of the apocalyptic Son of man sayings.[1] For the moment, however, we concern ourselves with a particular aspect of Lindars's own work, his convincing demonstration of the fact that the pericope on the question of David's son, Mark 12.35–37, is a product of early Christian exegetical traditions and not a reminiscence of the ministry of Jesus.

In a brilliant analysis of Peter's Pentecost speech in Acts 2, Lindars shows that its present structure reveals a combination of two different Old Testament passages, each accompanied by the Christian *pesher* on it: Joel 2.28–32 (Acts 2.14–21; 38f.) and Ps. 16.8–11 (Acts 2.22–36).[2] The Christian *pesher* on Psalm 16, like the *pesharim* from Qumran, uses both that Psalm itself and also other Old Testament passages in its interpretation, in this instance particularly Ps. 110.1, and Lindars offers a detailed, and completely convincing, analysis of

---

[1] See below, pp. 173–85.   [2] B. Lindars, *New Testament Apologetic*, pp. 36–38.

Acts 2.22–36 and the early Christian exegesis which underlies it.[1]
The point which concerns us here is that he is able to go on to show
that the argument in the pericope Mark 12.35–37 turns upon a claim
that 'Lord' is either inconsistent with, or greatly superior to, 'son of
David'. But such a claim depends upon the arguments that the 'Lord'
sits at the right hand of God whereas the 'son of David' sat upon an
earthly throne, i.e. it depends on the argument of Acts 2.34 ('For
David did not ascend into the heavens; but he himself says, "the Lord
said to my Lord, 'Sit at my right hand . . .' " '). 'Viewed in this
light,' concludes Lindars, quite correctly, 'the whole pericope is
evidently derived from the exegesis preserved in Acts 2.'[2] In other
words, the pericope about David's son is a 'historicization' of an early
Christian exegetical tradition and a product of the early Church; it is
not a historical reminiscence of the ministry of Jesus.

Still another factor to be adduced in a consideration of the nature
of the synoptic gospel tradition is the success with which this tradition
has been approached from the viewpoint of its exhibiting the theological concerns of the evangelists. Here the crux of the matter is the
gospel of Mark, for this is regarded by main-stream critical scholarship as the earliest of the gospels, and it has been used as the major
source in all attempts to achieve a historical presentation of the
ministry of Jesus. British scholars, such as T. W. Manson and C. H.
Dodd, for example, concerned to preserve the broad outline of the
ministry of Jesus as historical, must of necessity strenuously defend the
historicity of the Markan order. But recent scholarship has shown that
the Markan order in general represents the theologically motivated
order of events presented in early Christian preaching, and in its
detail the order represents the concerns of the evangelist himself. The
one thing it does not represent, either in general or in detail, is
historical reminiscence of the ministry of Jesus. The most one could
argue is that the order presented in early Christian preaching was the
result of historical reminiscence; but this is to make an assumption
about early Christian preaching, that it was interested in historical
reminiscence, for which we have absolutely no evidence. The opposite
view, that it was theologically motivated, is the one for which we have
evidence. The characteristics of the Markan order, and the order of
early Christian preaching, are precisely the things that we can explain
theologically, whereas it is doubtful whether they are, in fact, true
historically. Examples of this are the beginning with John the Baptist

[1] *Ibid.*, pp. 38–45.   [2] *Ibid.*, p. 47.

and the one visit to Jerusalem. Both of these clearly reflect a theological purpose, and although the former may also be historically true, the latter is against all probability. The Markan order in general, and the views of Manson and Dodd in particular, were discussed in the present writer's previous book[1] and the views of contemporary scholarship on the theological motivation of Mark, and of the other synoptic evangelists and their traditions, are readily available.[2] We do not, therefore, propose to discuss the matter further here; it is sufficient for our purposes to call attention to this aspect of the contemporary understanding of the nature of the Markan gospel material and to remark that what is true for Mark is true also for Luke and Matthew. They, too, are theologically motivated in the arrangement, presentation and even formulation of their material. Nor is this true only of the evangelists themselves; when we go behind the evangelists to the material they have used, for example, the account of the Temptation or Transfiguration or the source 'Q', we do not come to historical reminiscence, but still only to theologically motivated narrative or formulation and collection of sayings.[3]

The views that we are here presenting as to the nature of the gospel tradition are the results of what may loosely be called 'form criticism', although technically one would have to use a whole array of German words to describe the various aspects of the work: *Formgeschichte*, *Redaktionsgeschichte*, *Redaktionstheologie*, *Traditionsgeschichte*, etc. We will, however, follow the generally accepted usage and refer to them as 'form-critical' views. They have not, of course, escaped criticism and attempts at refutation. The arguments against them most often found are those characteristic of Roman Catholic and the more conservative Protestant biblical scholarship. They consist of three main points:[4] (1) The community would not have possessed the creative power which form criticism attributes to it in ascribing so much of the gospel material to the early Church. (2) The New Testament itself appeals to 'eyewitnesses and ministers of the word' as authorities for the tradition (Luke 1.2), thereby showing its concern for the historical ministry of Jesus. (3) During the period of the formation of the tradition, the

[1] N. Perrin, *Kingdom*, pp. 96f.

[2] See Annotated Bibliography No. 2: Theology of the Synoptic Evangelists and Their Tradition.

[3] For some recent examples of this kind of work on the tradition, see the books of H. E. Tödt and F. Hahn in Annotated Bibliography No. 2.

[4] We take them from a recent Roman Catholic work, J. R. Geiselmann, *Jesus der Christus* I. *Die Frage nach dem historischen Jesus* (München: Kösel-Verlag, 1965), 144–7.

first few decades of the Church's life, there were men living and active in the Church who had been eyewitnesses and earwitnesses of the ministry of Jesus, for example, James, Peter and John, the 'pillars' of the church in Jerusalem (Gal. 2.9). These are a strong guarantee for the accuracy of the tradition of Jesus' words and deeds.

Before discussing these three points in some detail, two things need to be said in general. The first of these is that we must strenuously avoid the assumption that the ancient world thought as the modern western world thinks. This is such a truism that one is almost ashamed to pen the words, and yet it remains a fact that, in a great deal of the more conservative biblical scholarship, it does seem to be assumed that the appeal to factual accuracy would be as valid and important a factor in the case of ancient Near Eastern religious texts as it would be in a modern western court of law or in a somewhat literally-minded western congregation. Against this it can only be stated that this is simply not the case. No ancient texts reflect the attitudes characteristic of the modern western world, and some of the difficulties we see in texts about Jesus could be matched by difficulties to be seen in texts about Pythagoras or Socrates. All this is obvious and yet it needs to be said, if only to clear the air for a consideration of the early Christian use of a word such as 'eyewitness'.

The second thing to be said in general is that we must constantly remind ourselves that the early Church absolutely identified the risen Lord of her experience with the historical Jesus and *vice versa*, as we pointed out earlier in this chapter. This becomes particularly important to us, in our present immediate context, when we consider the practice of the apostle Paul. He claims, as the basis for his apostleship, to have 'seen the Lord' (I Cor. 9.1), by whom he certainly means the risen Lord of the Damascus-road experience; and we should note that when he uses the technical formula for receiving and handing on tradition, and speaks of having received it 'from the Lord' (I Cor. 11.23), he also there means the Risen One, the Lord of the Church. Even if the Lord's Supper paranese which follows (I Cor. 11.23b–25) should ultimately be based upon a historical reminiscence of an actual Passover celebrated by Jesus with his disciples shortly before his death—and that is in itself a very considerable 'if'—there is no doubt but that the paranese represents an extensive development away from that original reminiscence. At the very least, all the Passover aspects have disappeared, the 'words of institution' have been reformulated in light of early Christian eucharistic practice ('Do this as often as you drink, in remembrance of me'), and the paranese concludes with an injunction (v. 26) which cannot have come from the earthly Jesus. Now, none of this would matter to Paul. Precisely because for him risen Lord and earthly Jesus are one and the same person, it would be a matter of complete indifference to him whether all, some, *or none*, of the words ascribed to the 'Lord Jesus' of the paranese had, in fact, been spoken by the earthly Jesus to his disciples at an actual Passover, since they were being spoken by the risen Lord to his Church at the Eucharist. But it would matter to a modern writer who concerned himself with the question of the teaching of Jesus about his death, to such a one it would matter very much indeed. This, again, is an obvious point, but it needs to be stressed: the modern distinction between historical Jesus and risen Lord is quite foreign to the early Church.

Now to the three arguments against the form-critical view of the gospels, of which the first was that it ascribes too great a creative power to the community. This argument breaks down on the fact that the contemporary form critic does not deal with a nebulous entity, 'the community', to which he ascribes all kinds of powers; he deals with specific groups, individuals and traditions which he isolates, identifies and delineates. Käsemann, for example, deals specifically with Christian prophecy, isolating it by references taken from the Pauline corpus and Revelation; Lindars with Christian exegetical traditions; Haenchen with the evangelist Mark, to mention only works we have used above. The force of this work is not to be denied by any generalization about 'the community' and its 'creative power', or lack of it. It could only be denied by offering an alternative and more convincing explanation of the actual phenomena in the New Testament texts to which these scholars are calling attention and with which they are dealing.

The second argument turned on the fact that the New Testament itself, and more especially Luke, appeals to the testimony of 'eyewitnesses and ministers of the word' (Luke 1.2). If we resolutely ban from our minds, however, what a modern writer would mean by an 'eyewitness' and ask ourselves what Luke meant by the expression, then this argument also breaks down. Luke considers Paul an eyewitness! The actual word used in Luke 1.2, *autoptai*, does not occur again in Luke–Acts,[1] but it is paralleled in meaning in the words

[1] It may have been a conventional word to use in a 'preface' to a Hellenistic 'historical' work. H. J. Cadbury, *Beginnings of Christianity*, ed. Foakes Jackson and Lake) London: Macmillan), II (1922), 498f.

which Luke has Ananias say to Paul in Acts 22.14f.: 'The God of our Fathers has appointed you . . . to see the Just One and to hear the voice from his mouth, that you may be a witness to him . . .', and the risen Lord to him in Acts 26.16: 'I am Jesus . . . for this reason I have appeared to you, to appoint you a minister and witness . . .' Any attempt to argue for accuracy of the tradition so far as the historical Jesus is concerned on the basis of Luke's use of 'eyewitness' is to fail to take into account the clear fact that he, like Paul, absolutely identifies risen Lord and earthly Jesus and so regards Paul as, in effect, an 'eyewitness and minister of the word'.

The third argument was an appeal to the fact that there were some people active in the early Church whom even we would have to call 'eyewitnesses', such as James, Peter and John. This argument would be effective if we could show that these men, unlike Paul and Luke, did feel that it was important to maintain the separate identity of the historical Jesus, and hence to preserve the Jesus tradition from changes under the influence of the risen Lord. It has always to be remembered that no one in the early Church regarded the changes going on in the synoptic-type Jesus-tradition as due to anything other than the influence of the risen Lord. The only man whose work we can trace in the synoptic tradition who ever concerns himself to remain reasonably true, in our sense of that word, to his sources is Luke, and even he does not hesitate to make very considerable changes indeed when he has theological reasons for doing so.[1] But where is there any evidence whatever that an attempt was made to preserve a narrative from theological development and change? Or, alternatively, where is there a narrative, the details of which are more readily explicable on the basis of an eyewitness's concern for historical accuracy and reminiscence than on that of evangelical and theological motives demonstrably at work in the tradition?

The influence of such eyewitnesses would be most evident in the case of narratives of events and occasions, as distinct from collections of sayings and teaching material. But if we consider the narratives in the gospels, we must note that many of them have been freely created within the early Church, especially the controversies, for example, the David's Son pericope we discussed above, and the ascension narrative (Luke 24.51 RSV margin)[2] and even ones in which the

---

[1] See below, pp. 176–79, for an example of this even more striking than his version of Mark 9.1 discussed above.

[2] On this as a creation of Luke himself, see below.

'eyewitnesses' play a considerable role: the Confession at Caesarea
Philippi, discussed above, and the Transfiguration.[1] Others have been
so modified in the course of their transmission in the tradition that
today we can know almost nothing about the details of the events
themselves, only the fact that they happened. The details have been
supplied, often from the Old Testament, but also from other sources,
to serve the theological, apologetic and interpretative motives of the
Church. In this connection we think particularly of the narratives of
the Baptism and the Crucifixion.[2] The most that the present writer
believes can ever be claimed for a gospel narrative is that it may
represent a typical scene from the ministry of Jesus, for example the
narrative of the Paralytic at Capernaum, Mark 2.1–12 par. Here, we
can argue, is something the like of which must have happened in the
ministry of Jesus; here are elements that must have been a feature of
that ministry.[3] But we can argue this on the basis of the 'criterion of
dissimilarity', to be described below, i.e. on the basis of differences
between these stories and those to be found in Judaism, Hellenism or
later Christianity, not on the basis of the veracity of eyewitnesses and
the tenacity of their influence. Against this latter argument there is
one decisive factor: the fact that the 'eyewitnesses' would have had to
be quite different in interest and concern from any men whose influence we can trace in the synoptic tradition. In the instance of the
story of the Paralytic at Capernaum, the evangelists have used the
tradition to serve their own purposes, Mark (followed by Luke) as a
demonstration of the authority of the Son of God (Mark 2.12), and
Matthew as a basis for the Church's authority to forgive sins (Matt.
9.8). As we argued was the case with some of the parables, it is the
fact that the evangelists were able to use the story to serve their purposes that has caused it to be preserved, not an interest in historical
reminiscence as such. If the 'eyewitnesses' are to be regarded as

[1] For an excellent study of the christological motives at work in the formation
and transmission of the Transfiguration narrative, with references to and discussion
of the literature, see F. Hahn, *Christologische Hoheitstitel* (Göttingen: Vandenhoeck & Ruprecht, [2]1964), pp. 334–40.

[2] On the narrative of the Baptism, see again F. Hahn, *op. cit.*, pp. 340–6.
Attention was decisively called to the role of the Old Testament in the Crucifixion
narrative by Martin Dibelius, *From Tradition to Gospel* (ET by B. L. Wolf of *Die
Formgeschichte des Evangeliums* [[2]1933]); London: Lutterworth, and New York:
Scribner's, 1935.

[3] See below, pp. 130–37, for a discussion of exorcism and healing narratives from
the gospels and their authenticity, or more accurately, the authenticity of certain
elements within them.

different in this regard from Matthew, Mark and Luke, then we need some evidence that they were, evidence which the New Testament narratives themselves do not seem to offer. No single man whose work and influence on the tradition we can trace shows any signs of the interest in historical reminiscence and accuracy which the opponents of form criticism ascribe to the 'eyewitnesses'. We may, therefore, be forgiven for being sceptical of the possibility that these were different in their fundamental attitude from those men whose work we do know and whose attitude we can determine.

This brings us to the most determined recent effort to overturn the results of form-critical work on the gospels, namely, the Scandinavian reaction against form criticism culminating in B. Gerhardsson, *Memory and Manuscript* (Acta Seminarii Neotestamentici Upsaliensis XXII [Lund: C. W. K. Gleerup, 1961, ²1964]). This work attempts to show that Jesus taught, and the early Church handed on his teaching, in a manner analogous to that of the later rabbis, and that the synoptics have recorded condensed memory texts of Jesus' teaching, and also interpretative expositions of his sayings which go back in principle to him.

The most successful part of the work is the study of 'oral tradition and written transmission' in rabbinic Judaism, to which Gerhardsson has clearly devoted a great deal of time. His claim, however, that this is to be found before AD 70 in Judaism, and his study of the same processes in early Christianity have not been so well received. Indeed, the reviews which the book received were of such a nature as to provoke Gerhardsson to take the unusual step of publishing a specific reply to his reviewers: *Tradition and Transmission in Early Christianity* (Coniectanea Neotestamentica XX [Lund: C. W. K. Gleerup, 1964]). Most damaging to his cause, as he himself recognizes, are two lengthy reviews by scholars who are not particularly devotees of form criticism and who are experts in the Jewish materials of which he makes so much: Morton Smith and W. D. Davies.[1] Smith is able to show that Gerhardsson misrepresents both rabbinic and Christian tradition by reading back into the period before AD 70 the conditions *circa* AD 200, and that the differences between rabbinic and New

---

[1] Morton Smith, 'A Comparison of Early Christian and Early Rabbinic Tradition', *JBL* 82 (1963), 169–76. W. D. Davies, 'Reflections on a Scandinavian Approach to "the Gospel Tradition"', in *Neotestamentica et Patristica. Freundesgabe Oscar Cullmann* (Supplements to *Novum Testamentum* VI [Leiden: E. J. Brill, 1962]), pp. 14–34, now reprinted in his book *The Setting of the Sermon on the Mount* (Cambridge: University Press, 1964), pp. 464–80.

Testament materials themselves are such as to refute his theory. W. D. Davies is himself sympathetic to Gerhardsson's basic concern in that he believes that Jesus' disciples would have treasured the memory of his works and words with reverent tenacity,[1] and this makes his searching criticism of the work the more telling. Two particularly important points that he makes are that there is no evidence in the New Testament for the importance Gerhardsson has to ascribe to the Twelve in Jerusalem and the teaching emanating from them, and that there is every indication that the centre of gravity for primitive Christianity was not a transmitted body of words and works, but Jesus Christ, past, present and to come.

This last point reaches the heart of the matter, for the most characteristic feature of the gospel tradition, especially in contrast with Jewish rabbinical tradition, is the remarkable freedom which the transmitters of that tradition exercise in regard to it. The almost cavalier manner in which sayings are modified, interpreted and rewritten in the service of the theology of the particular evangelist or editor is quite without parallel in Judaism, and is only possible in Christianity because of the basic Christian conviction that the Jesus who spoke is the Jesus who speaks, i.e. because of the absolute identification of earthly Jesus of Nazareth and risen Lord of the evangelist's or editor's Christian experience. The strength of the form-critical approach to the gospels is that it does justice to this basic and fundamental aspect of earliest Christianity; the weakness of Gerhardsson's approach is that it does not.

Catastrophic so far as the overall impact of Gerhardsson's work is concerned is that in a book having some 325 pages of text, only twelve of those pages are devoted to a discussion of the gospel tradition itself (pp. 324–35), and these pages include no exegesis whatever of the text of the synoptic tradition on the basis of his hypothesis. In sharp contrast to form criticism, which takes its point of departure from the observable phenomena in the texts, which it seeks to explain, Gerhardsson is content to offer a string of hypothetical possibilities with regard to the variations between different parallel traditions, including the reminder that we may be dealing with sayings 'delivered by Jesus himself in more than one version'.[2] In view of the exegesis we have offered above of Mark 9.1 and its parallels, and in view also of what we have claimed to be the success of the total

---

[1] W. D. Davies, *Setting of the Sermon on the Mount*, p. 466.
[2] B. Gerhardsson, *Memory and Manuscript*, p. 335.

contemporary approach to the synoptic tradition in which these variations are accounted for on the assumption that they are due to, and a source of knowledge of, the theology of the evangelist or redactor concerned, we claim that we are entirely justified in challenging Gerhardsson to produce an exegesis of some sets of parallel sayings as evidence for his hypothesis, as we are prepared to do as evidence for ours. When he has done this, and the final pages of his book promise such a work at some future date, then further debate will become possible on this point. But we must insist that the crux of the matter is to explain the phenomena present in the texts.

Given the form-critical view of the tradition, it is evident that the way back from the tradition as we have it to the historical Jesus will be a long and arduous way, and there will be many instances where it will simply not exist, since much of the tradition will have been created in the early Church and will lead us at most to an aspect of the Church's understanding of the risen Lord. Indeed, on accepting this view of the tradition, one's first impulse is simply to give up the ghost and content oneself with selecting from the earlier strata of the tradition such teaching as is in keeping with one's overall view of the historical Jesus, making no systematic attempt to defend the authenticity of each saying used. But this could lead to a multiplicity of pictures of Jesus of Nazareth and could amount to an abandoning of any scientific historical research upon him and his teaching. What we must attempt to do is to recognize that the problem is more difficult than we first expected, but to allow this to act as a spur rather than a deterrent. It is much too soon, and the subject-matter is much too important, for us to abandon the task as hopeless.

If we are to establish any sayings attributed to Jesus in the tradition as authentic, then the first thing we must be able to do is to write a history of the tradition of which a given saying is a part, establishing so far as we are able to do so the earliest form of the saying known in the tradition. The synoptic tradition as we have it is the culmination of a long and complex process of transmission according to the needs, interests, and emphases of the Church. It follows, therefore, that only the earliest form of any saying known to us, and a form not reflecting these needs, interests or emphases, has a claim to authenticity.

In our earlier mention of the work of Jeremias on the parables we pointed out that one of the reasons for its success is that he achieves a history of the parabolic tradition; he is able to show how the parabolic tradition reached its present form and what that tradition was like in its earlier and earliest forms. In particular, he is able to isolate considerations at work on the tradition at various points: the change of situation and audience, the loss of the original eschatological setting, the introduction of allegory, and so on.[1] Then he is able to move from this to the conditions of the ministry of Jesus itself as they differed from these, in particular, the use of parable as distinct from allegory and the relationship to the Kingdom of God proclamation. This remains a classic example of the prime necessity in the reconstruction of the teaching of Jesus: the ability to write a history of the aspect of the tradition with which we are concerned.

The achievement of Jeremias in respect of the parabolic tradition only is that of Bultmann in respect of the synoptic tradition as a whole, and his *History of the Synoptic Tradition*[2] is the pioneer work in attempting a history of the synoptic tradition. All of us currently working in this field are immeasurably indebted to him for his demonstration of both the necessity and the possibility of doing this, and for a thousand invaluable insights into that history itself.

Other work on the history of the synoptic tradition will be mentioned in the course of our own work; at this point our concern is simply to argue that the reconstruction of the teaching of Jesus *must* begin by attempting to write a history of the synoptic tradition. Not that we must produce over and over again works of the scope of Bultmann's or Jeremias's; but we must be prepared ever to learn from them and to consider any and every saying in the light of the history of the particular branch of tradition of which it is a part. Only the earliest, most primitive form of the saying will concern us. Also, we must be prepared to keep learning things about the tradition from the work that has been done on various parts of it. An insight derived from work on one part of the tradition will often help us in our consideration of another part. For example, the work of Käsemann on what he calls 'Säze heiligen Rechtes' and what we call 'an eschatological judgement pronouncement tradition' will help us in our consideration of the apocalyptic Son of man tradition.[3] Further, our work upon the history of the tradition will enable us to recognize

---

[1] J. Jeremias, *Parables of Jesus* (rev. ed., 1963), pp. 23–114.
[2] R. Bultmann, *History of the Synoptic Tradition*; ET by John Marsh of *Geschichte der synoptischen Tradition*, first published in 1921, ET from the third German edition of 1958; Oxford: Basil Blackwell, and New York: Harper & Row, 1963. M. Dibelius, *From Tradition to Gospel*, does not deal with the history of the tradition as a whole, as does Bultmann.
[3] See below, pp. 185–91.

the characteristic interests and emphases of the Church and the evangelists, which we must always be prepared to recognize and to remove.

A consideration of the history of the synoptic tradition must proceed on the basis of an assumption with regard to the literary relationships between the gospels. The era of literary criticism, which culminated in B. H. Streeter's *The Four Gospels*, published in 1924, led to the general acceptance of the two-source hypothesis, i.e. that Mark and a sayings source ('Q') used by Luke and Matthew are basic sources for the three synoptic gospels, that Mark and Q are prior to Matthew and Luke, and that, so far as we can tell, Mark and Q are independent of one another, as are Matthew and Luke. From time to time attempts are made to overturn this basic hypothesis, usually in favour of the theory that Matthew is prior to both Mark and Luke, and that Luke used Matthew, and Mark used both Matthew and Luke.[1] These attempts to overturn the work of a previous era of scholarship must be regarded as unsuccessful, because the most they achieve is a demonstration that the literary relationships between the texts of the gospels as we have them are more complex than the older form of the two-source hypothesis imagined. This may be granted at once, but then the point has to be made that the literary relationships between the texts of the synoptic gospels are more complex than any theory of direct relationship imagines. First of all, we must recognize that the era of literary criticism was also an era of optimism about establishing the original texts of the gospels to a degree of high probability; that any theory of literary dependence is a theory of literary dependence between texts established by the process of textual criticism; and that such optimism is not as widespread today as it was in the era of Westcott and Hort. This tends to diminish the importance of verbal relationships as a decisive factor in themselves, and to emphasize the importance of more purely theological factors. Another point not recognized in the era of literary criticism as it would be today is that we must conceive of the existence of a living, free tradition of sayings of Jesus, out of which the gospels have come. But this tradition did not come to an end with the writing of the gospels. To the contrary, a careful study by Köster[2] has shown that even as late as the first half of the second century such free tradition was a strong factor in the

---

[1] See most recently W. R. Farmer, *The Synoptic Problem*; New York, and London: Macmillan, 1964.

[2] H. Köster, *Synoptische Überlieferung bei den apostolischen Vätern* (Texte und Untersuchungen 65); Berlin: Akademie Verlag, 1957.

Church, and this must be considered even more the case for the second half of the first. So, in any single instance, or in any number of instances, it must always be considered possible that the tradition which the first written gospel source has used has lived on to affect the later gospel traditions in cases where they have used the earlier written source.

The effect of all this is to throw into relief the results, and especially the theological results, of the work done on the basis of a given hypothesis of gospel interrelationships as the only effective test of the validity of that hypothesis. Here the two-source hypothesis establishes itself beyond reasonable doubt. We can appeal to the work of Bultmann and Jeremias on the history of the tradition; we can appeal to the recent work on the theology of the synoptic evangelists and their tradition; and, as we shall see in our work below, the acceptance of this hypothesis as a working hypothesis is validated over and over again by the results achieved in individual instances. If Farmer or others wish to return to the hypothesis of the priority of Matthew, then they must show us that this contemporary work is producing false results, and that better results would be attained on the basis of their hypothesis. They must also be prepared to show us how they believe the theological characteristics of the various evangelists are to be accounted for on the basis of their hypothesis, something we are constantly prepared to do on the basis of ours. We, at any rate, have no hesitation in basing our work on the two-source hypothesis, with suitable recognition of the possibility of the continuing existence and influence of synoptic-type tradition alongside the synoptic gospels themselves all through the period that concerns us.

Any discussion of the history of the synoptic tradition today must take into account the newly discovered Coptic gospel of Thomas,[1] for here we have a gospel radically different from the synoptic gospels. It contains no narrative of any kind and consists entirely of synoptic-type teaching material, i.e. sayings and parables with very simple introductions. Much of this material parallels material already to be found in the canonical synoptic gospels, while other parallels material already known to us from extra-canonical sources, especially the Oxyrhynchus papyrus sayings,[2] and some is quite new. The gospel

[1] *The Gospel According to Thomas*, ed. A. Guillaumont *et al.*; Leiden: E. J. Brill, and New York: Harper & Bros., 1959.

[2] See E. Hennecke–W. Schneemelcher, *New Testament Apocrypha*, I *Gospels and Related Writings* (London: Lutterworth Press, and Philadelphia: Westminster Press, 1963), 97–113.

itself in its present form is heavily gnostic in tone, and much of the material in it has clearly been either modified or created to serve gnostic Christian purposes. In this respect, it is like the canonical gospels, for, as we argued above, much of the material in them has been either modified or created to serve orthodox Christian purposes. The crucial question is that of the relationship between Thomas and the canonical synoptic tradition. That is a question to which there is at the moment no agreed answer,[1] and which perhaps cannot definitely be answered. But we do not need a definite answer; we need a working hypothesis. As a working hypothesis, we have chosen to treat the Thomas material as independent of our gospels in their present form.

This working hypothesis seems to us to be justified, simply because of the complete lack of anything except verbal similarities to indicate possible dependence of Thomas upon the canonical tradition. We pointed out above that this is a difficult factor to assess in the case of gospel relationships because of the difficulty of establishing original texts, and because of the possibility of parallel free tradition living on side by side with the written gospels and influencing them at various stages. In the case of Thomas, these difficulties are multiplied because we have no Greek text of the gospel, except to the limited extent to which the Oxyrhynchus sayings may be said to be part of a text of Thomas, and because of the additional possibility that the Thomas tradition has been influenced by the Coptic gospel tradition. Verbal similarities are not therefore a strong argument for the dependence of Thomas upon the canonical gospel tradition, and all other factors are against such dependence. The fact is that canonical tradition is scattered about in Thomas 'as if it had fallen from a pepperpot' (R. McL. Wilson); that sayings appear in totally different combinations and a totally different order from that found in the canonical tradition; that almost invariably what the canonical traditions join together Thomas puts asunder, and *vice versa*; that although Thomas reproduces the parables in the Matthaean tradition, he scatters them throughout his gospel for no conceivable reason; and so on. In addition to this, and most significant, is the fact that over and over again the text of a parable in Thomas will be different from that of the canonical tradition, and often it will be closer to a form which on Jeremias' form-critical grounds is to be regarded as earlier than that of the canonical tradition. This may not justify the absolute claim that

[1] See Annotated Bibliography No. 3: Thomas and the Synoptic Gospels.

Thomas is independent of the canonical synoptic tradition, but it certainly justifies the acceptance of this as a working hypothesis, and hence the use of Thomas material, where relevant, in addition to the canonical material in an attempt to reconstruct the history of the tradition and to arrive at the earliest form of a saying or parable. This will be our procedure in the central chapters of this work.

An important factor in the writing of a history of the tradition is the use of linguistic features, especially the observation of Aramaisms. We must note that Aramaic and Greek are radically different languages, so that it is often possible to say that a given construction or use of vocabulary is Aramaic and not Greek. Of course, we must always remember that many early Christians must have been bilingual and, moreover, more at home in Aramaic than Greek, and that many early Christian congregations were Aramaic speaking. All in all, however, it is true to say that the observation of Aramaisms can help to reach an earlier stratum of tradition than the Greek one in the text before us. In the past, this has tended to be overstated; on the basis of the fact that Jesus certainly taught in Aramaic, and on the assumption that when we had reached one step behind the tradition in our synoptic sources we had reached the teaching of Jesus, it was sometimes assumed that an Aramaism represented the voice of Jesus. This is certainly not necessarily the case. But it is the case, as Jeremias always insists, that an Aramaism can help us to reach an earlier stratum of the tradition, and an example of this in our own work will be found below in our discussion of the apocalyptic Son of man sayings.[1]

A particularly interesting Aramaism is the use of a passive voice of the verb to represent the activity of God. This is very common in Palestinian Aramaic of New Testament times, where the passive voice of the verb is very frequently used for this purpose, and it is often to be found in the New Testament. In our discussion of Käsemann's 'Sätze heiligen Rechtes' we noted an example from I Cor. 14.38, and some examples from the gospels would be: Mark 4.11 par.; Matt. 5.7, 7.1 par.; 7.7f. par.; 12.31 par., 32; 21.43. The fact that the construction is found in the eschatological judgement pronouncement tradition must warn us against ready assumptions that a saying using this construction is from Jesus. But certainly Jesus must have used it, since in Palestinian Aramaic nothing else would be possible; and it is obviously true that the increasingly Hellenistic tradition of the

[1] See below, p. 188.

Church loses its feeling against the direct mention of God, witness the widespread 'Kingdom of God' which would never be found in Aramaic. So it is reasonable to assume that, other things being equal, this construction will belong to Palestinian and probably earlier strata of the tradition, and it may be expected to be found in preference to other constructions in genuine sayings of Jesus. It must have been a feature of his teaching, but that does not mean that a saying containing it must necessarily be dominical.

In what we are saying here, we are particularly indebted to Jeremias' work on *ipsissima vox Jesu*.[1] In many ways the most interesting aspect of that work is the argument that the formula-like turn of phrase, 'Amen, I say to you . . .' is a feature of the teaching style of Jesus. It must be said at once that he has one decisive argument on his side: that it is a phrase unique in Judaism, where Amen signifies assent to something said, or links one to a prayer, but never introduces sayings, and that the developing Christian tradition tends to modify it to something much less startling.[2] This is an example of the 'criterion of dissimilarity' that will concern us below, and it is the strongest criterion for authenticity that contemporary research has found. So strong is this argument that Jeremias must be granted his point: the turn of phrase comes from Jesus and is a feature of his teaching. But this does not necessarily guarantee the authenticity of any saying featuring it. We saw above that Mark 9.1, although introduced by it, owes its present form to Mark, and we must recognize the very real possibility that the characteristic early Christian conviction that the Lord who spoke is the Lord who speaks has led to an imitation of the very style of that speech, at any rate to a limited extent. The presence of the formula may indicate, therefore, either a dominical element in the saying, or it may indicate a particularly solemn feeling that here the Lord who had spoken was speaking, as we would be prepared to argue is the case in the eucharistic sayings Mark 14.18b, 25. Each saying will have to be judged on its own merits; the most the presence of this formula will do is to increase the possibility that the saying concerned contains a certain genuine dominical element.

In our attempts to reconstruct the teaching of Jesus, then, we must first seek to write a history of the tradition with which we are con-

---

[1] J. Jeremias, 'Kennzeichen der ipsissima vox Jesu', *Synoptische Studien* (Festschrift A. Wikenhauser [München: Karl Zink Verlag, 1953]), pp. 86–93.

[2] For the many examples, see Jeremias, *ibid.*, pp. 90f.

cerned and to arrive at the earliest form of the saying in the tradition, or the earliest form of the saying we can reconstruct from the tradition. What next? Well, clearly, we have to ask ourselves the question as to whether this saying should now be attributed to the early Church or to the historical Jesus, *and the nature of the synoptic tradition is such that the burden of proof will be upon the claim to authenticity.* This means in effect that we must look for indications that the saying does not come from the Church, but from the historical Jesus. Actually, our task is even more complex than this, because the early Church and the New Testament are indebted at very many points to ancient Judaism. Therefore, if we are to ascribe a saying to Jesus, and accept the burden of proof laid upon us, we must be able to show that the saying comes neither from the Church nor from ancient Judaism. This seems to many to be too much to ask, but nothing less will do justice to the challenge of the burden of the proof. There is no other way to reasonable certainty that we have reached the historical Jesus.

Thus we reach the fundamental criterion for authenticity upon which all reconstructions of the teaching of Jesus must be built, which we propose to call the *'criterion of dissimilarity'*. Recognizing that it follows an attempt to write a history of the tradition concerned, we may formulate it as follows: the earliest form of a saying we can reach may be regarded as authentic if it can be shown to be dissimilar to characteristic emphases both of ancient Judaism and of the early Church, and this will particularly be the case where Christian tradition oriented towards Judaism can be shown to have modified the saying away from its original emphasis.

The first part of this formulation follows from what we have said above; the second needs a word of explanation. The teaching of Jesus was set in the context of ancient Judaism, and in many respects that teaching must have been variations on themes from the religious life of ancient Judaism. But if we are to seek that which is most characteristic of Jesus, it will be found not in the things which he shares with his contemporaries, but in the things wherein he differs from them. Now those circles of early Christians who were most concerned with the Jews, now represented for the most part by traditions to be found in Matthew,[1] tended both to 'tone down' the startlingly new element in the teaching of Jesus, as we shall see in some examples below, and also to develop new traditions specifically related to emphases in

---

[1] This remains true irrespective of whether or not Matthew's gospel is to be regarded as 'Jewish Christian' in any stricter sense.

Judaism.[1] So far as our criterion of dissimilarity is concerned, the former tendency in these traditions will be very important, for it will help us to focus our attention on elements in the teaching of Jesus which were, in fact, new and startling to Jewish ears, and it is for this reason that we called attention to it in the formulation above.

The criterion of dissimilarity we have formulated was not reached on the basis of theoretical considerations, although it can be defended on this basis, but in the course of practical work on the synoptic tradition. It was, in fact, first used by Bultmann, who, in discussing the parables, reached the conclusion: 'We can only count on possessing a genuine similitude of Jesus where, on the one hand, expression is given to the contrast between Jewish morality and piety and the distinctive eschatological temper which characterized the preaching of Jesus; and where on the other hand we find no specifically Christian features.'[2] The subsequent discussion has simply taken up the principle and applied it to other forms of the teaching, as, of course, may quite legitimately be done.

The use of this criterion has always been a feature of the work of Jeremias. We called attention above to the way in which it is used in connection with the formula, 'Amen, I say to you . . .', introducing sayings of Jesus. Another striking example from his work is in connection with his investigation of the use of *abba* in addressing God. First announced in a paper read to a *Theologentag* in Berlin in January 1954, and since published in several forms as the work progressed, this is now to be found in English in his book, *The Central Message of the New Testament* (London: SCM Press, and New York: Scribner's, 1965), presented in rather a general form, and in his collected essays entitled *Abba* (Göttingen: Vandenhoeck & Ruprecht, 1965) in a more academic form. The crux of the matter is that we find in the New Testament tradition that Jesus addresses God as *abba* in Gethsemane, Mark 14.36: 'Abba, Father . . .', where 'Father' is simply a translation of the Aramaic word. In the parallels, Luke 22.42 simply echoes Mark, but omits the Aramaic word; Matt. 26.39 also omits the Aramaic word, but offers an alternative translation of it: 'My Father . . .' Both 'Father' and 'My Father' are correct translations of *abba*, since this particular form of the word served both as the sub-

---

[1] See, for example, the very interesting suggestion by W. D. Davies that the Matthaean Sermon on the Mount may represent a Christian answer to Jamnia. *Setting of the Sermon on the Mount*, p. 315.

[2] R. Bultmann, *History of the Synoptic Tradition*, p. 205.

stantive and as the substantive with the first person singular suffix. In the Lord's Prayer tradition, Luke 11.2 again has the simple 'Father' clearly representing *abba* here, as it did in 22.42, whereas Matt. 6.9 has 'Our Father who art in heaven', a very considerable modification. An intensive investigation of the Jewish traditions has shown that to address God as Father is by no means a commonplace of ancient Jewish piety, and that when it does happen the form *abba*, 'Father' or 'My Father', is *never* used. An equivalent of the Matthaean 'Our Father who art in heaven' is the most common form, and this is especially the case during the time of Johanan ben Zakkai (*circa* AD 50–80), which is also approximately the time of the fashioning of the Matthaean tradition.

The reason for the avoidance of *abba* in address to God in the ancient Jewish piety is that this is the form of the word used by a child in first learning to speak to his earthly father. Aramaic, unlike English, does not have an onomatopoeic word to be taught to children (Dadda or the like) and then a quite different root for the formal word. In Aramaic, the root *ab* has to serve for both. Thus, the ancient Jews maintained the dignity of God, in so far as they addressed him as Father at all, by scrupulously avoiding the particular form of the word used by children.

The New Testament tradition represents Jesus as addressing God as *abba* (Mark 14.36) and as teaching his disciples to do so (Luke 11.2). In the first instance Matthew maintains the tradition also, but in the second he modifies it to a form more acceptable to Jewish ears, to the form that indeed in his day flowered in Jewish circles. This is a good example of the things for which the criterion of dissimilarity seeks: radical difference from Judaism and later modification towards Judaism. Since, however, *abba* is also found in Rom. 8.15 and Gal. 4.6, it could be argued that the Jesus tradition is not here dissimilar to that of the early Church. But these may not be regarded as representing early Christian tradition as such. They are the only examples of it, and the Lord's Prayer is universally known with its Matthaean form of address, even in most texts of Luke! The most reasonable explanation is that it is characteristic of Jesus rather than the early Church, but that Paul knows the tradition preserved in Luke and, as a bilingual Jew, fully appreciates its significance. All in all, therefore, we may regard it as established, on the basis of the criterion of dissimilarity, that Jesus addressed God as *abba* and taught his disciples to do so.

A particularly effective presentation of the criterion of dissimilarity is that by Ernst Käsemann in the essay which sparked the intensive discussion of the question of the historical Jesus which has been such a prominent feature of recent New Testament scholarship, 'Das Problem des historischen Jesus'.[1] Here he writes, in connection with the question of reconstructing authentic teaching of Jesus, 'we have reasonably secure ground under our feet only in one particular instance, namely, when there is some way of showing that a piece of tradition has not been derived from Judaism and may not be ascribed to early Christianity, and this is particularly the case when Jewish Christianity has regarded this tradition as too bold and has toned it down or modified it in some way'.[2]

In the most recent discussion this criterion has been widely used, especially by members of the 'Bultmann school', who are indebted for it to Bultmann himself. We will mention only one example, that in Hans Conzelmann's most important article 'Jesus Christus' in the third edition of the German encyclopedia, *Religion in Geschichte und Gegenwart*.[3] The importance of this article is that Conzelmann successfully attempts a presentation of the current situation in life of Christ research, as seen from the perspective of the radical acceptance of the form-critical view of the sources characteristic of the Bultmann school, and so achieves a presentation of the factors involved in this research that should become a standard, a basis for future work as the perspective from which he starts becomes even more widely accepted. In passing, may we say that it is an article which demands both translation into English and presentation in a form more readily accessible than that of an article within the pages of a multi-volume learned encyclopedia. So far as our criterion of dissimilarity is concerned, Conzelmann formulates this as follows: 'What can, therefore, be accepted as authentic [on the basis of the radical form-critical view of the sources] ? . . . we do have some starting points. . . . So far as the reconstruction of the teaching is concerned the following methodological basis is valid: we may accept as authentic material which

[1] Originally published in *ZTK* 51 (1954), 125–53, and then in Käsemann's collected essays *Exegetische Versuche und Besinunngen* (Göttingen: Vandenhoeck & Ruprecht) I (1960), 187–214. An English translation by W. J. Montague is to be found in E. Käsemann, *Essays on New Testament Themes* (Studies in Biblical Theology 41 [London: SCM Press, 1964]), pp. 15–47.

[2] E. Käsemann, *Exegetische Versuche und Besinnungen* I, 205, cf. *Essays*, p. 37. The above translation is our own and we are glad to acknowledge our indebtedness to Käsemann's formulation in the one we have ourselves attempted.

[3] *RGG*3 (Tübingen: J. C. B. Mohr [Paul Siebeck]) III (1959), 619–53.

fits in with neither Jewish thinking nor the conceptions of the later [Christian] community.'[1]

This, then, is the criterion of dissimilarity, and it must be regarded as the basis for all contemporary attempts to reconstruct the teaching of Jesus. Of course, it is limited in scope—by definition it will exclude all teaching in which Jesus may have been at one with Judaism or the early Church at one with him. But the brutal fact of the matter is that we have no choice. There simply is no other starting-point that takes seriously enough the radical view of the nature of the sources which the results of contemporary research are forcing upon us.

With the criterion of dissimilarity as our starting-point, and with the results of the application of this criterion as the only foundation upon which we can build, the next step is to find a criterion by means of which we can move carefully into areas of tradition where this criterion would not be applicable. Here we propose a second criterion, which we will call '*the criterion of coherence*': material from the earliest strata of the tradition may be accepted as authentic if it can be shown to cohere with material established as authentic by means of the criterion of dissimilarity.[2]

Like the criterion of dissimilarity, the criterion of coherence was first reached in the course of practical work on the synoptic tradition, and again by Bultmann. In his *History of the Synoptic Tradition*, we find him accepting as authentic 'such sayings as arise from the exaltation of an eschatological mood', or, 'sayings which demand a new disposition of mind'.[3] He accepts them because they 'contain something characteristic, new, reaching out beyond popular wisdom and piety and yet are in no sense scribal or rabbinic nor yet Jewish apocalyptic'.[4] In other words, they satisfy the criterion of dissimilarity. But once characteristics of the teaching of Jesus are established in this way, these characteristics can be used to validate sayings which themselves would not meet the requirements of the criterion of dissimilarity. Already in the *History of the Synoptic Tradition* we find traces of this, because it is noticeable that when he is grouping

---

[1] Conzelmann, *RGG*[3] III, 623.

[2] We are using the word 'coherence' in the sense given in the dictionaries: 'Harmonious connexion of the several parts so that the whole "hangs together"' (Oxford English Dictionary).

[3] R. Bultmann, *History of the Synoptic Tradition*, p. 105. Cf. p. 125 ('. . . passages . . . which express the acute eschatological consciousness with its combined gladness and gravity in the face of decision').

[4] *Ibid.*

together sayings which reflect one of these characteristics, Bultmann shows no great concern if some of them are dubious on other grounds, although he will note the possibility in passing. In his *Jesus and the Word*,[1] however, he goes beyond this, for in that book he by no means restricts himself, in his presentation of the message of Jesus, to sayings which he had found to be authentic in the course of the discussion in the *History of the Synoptic Tradition*. What he does is to use any saying from the earliest stratum of the tradition which expresses something he has previously determined to be characteristic of the teaching of Jesus.[2] This is in practice the criterion we have sought to formulate in principle.

As was the case with the criterion of dissimilarity, this second criterion has also been used by Jeremias. It is particularly to be found in his work on 'unknown sayings of Jesus', i.e. sayings to be found in sources outside the gospels, both canonical and extra-canonical.[3] He formulates it as follows: 'By a process of elimination we are left with twenty-one sayings whose attestation and subject matter do not give rise to objections of weight, *which are perfectly compatible with the genuine teachings of our Lord*, and which have as high a claim to authenticity as the sayings recorded in our four gospels.'[4]

In the body of the work he then argues the authenticity of these twenty-one sayings on the basis of this criterion. A good example of his methodology is his discussion of a saying preserved by Origen and now also found in the gospel of Thomas:

Thomas 82. He that is near me is near the fire;
he that is far from me is far from the Kingdom.

This can be accepted as authentic because, among other things, it has 'the ring of a genuine saying of Jesus', it 'echoes Mark 9.49 and 12.34',

---

[1] ET by L. P. Smith and E. Y. Lantero of *Jesus* (1926); New York: Scribner's, 1934, 1958; London: Nicholson and Watson, 1935. The first German edition was, therefore, published five years after the first German edition of the *History of the Synoptic Tradition*.

[2] Note the partial explanation of this, *Jesus and the Word*, pp. 12ff. There he explains that he will use sayings from the earliest stratum of the tradition. That he uses them in so far as they reflect previously determined characteristics of the teaching of Jesus follows from the structure of the book itself, for its divisions correspond to the characteristics of the message of Jesus determined in the *History of the Synoptic Tradition*.

[3] J. Jeremias, *Unknown Sayings of Jesus*; ET by R. H. Fuller of *Unbekannte Jesusworte* ([2]1951); London: SPCK, 1957.

[4] *Ibid.*, p. 30, italics ours. In the German, the last part is italicized: 'which have as high a claim . . . gospels'.

its purpose is to 'convey a stern warning' as to the cost of discipleship, as does Matt. 8.19f.[1]

Jeremias' concern is to establish that these sayings have the same claim to authenticity as those in the gospels, but in his discussion he tends to assume that to do this and to establish their authenticity as sayings of Jesus are one and the same thing. He can do so because the twenty-one sayings are selected from a much greater number, and no doubt were selected because they were compatible with elements in the gospel tradition which Jeremias regards as authentic. In effect, then, his criterion is ours (or, better, our criterion is his!), except that we have preferred 'to cohere with' to the 'to be perfectly compatible with' chosen by R. H. Fuller to represent Jeremias' German *sich einfügen*. However, where Jeremias has applied it to sayings from outside the gospels, we propose to apply it also to sayings within the gospel tradition, since we are convinced that, in this regard, no distinction should be made between canonical and extra-canonical sayings. As Köster has shown,[2] they are all part of a living tradition in the Church, and no distinction was made between them at all before the second half of the second century.

In regard to the actual formulation of the criterion we have attempted, it should be noted that we are still insisting on the importance of establishing a history of the tradition and of restricting ourselves to the earliest stratum of that tradition; in our view, material dependent upon other material already present in the tradition is necessarily a product of the Church. What we are proposing, in effect, is to use material established as authentic by the one sure criterion as a touchstone by means of which to judge material which itself would resist the application of that criterion, material which could not be established as dissimilar to emphases of Judaism or the early Church.

Before leaving the question of criteria, we must mention one further one: *the criterion of multiple attestation*.[3] This is a proposal to accept as authentic material which is attested in all, or most, of the sources which can be discerned behind the synoptic gospels. It is a criterion

[1] *Ibid.*, pp. 54f.

[2] H. Köster, 'Die ausserkanonischen Herrenworte', *ZNW* 48 (1957), 220–37; and *Synoptische Überlieferung bei den apostolischen Vätern, passim.*

[3] We are here using the terminology suggested by Harvey K. McArthur in his 'Survey of Recent Gospel Research', *Interpretation* 18 (1964), 39–55, especially 48. See Annotated Bibliography No. 1, below, for a brief comment on this article and the various criteria McArthur proposes.

much used in England, as McArthur points out, and he claims that it is the most objective of the criteria which can be used.[1]

We must admit to some reservations about this criterion, reservations which McArthur shares in part. It was first used in England in an atmosphere in which it was felt that the sources of the synoptic gospels came very close to being actual historical reminiscence. This is particularly evident in the work of T. W. Manson, who uses the criterion extensively. In his view, when a saying is found in Mark and Q the two versions can be compared and the voice of Jesus recovered; but then he believed that Peter stood directly behind Mark and that Q was the work of the apostle Matthew.[2] If we cannot accept the basic presupposition that to take one step behind the sources is to arrive at firm historical tradition about Jesus, then this criterion becomes much less effective. Again, we must always take into account the possibility that something may have multiple attestation because of the role it played in primitive Palestinian Christianity, or in early Christian liturgy. We do tend to agree with McArthur, however, that this criterion does have a usefulness in terms of establishing the authenticity of motifs from the ministry of Jesus, although rarely that of specific sayings,[3] and particularly when we think in terms of strands and forms of tradition rather than in terms of synoptic gospel sources. We may say that a motif which can be detected in a multiplicity of strands of tradition and in various forms (pronouncement stories, parables, sayings, etc.) will have a high claim to authenticity, always provided that it is not characteristic of an activity, interest or emphasis of the earliest Church. So, for example, we may accept the authenticity of Jesus' special concern for 'tax collectors and sinners', which certainly has multiple attestation in this sense,[4] and this is so clearly the case that we shall not argue the authenticity of this aspect of Jesus' ministry in our work below, but only concern ourselves with its meaning.

The usefulness of this criterion is somewhat restricted. It will not often help with specific sayings, but rather with general motifs, and

[1] H. K. McArthur, *Interpretation* 18 (1964), 48.

[2] On the criterion, T. W. Manson, *Teaching of Jesus* (Cambridge: University Press, 1935 [many subsequent unrevised reprints]), pp. 10f. On the roles of Peter and Matthew, T. W. Manson, *Studies in the Gospels and Epistles* (a posthumously published collection of Manson's Rylands lectures, ed. Matthew Black [Manchester: University Press, 1962]), pp. 33f. (Peter), 82f. (Matthew).

[3] H. K. McArthur, *Interpretation* 18 (1964), 48.

[4] *Ibid.*

consequently will tend to be more useful in arriving at general characteristics of the ministry and teaching of Jesus than at specific elements in the teaching itself. Our procedure will be to attempt to arrive at elements in the tradition which have a high claim to authenticity and then to move out from there, going from the specific to the general rather than *vice versa*. We shall therefore have only limited occasion to use the criterion of multiple attestation, preferring to work upon the basis of the establishment of the history of the tradition and the criteria of dissimilarity and coherence.

We are ourselves convinced that there are three aspects of the tradition where the establishment of the history of the tradition and the application of the criterion of dissimilarity enable us to reconstruct major aspects of the teaching of Jesus beyond reasonable doubt: the parables, the Kingdom of God teaching and the Lord's Prayer tradition. In the case of the parables, Jeremias achieves a history of the tradition, and then is able to show that the earliest forms of the parables are dissimilar to emphases of the early Church (they are parables and not allegories, they reflect Palestinian peasant life, etc.) and of ancient Judaism (above all the eschatology). The Kingdom of God teaching differs from both the early Church and ancient Judaism in its use of the key concept, Kingdom of God, and in aspects of its eschatology, where, incidentally, it is in agreement with the eschatology of the parables. The Lord's Prayer is dissimilar to both the early Church and ancient Judaism in the address to God and in the linking of a petition for forgiveness with a preparedness to forgive (which ancient Judaism does not have in a prayer and which the early Church legalizes, Matt. 6.14), is strongly Aramaic (the word play 'debt/sin' is possible only in Aramaic), and has a characteristic brevity and a strongly personal element in its phraseology which is derived from the spirit of the use of *abba*. We would argue that any attempt to reconstruct the teaching of Jesus today must build upon the foundations laid by the application of the criterion of dissimilarity in these three areas. Then, by the application of the criterion of coherence, it is possible to go on to accept as authentic that material from the earliest strata of the traditions, the tendencies of the tradition having been taken into account, which coheres with the emphases to be found there. Similarly, any new material established as authentic on the basis of the criterion of dissimilarity will carry with it new possibilities with regard to the use of the criterion of coherence.

In accordance with these views, it will be found that in the central section of this work we have relied heavily upon the parables, the Kingdom teaching and the Lord's Prayer. So far as the last two are concerned, we have assumed the results of our previous work in *The Kingdom of God in the Teaching of Jesus*, except that we have modified them where necessary in view of the more stringent criteria for authenticity which we have come to accept in the period between the two works. So far as the parables are concerned, it will be found that, where applicable, they are always the starting-point for our discussion, except in the case of the Kingdom teaching.

Thus far we have assumed that we are dealing with material where it is possible to write a history of the tradition; what are we to do in the case of material where this is not possible, that is, in the case of isolated and independent sayings which have no history in the tradition? If they can be ascribed to an early stratum of tradition by reason of their content or association, then we may treat them as belonging to that stratum and, of course, if they have to be ascribed on the same grounds to a comparatively late stratum, then we have to treat them as belonging to that. The first possibility will bring them into serious consideration by the criteria of dissimilarity and coherence. The second will mean that we will have to have extraordinarily strong grounds for accepting them. In the case of completely isolated and independent sayings, then, the only thing to do is to apply the criteria even more carefully; such sayings will not inspire the same confidence as those demonstrably from the earlier strata, but we may certainly not forejudge them.

In our discussion so far we have made no mention of the gospel of John, the fourth gospel, and its possibilities as a source for knowledge of the teaching of Jesus. The reason for this is simple: as far as our present knowledge and methodological resources go, the gospel of John is not a source of knowledge of the teaching of Jesus. It is generally recognized that it represents a reinterpretation of the ministry and teaching of Jesus along markedly theological lines, witness the fact that it has been widely accepted as the 'spiritual' gospel since the time of Clement of Alexandria, and contemporary research has scarcely modified this opinion. What has happened in contemporary research is that opinion with regard to the synoptic gospels has moved nearer, concerning their theological motivation, to what opinion with regard to the fourth gospel always has been, without opinion with regard to that gospel changing significantly. In the case of the synoptic gospels, however, we find that we are dealing with a number of authors and complexes of tradition, and that the multiplicity of influences at work on the tradition tend to cancel one another out, to call attention to one another and, in short, to enable us to write a history of the tradition and work our way back through it. But in the case of the fourth gospel we are dealing with a single entity exhibiting a marked degree of unity in theological emphasis such that no attempt to divide the gospel into different sources and to begin to write a history of the Johannine tradition has commanded anything like a common consent among scholars. One has only to compare the very different results exhibited in the works of the two greatest contemporary commentators on the gospel, R. Bultmann and C. H. Dodd,[1] to realize how far we are from being able to write a history of the Johannine tradition. But until we can write a history of that tradition and learn to work our way back through it, there is not very much that we can do with the gospel of John as a source for knowledge of the teaching of Jesus.

The work of C. H. Dodd on the historical tradition in the fourth gospel does not help us appreciably here, because, even if we grant his case (and we could not accept his basic premise that early tradition and historical tradition are synonymous),[2] all that we then have is a series of historical allusions in some of the events recorded in the gospel, especially in the passion narrative, with little or no teaching material involved. All in all, the problems are such that we have felt it necessary to ignore the Johannine material altogether, even in the case of the Son of man teaching, and the only major reference to be found on the fourth gospel in what follows is one of the account of the crucifixion where it does seem apparent that John is referring to a Christian exegetical tradition. On the basis of a surer knowledge of the synoptic tradition, and of more and more work on the Johannine, it may one day be possible to make use of the fourth gospel in the reconstruction of the teaching of Jesus, but that day is not yet.

THE INTERPRETATION OF THE TEACHING OF JESUS

Once we have arrived at a reconstruction of an aspect of the

---

[1] R. Bultmann, *Das Evangelium des Johannes;* Göttingen: Vandenhoeck & Ruprecht, 1956. C. H. Dodd, *The Interpretation of the Fourth Gospel*; Cambridge: University Press, 1953. *Historical Tradition in the Fourth Gospel*; Cambridge: University Press, 1963.

[2] See our review of the book in *JR* 44 (1964), 335.

teaching of Jesus, our next task is to seek to understand it, by which we mean to interpret it in its original setting and to arrive as closely as we can at its original meaning. Here we are at once confronted by a whole series of problems. Most serious of them all is the fact that we are simply not first-century Palestinian Jews, and that no effort of historical imagination can make us become such. Thus, there will always be a barrier between us and the original meaning of the teaching of Jesus, the barrier of two millennia and radically different *Weltanschauungen*. But it remains a fact that we have no choice but to attempt to surmount this barrier, at any rate to achieve some sort of a glimpse over it, if we are to arrive at the teaching of Jesus.

One of the most disturbing things about the history of the life of Christ research is the way in which the teaching of Jesus has been seen in categories of nineteenth-century liberalism, of twentieth-century existentialism, or of some other 'modern' way of thinking. None of this would be disturbing in devotional works, but the thing is that it happens over and over again in academic works. The problem is not one of wilfulness on the part of the scholars concerned; it is simply that any historian tends to see the past in terms which are most real to him personally, perhaps, indeed, in some sense it is impossible to see the past at all except when it can be seen in such terms. This is particularly the case with research into Jesus of Nazareth, who, as a historical figure, certainly transcended the categories of his own day, and therefore, so to speak, invites consideration in terms of the categories of another day. Again, most serious research into the teaching of Jesus is carried on by historians who are also Christians, and who, therefore, by definition have some concept of the risen Lord of their faith and experience, and of his teaching to them. This naturally, even unconsciously, influences them, and can lead to the situation where a historian carefully disentangles the original Jesus of history from the Christ of faith of the first-century Church only to re-identify him with the Christ of his own faith and so reinterpret the teaching all over again.

So it is that we have, so to speak, two problems: a barrier which is almost insurmountable on the one hand, and a figure who can all too easily be drawn into our own time and categories on the other. It is little wonder that we often do this latter thing, and in so doing think we are overcoming the former. These problems are perhaps insoluble in the work of any one scholar, but there are certain precautions that he can and should take.

In the first place, he should demand of himself that the understanding of the teaching of Jesus he reaches should do justice to the categories of first-century Judaism in terms of which that teaching was originally expressed. In itself this is an extraordinarily difficult task because of the intrinsic difficulty in comprehending the meaning of those categories to the men of first-century Judaism. To give an example from a matter that will concern us later, the eschatology of Jesus demands that we wrestle with the problem of the meaning of the element of futurity in the hope of first-century Judaism, and at the same time that we do justice to the new element in the teaching of Jesus in this regard. But now all kinds of questions arise. Many first-century Jews certainly expected God to act, to visit and redeem them through a concrete individual figure and by means of actual historical events at a chronological moment in time. If this had not been the case, then there could not have been the almost constant revolts against Rome led by messianic pretenders who began a war in the expectation that God would end it which are a feature of the history of this period. But at the same time, a reading of the apocalyptic literature from the period discovers such a bewildering variety of imagery, such a complex mixture of historical and mythical expectation,[1] that it becomes a real problem as to how much of this is to be taken literally. Some scholars have suggested that there were two distinct kinds of expectation, a nationalistic historical one based upon the expectation of a human messiah, and a trans-historical one based upon the expectation of a heavenly redeemer. This is possible, but one suspects that it is an oversimplification of the matter, especially when one notes the ease with which language from a text which, on this theory, reflects the historical expectation can be used in a text which reflects the trans-historical.[2] The problem is intensified when we come to the teaching of Jesus. He certainly added a new note and a new dimension to the Jewish eschatology in terms of which he expressed his hope for the future. But did he, in effect, 'demythologize' it so that we may properly express *his* teaching in existentialistic categories, or speak of the present and future elements in his teaching in terms of the nearness and distance of God? Or must we conclude that he was as literalistic in this matter as the early Church, and expected a world-historical act of God at a chronological point of time in the near future, as the Church expected her Lord's return? So the problems

[1] On this see N. Perrin, *Kingdom*, pp. 164ff.
[2] For an example of this, see our discussion of IV Ezra 13, below, pp. 170f.

multiply, both the difficulty of determining the meaning of first-century categories to first-century man and the natural tendency of a twentieth-century man to read them in terms of his own understanding, literalistic, existentialistic or whatever, adding to their number. Yet these are problems with which we must wrestle, for unless we are prepared to do justice to the categories of the first century in our interpretation, we are not going to reach the historical Jesus and his teaching. A prerequisite of historical research of this kind is constant wrestling with, and reference to, the literature, idioms and categories of the social, cultural and historical context of the subject.

A second point, closely related to this first one, is that we must always set the teaching of Jesus in the context of the circumstances and situation of his ministry. It is no accident that research into the parables came alive with the attempt to set them systematically into the situation of the ministry of Jesus. It was C. H. Dodd and J. Jeremias, above all, who achieved this,[1] and the result was a new era, not only in the understanding of the parables, but also in the whole field of research into the teaching of Jesus. What was found to be true of the parables is true of every aspect of the teaching of Jesus. That teaching is always directed to specific circumstances, to a concrete situation, to a definite person or group of people; and it is, if not unintelligible, certainly all too easily misunderstood if it is not first seen in the historical context to which it was directed or in which it was given. No understanding of the teaching of Jesus is possible without the recognition of the significance of its original historical context, and the precaution of constantly seeking to discover that context and to take it into account is one that is most necessary for us to take. This is the way to a true historical understanding and it is a major protection against the ever-prevalent danger of eisegesis.

A third precaution concerns the work on the sources, in this instance the synoptic gospels: the methodology should be appropriate to the nature of the sources. In order to work adequately with the sources, we must use a methodology which arises out of the nature of those sources and not one which is imposed upon them from outside. It is for this reason that we have insisted so strenuously upon the necessity of using what is loosely and somewhat inappropriately called the 'form-critical approach' to the gospels. No other approach does justice to the special nature of the synoptic tradition and the synoptic gospels. If we use a methodology derived from a study of rabbinic

[1] See Annotated Bibliography No. 6: Modern Research on the Parables.

Judaism, we shall fail. Rabbinic Judaism has a respect for the text and content of that which was being passed on, and in this respect is absolutely different from the freely creative nature of the synoptic tradition. If we work only with source and literary criticism, we shall fail. This approach assumes that if we can take one step behind the sources we can observe, then we reach historical reminiscence of Jesus and his ministry; but this is not the case. One step behind Mark or Q, indeed several steps behind Mark or Q, we are still only reaching the preaching, teaching or apologetic of the early Church; and the main source for the content of this is not historical reminiscence of Jesus, but present experience of the risen Lord. Of course, it is not a question of either/or. Some things we learn from a study of rabbinic traditions will help us, and source criticism is a starting-point for the attempt to write a history of the tradition so integral to the form-critical method. But the cutting edge of our method must always be that which does justice to the special nature of our sources. This is an essential aspect of any historical research.

But perhaps the most important thing in this regard is the consensus of scholarly opinion, granted that the scholars concerned are doing justice, so far as they are able, to the categories of first-century Judaism and the nature of the synoptic gospels. Then a consensus reached by scholars of different confessional and theological viewpoints becomes the really significant thing. It is unlikely that they will all make the same mistakes and impossible that they should all have the same presuppositions, and in this lies our only hope for true progress. In the historical sciences, we cannot, as in the natural sciences, achieve the clarity of observation that will enable all observers to describe the same phenomenon in the same way, but we can enter into debate with one another with regard to our findings and so strive for a consensus that will take us all further forward. It is in this spirit that this present work is offered, as one man's contribution to the ever-continuing task of research into the teaching of Jesus.

II

THE KINGDOM OF GOD

INTRODUCTION

THE CENTRAL ASPECT of the teaching of Jesus was that concerning the Kingdom of God. Of this there can be no doubt and today no scholar does, in fact, doubt it. Jesus appeared as one who proclaimed the Kingdom; all else in his message and ministry serves a function in relation to that proclamation and derives its meaning from it. The challenge to discipleship, the ethical teaching, the disputes about oral tradition or ceremonial law, even the pronouncement of the forgiveness of sins and the welcoming of the outcast in the name of God—all these are to be understood in context of the Kingdom proclamation or they are not to be understood at all. Of all the descriptive titles that have been applied to Jesus through the centuries, the one that sums up his historical appearance best is the one whose currency owes so much to Bultmann: Jesus is the Proclaimer of the Kingdom of God.

Having recognized this, the immediate question is that of determining what Jesus meant by his Kingdom of God proclamation, and this is a question to which New Testament scholarship has directed a major share of its attention in recent times. The present writer discussed it at length in his previous book[1] and does not propose, therefore, to repeat here either the review of the discussion in general or the evidence and arguments for some of the points of detail which are to be found in that work. However, a summary of the interpretation there offered will be given and where necessary modifications will be noted and other viewpoints discussed. In particular, crucial sayings will be rediscussed in accordance with the methodology outlined in the first chapter and in the light of recent contributions to the scholarly discussion.

[1] N. Perrin, *Kingdom*. For work on the Kingdom of God in the teaching of Jesus published since 1962 see Annotated Bibliography No. 4: Recent Work on the Kingdom of God.

So far as the actual meaning of the expression translated Kingdom of God (Hebrew: *malkuth shamayim* and its cognates and their Aramaic equivalents) is concerned there is no doubt but that the primary and essential reference is to the sovereignty of God conceived of in the most concrete possible manner, i.e. to his *activity* in ruling. We can see this in the contexts in which reference is made to God as king or to the Kingdom of God in the Old Testament. So, for example, the earliest reference is in Ex. 15.11–13, where the fact that God reigns is celebrated in a recital of what he has done to deliver Israel from Egypt. Absolutely characteristic, and crucial to a grasp of the real meaning of the expression, is the way in which Ps. 145.11f. uses as parallels to 'thy (God's) Kingdom' the expressions 'thy power' and 'thy mighty deeds'. The Kingdom of God is the power of God expressed in deeds; it is that which God does wherein it becomes evident that he is king. It is not a place or community ruled by God; it is not even the abstract idea of reign or kingship of God. It is quite concretely the activity of God as king. The English translation of Schnackenburg's *Gottes Herrschaft und Reich* expresses it very well: it '. . . is characterized not by latent authority but by the exercise of power, not by an office but a function. It is not a title but a deed.'[1] It is an idea absolutely impossible to express in any one English word: 'reign' or 'kingship' would be too abstract and 'theocracy' puts the emphasis in the wrong place. Perhaps 'rule' or, better, the active participle 'ruling' would come nearest to the original, but constant reference to the 'ruling of God' would be both clumsy and subject to the facetiousness of reading the genitive as a genitive of object! Since any English word is wrong, we have preferred to retain the familiar 'Kingdom', but to capitalize it to indicate that we are using it as a proper name to designate the *malkuth shamayim* which Jesus proclaimed and not in its normal English sense.

The Kingdom of God is, of course, for the Jew an everlasting Kingdom: God always was, is, and always will be king, and the activity wherein he manifests himself as such is everlastingly to be experienced and expected. The two passages from the Old Testament quoted above both end on this motif, Ex. 15.18; Ps. 145.13. It is also found in apocalyptic, e.g. this verse from the Psalms of Solomon which we quote as a typical example from a time very near to that of Jesus:

[1] R. Schnackenburg, *God's Rule and Kingdom* (ET by John Murray; New York: Herder and Herder, 1963), p. 13.

Ps. Sol. 17.3. But we hope in God, our Saviour;
For the might of our God is forever with mercy,
And the Kingdom of our God is forever over the nations in judgment.

And it is common in rabbinical writings, e.g. Targum of Onkelos on Ex. 15.18 which has 'God . . . his kingdom (*malkuthēh*) endures for ever' for the 'God will reign for ever and ever' of the MT.[1] But it also comes to be regarded as an eschatological Kingdom. It is with this development that we are particularly concerned, since Jesus certainly proclaimed the *eschatological* Kingdom of God. To summarize what we have argued in more detail elsewhere,[2] it is in the message of the prophets that we first meet this conception, for it is in their message that we find the idea of a future act of God which will be decisive for the salvation of the people in a way in which his past acts on their behalf were not. This future act of God is conceived in terms analogous to those used of his past acts, but different in that it will be final and decisive, the last and completely effective act, and thus it is the eschatological act of God. So we may speak of a new or eschatological covenant (Jeremiah) or of a new or eschatological Exodus (Deutero-Isaiah), and so on. Naturally we find here references to God acting as king (Micah 2.12f.; 4.1–7; Isa. 24.21–23; 33.22; 52.7–10; Zeph. 3.14–20; Obad. 21), and it is here, therefore, that we have the beginning of the concept of the eschatological Kingdom of God: the eschatological Kingdom of God is that final and decisive act of God wherein he manifests himself as king as he visits and redeems his people. As time went on and the concept developed, all kinds of pictures and ideas were associated with it, especially in the apocalyptic literature: the transformation of the earth, the end of history, the resurrection of the dead, and many others. But none of these ideas are essential to the nature of the expectation as an eschatological expectation; what is essential to that is the idea of a last, decisive, all-transforming act of God on behalf of his people. All the particular forms in which we find this expressed are simply varied attempts to express the essentially inexpressible, and all the myths and symbols

---

[1] Taken from G. Dalman, *The Words of Jesus* (hereinafter *Words*) (ET by D. M. Kay of *Die Worte Jesu*; Edinburgh: T. & T. Clarke, 1902), p. 96, where further rabbinical references are given.

[2] N. Perrin, *Kingdom*, pp. 160–8, with heavy dependence upon Gerhard von Rad, *Theologie des Alten Testaments: II Die Theologie der prophetischen Überlieferungen Israels*; München: Chr. Kaiser Verlag, 1960; ET by D. M. G. Stalker is now available as *Old Testament Theology: II The Theology of Israel's Prophetic Traditions*; Edinburgh and London: Oliver and Boyd, 1965.

associated with it in the literature are simply being pressed into the service of this attempt. When we say, then, that Jesus proclaimed the eschatological Kingdom of God, we mean that he proclaimed the final and decisive activity of God in visiting and redeeming his people; no particular form of this activity is necessarily implied and no particular accompanying phenomena must necessarily be present. Indeed, in view of the extraordinary variety of forms in which this concept is expressed in ancient Judaism, and the endless variety of phenomena expected to be a feature of its manifestation,[1] there could be no particular form or content necessarily implied by a proclamation such as 'the Kingdom of God is at hand'; each hearer would supply his own, and it would be up to the proclaimer to make clear in what terms he conceived of the eschatological activity of God as king, which, as we shall see, is what Jesus did.

The best and most important evidence for the currency of the eschatological Kingdom of God expectation at the time of Jesus and its lack of definite form is the Kaddish prayer of the ancient synagogue. This prayer is in Aramaic and certainly was in use at the time of Jesus, forming then, as now, an integral part of the regular synagogue worship. Indeed, it may very well have been known to Jesus, since the first two petitions of the Lord's Prayer appear to be a significantly modified version of it. In a translation by the present writer of the oldest text as reconstructed by G. Dalman, it runs: 'Magnified and sanctified be his great name in the world which he has created according to his will. May he establish his kingdom in your lifetime and in your days and in the lifetime of all the house of Israel even speedily and at a near time.'[2] The parallel between this and the 'Hallowed be thy name, thy Kingdom come' of the Lord's Prayer is so marked that it is difficult to conceive of it as accidental. Moreover, the changes from wordiness to brevity, and from the impersonal third person to the personal second, are absolutely in accord with the differences between the Lord's Prayer and other first-century Jewish prayers noticeable throughout the former. It is entirely reasonable to suppose that 'May he establish his kingdom' and 'Thy kingdom come' represent essentially the same hope, the one characteristic of first-century Judaism in general and the other of Jesus in particular.

[1] Illustrated in N. Perrin, *Kingdom*, pp. 164–7.
[2] Originally given in N. Perrin, *Kingdom*, p. 19. This version is not, in fact, significantly different from that used regularly today in Jewish worship, which illustrates the conservative tendency of liturgical texts.

But if this is the case, then a difference becomes immediately apparent: the one speaks of the kingdom being 'established', the other of its 'coming'. Is this difference significant?

Liturgical prayers are usually very carefully composed and it would be strange if this were not the case here. Further, the difference is characteristic in that ancient Jewish texts normally use a verb such as 'to establish' in connection with the kingdom, very rarely 'to come'.[1] What 'comes' in the ancient Jewish texts is not the Kingdom but the New Age.[2] The opposite is the case in the teaching of Jesus where the Kingdom is regularly spoken of as 'coming', e.g. Matt. 12.28 par.; Luke 17.20f., but never as being 'established' or 'manifest'.

This point is so important that we must make it in some detail. The immediate background to Jesus' use of Kingdom of God is certainly the use in the ancient Jewish prayers and in the apocalyptic literature.[3] In both cases we can see the same significant difference. The Kaddish prayer, as we saw, uses Kingdom, but with the verb 'establish', not 'come'. Two other ancient prayers, the eleventh of the Eighteen Benedictions, from the period before the destruction of the Temple in AD 70, and the Alenu prayer, probably from the third century AD, both use a form of the verb *mlk*, 'to reign, be king', with God as the subject. In the apocalyptic literature the Kingdom 'is forever over the nations' (Ps. Sol. 17.3), 'shall appear' (Sib. Orac. 3.46f.; As. Mos. 10.1) or God 'will raise up his Kingdom' (Sib. Orac. 3.767), but it is never referred to as 'coming'. Also, as in the prayers, there are references to God appearing as king, usually, of course, expressed elliptically, e.g. 'the Lord will appear' (Jub. 1.28); 'the Heavenly One will arise from his royal throne' (As. Mos. 10.3; cf. v. 7: 'he will appear'). See further: I Enoch 1.3, 9; 102.3; IV Ezra 8.51; Apoc. Bar. 21.23, 25. The teaching of Jesus, on the other hand, not only regularly uses the verb 'to come' in connection with the Kingdom and avoids the other verbs more characteristic of ancient Judaism, it also never speaks of God 'appearing' as king as do the Jewish texts. While Jesus is concerned with essentially the same eschatological hope as is

---

[1] G. Dalman, *Words*, p. 107, gives only one example and that from a Targum on Micah 4.8, which is late and where the presence of the verb is certainly due to the Hebrew original. We have not found another example ourselves.

[2] E.g. Apoc. Bar. 44.12; G. Dalman, *Words*, p. 107.

[3] That there is a close relationship between the teaching of Jesus and Jewish apocalyptic in this matter is the consensus of contemporary scholarship reached after half a century of vigorous discussion. See N. Perrin, *Kingdom, passim*, but especially pp. 158f.

found in the ancient prayers and apocalyptic literature, both in preferring 'Kingdom' to direct references to God[1] and also in using the verb 'to come' in connection with the Kingdom, he differs significantly from his immediate background.

On these points, however, not only does Jesus differ from ancient Judaism—the early Church also differs from him. Outside the synoptic gospels we never find the verb 'to come' used with Kingdom,[2] for what is to come, in the view of the early Church, is not the Kingdom but the Lord Jesus (I Cor. 16.22; Rev. 22.20) and, especially, of course, the Lord Jesus as Son of man, whereas we do find the verb 'to reign' with God as subject, albeit only in the book of Revelation (11.17).

There is a further difference between Jesus and ancient Judaism in respect to their usages of Kingdom of God, a difference hinted at above where we called attention to the fact that in the Jewish texts it is not the Kingdom that 'comes' but the New Age. The Jewish expectation was of the eschatological activity of God, of a final and decisive intervention by God in history and human experience whereby his people would be redeemed. As such, it was also an eager anticipation of the blessings, joy, and peace which would thereby be secured for them. They looked for the activity of God and they anticipated the blessings that would thereafter be theirs. These blessings could be conceived of in a hundred different ways,[3] and the state of things in which they would be enjoyed could be given many different names. Gradually, however, one term became dominant; the future blessed state came more and more to be called the 'age to come', and this became, therefore, '. . . a comprehensive term for the blessings of salvation . . .'[4] Now, in the teaching of Jesus, this term has no secure place,[5] but the same function is served by 'Kingdom of God', which is clearly used by Jesus to denote the blessings secured to men by God's intervention;[6] 'Kingdom of God' is Jesus' 'comprehensive term for the blessings of salvation',[7] and although

---

[1] The expression 'Kingdom of God' is in fact surprisingly rare in the apocalyptic literature. See N. Perrin, *Kingdom*, p. 168.

[2] In Rev. 12.10, which RSV translates, 'Now the salvation . . . and the Kingdom of our God . . . have come', the verb is not *erchomai* or *phthanō* but *ginomai*.

[3] N. Perrin, *Kingdom*, pp. 166ff.   [4] G. Dalman, *Words*, p. 135.

[5] N. Perrin, *Kingdom*, p. 164, n. 1.

[6] *Ibid.*, pp. 178–85. References will be given below.

[7] This parallel between Jesus' use of 'Kingdom of God' and the Jewish use of 'age to come' was first pointed out by G. Dalman, *Words*, p. 135, and attention has been called to it many times since then, e.g. recently by S. Aalen, ' "Reign" and "House" in the Kingdom of God in the Gospels', *NTS* 8 (1961/2), 227.

this use of the term is possible in Judaism,[1] it is there rare and quite untypical.

According to the evidence of the synoptic tradition, therefore, Jesus may be said to use 'Kingdom of God' in two ways, both derived from the eschatological expectation which begins in prophecy and continues through apocalyptic: he uses it in reference to God's decisive intervention in history and human experience and he uses it in reference to that state secured for the redeemed by this intervention. In this he differs from Judaism, especially by making normative for his teaching the second usage which is rare and untypical in Judaism. We have to ask now whether these differences are characteristic of Jesus or of the early Church. Pursuing our criterion of dissimilarity, we must seek to determine whether these elements of difference between the synoptic tradition and Judaism are also differences between the synoptic tradition and the remainder of the New Testament. We note at once that outside the synoptic tradition there is no place in the New Testament where Kingdom of God is used in the first of the ways noted above, and very few where it is used in the second. Moreover, where it is used in the second way, there are still differences from the synoptic tradition. Since this point is crucial to our argument, we must list the occurrences and our interpretation of them.

John 3.3, 5

Here the term is being used as in the synoptic tradition to denote the blessings of salvation and is equivalent to eternal life, cf. 3.36. The verb 'to enter' (v. 5) in this context is quite in the synoptic manner, but 'to see' (v. 3), although a good Jewish and New Testament idiom for experiencing something, e.g. Luke 2.26 (death); Acts 2.27 (corruption); I Peter, 3.10 (good days), is never used with Kingdom of God in the synoptic tradition. The most reasonable explanation is that we have here a traditional saying of the synoptic type partially translated into a Johannine idiom. This is the only place where John uses Kingdom of God; he normally prefers eternal life, an equivalent term for the blessings of salvation.

Acts 1.3, 6; 8.12; 14.22; 19.8; 20.25; 28.23, 31

The majority of these references are to 'proclaiming' the Kingdom (using several different verbs), where Kingdom of God is equivalent to the Christian message (1.3; 8.12; 19.8; 20.25; 28.23, 31). This is a

---

[1] N. Perrin, *Kingdom*, pp. 178–81.

characteristically Lukan usage, e.g. Luke 9.11, cf. Mark 6.34 (Jesus);
Luke 9.2, cf. Mark 6.7 (the Twelve); Luke 9.60, cf. Matt. 8.22 (part
of the challenge to discipleship). The other two echo traditional
usages of the Jewish and synoptic traditions respectively: 1.6 the
Jewish use as 'dominion' (e.g. 1QM xvii. 7), and 14.22 a use found in
the synoptic tradition, 'to enter the Kingdom'.

Pauline Corpus

Here there are several different uses. In I Cor. 4.20 it means the
Christian life, and in Col. 4.11 the Christian Church. In I Thess. 2.12
it is the sphere in which the grace and power of God are known, a
usage parallel to the 'Kingdom of the son of his love' in Col. 1.13, and
in II Thess. 1.5 it is the final blessed state which will be established at
the parousia and for which present sufferings are a preparation.
Further, there is a group of references to 'inheriting the Kingdom'
(I Cor. 6.9–10; 15.50; Gal. 5.21; Eph. 5.5) which exactly parallel a
common Jewish usage, except that there the synonyms 'age to come'
or 'eternal life' would be used rather than Kingdom of God, as, for
example, in the question in Mark 10.14 or the promise in Matt. 19.29.
There is only one reference to 'inheriting the Kingdom' in the synoptic tradition and that is in the context of the markedly Matthaean
parousia parable of Matt. 25.34. The best explanation of this group of
references would seem to be that Paul[1] is using the common Jewish
expression, but substituting Kingdom of God for the more normal
expression under the influence of the synoptic tradition. Finally, there
is a unique use in Rom. 14.17 where it refers to the Age to Come as
something enjoyed in an anticipatory manner in the present. Such an
understanding of the Spirit as bringing an anticipatory enjoyment of
the life of the Age to Come is markedly Pauline, cf. Rom. 8.23; Gal.
6.15, but the equivalence of Kingdom of God and joys of the Age to
Come is certainly parallel to the use of the Kingdom of God in the
synoptic tradition as a comprehensive term for the blessings of salvation. Here again, therefore, we may see an influence of the synoptic
tradition upon Paul in his use of the term, this time in connection
with the expression of an element typical of his theology.

Revelation

In the book of Revelation, as we would expect, we have the regular

---

[1] As always in such contexts, we are using names for convenience and without
prejudice as to the question of actual authorship, here of Ephesians.

idioms of Jewish apocalyptic: 11.17 has God as the subject of the verb 'to reign'; 11.15 is a summary allusion to the imagery of Dan. 7; and 12.10 is part of the verbal summary and interpretation of the regular apocalyptic myth of the War in Heaven.

It can be seen from the above that there are real differences between the synoptic tradition on the one hand and the remainder of the New Testament on the other, as far as the usage of Kingdom of God is concerned. The only places where anything like a usage parallel to those characteristic of the synoptic tradition are to be found are John 3.3, 5; Acts 14.22; and the references to inheriting the Kingdom or enjoying the blessings of the Age to Come in the Pauline corpus. Here we have some influence of the synoptic tradition on John, Luke (in Acts) and Paul. However, John normally prefers a different idiom; Paul is clearly indebted to Judaism rather than the synoptic tradition for his basic conception of 'inheriting' the blessings, and to his own theology for that of the Spirit bringing the anticipatory joys of the Age to Come; and the Acts reference is only one among eight.

These few instances, therefore, serve to emphasize the differences rather than to diminish them. When we add the obvious point that the term itself is very frequently to be found in the synoptic tradition and comparatively infrequently outside it, then it becomes clear that we are fully entitled to claim that the real and significant differences between the use within the synoptic tradition and outside it call for an explanation. A reasonable explanation is that usages of Kingdom of God characteristic of the teaching of Jesus and not of the early Church live on in the synoptic tradition. This does not mean, of course, that even in the Kingdom sayings the tradition suddenly becomes historically reliable. If the Church had not had her own use for the sayings, she would not have preserved them, and if they could not have been made expressive of his purposes, no evangelist would have used them. But it does mean that we are entitled to posit an original *Sitz im Leben Jesu* for Kingdom sayings and to regard as real the possibility of recovering an original form in some limited number of instances. In particular, we may note that there are three points at which the Kingdom teaching of the synoptic tradition tends to differ both from Judaism and from the early Church as represented by the remainder of the New Testament: in the use of the expression Kingdom of God for (1) the final act of God in visiting and redeeming his people and (2) as a comprehensive term for the blessings of salvation, i.e. things secured by that act of God, and (3) in speaking of the Kingdom as 'coming'. At these points it is reasonable to suppose that we have emphases deriving from the teaching of Jesus.

With this in mind, let us turn to a discussion of three crucial sayings: Luke 11.20 par.; Luke 17.20f.; Matt. 11.12. These are sayings for the authenticity of which it is possible to offer strong arguments, and they present the fundamental emphases of the teaching of Jesus concerning the Kingdom.

EXEGESIS I. LUKE 11.20 PAR.; LUKE 17.20F.; MATT. 11.12. KINGDOM SAYINGS

Luke 11.20 = Matt. 12.28

But if it is by the finger of God [Matt.: spirit of God] that I cast out demons, then the Kingdom of God has come upon you.

The present setting of this saying is editorial, as are all settings in the tradition, and in this instance the setting is at least as old as Q, since both Matthew and Luke use the saying and its setting in different ways: Matthew to interpret the exorcisms of Jesus as a present manifestation of the eschatological future, 'spirit' being 'in primitive Christianity, like the "first-fruits" (Rom. 8.23) or the "guarantee" (I Cor. 1.22) of the eschaton, a technical term for the present manifestation of the Kingdom';[1] and Luke to present an aspect of the ministry of Jesus which fulfils the purpose of that ministry as set out in Luke 4.18–21.[2] That it is Matthew who changed 'finger' to 'spirit' was argued by T. W. Manson[3] and the fact that 'spirit' is a favourite Lukan word makes it difficult to conceive of it having been changed by him into something else, especially in light of Luke 4.18.

The two verses, Matt. 12.27 and 28, cannot have originally stood together at this point, since the connection makes the activity of the Jewish exorcists also a manifestation of the Kingdom.[4] Further, the Matthaean form of the pericope bears marks of an original connection

---

[1] James M. Robinson, 'The Formal Structure of Jesus' Message', *Current Issues in New Testament Interpretation*, ed. William Klassen and Graydon F. Snyder (New York: Harper and Bros., and London: SCM Press, 1962), p. 101, n. 28 (on p. 279.)

[2] H. Conzelmann, *Theology of St Luke*, p. 107, n.2.

[3] T. W. Manson, *Teaching of Jesus*, pp. 82f.

[4] R. Bultmann, *History of the Synoptic Tradition*, pp. 14, 162.

between vv. 26 and 29[1] and certainly the narrative makes perfect
sense with the omission of vv. 27 and 28. So it may be that we must
reckon with an original tradition encompassing the present Matt.
12.25, 26, 29, 30, to which were added, probably at different stages,
vv. 27 and 28. Verse 28, therefore, with which we are particularly
concerned, must be regarded as having existed as an isolated logion
before it was inserted into its present context, and since, as we have
seen, the probability is that the Lukan version is nearer to the original
form, we must, in fact, regard the saying as having so existed in very
much the form it now has in Luke 11.20.

Considered as an isolated logion, the saying has high claims to
authenticity. '. . . it is full of that feeling of eschatological power
which must have characterized the activity of Jesus',[2] and it has two
of the hallmarks of the differences between the synoptic tradition and
Judaism and the early Church respectively, which we have argued
are derived from the teaching of Jesus: a use of Kingdom of God in
reference to the eschatological activity of God[3] and the use of the
verb 'to come' in connection with it. Further, the relating of the
presence[4] of the Kingdom to the present experience of a man is an
emphasis unparalleled in Judaism. The saying is, in fact, one of the
very few sayings in the tradition, the authenticity of which has not
been seriously questioned in more than half a century of intensive
discussion of Jesus' eschatological teaching. What has been in question is not its authenticity but its interpretation and, specifically,
whether it can be held to be evidence for an element in the teaching
of Jesus in which the Kingdom is regarded not merely as imminent
but as actually present.[5]

[1] Verse 26 'how will . . .' and v. 29 'how can. . . .' E. Klostermann, *Das
Matthäusevangelium* (Handbuch zum Neuen Testament 4 [Tübingen: J. C. B.
Mohr (Paul Siebeck), ²1927]), p. 243.

[2] R. Bultmann, *History of the Synoptic Tradition*, p. 162.

[3] S. Aalen, ' "Reign" and "House" . . .', *NTS* 8, 229ff., argues that the reference in this saying is not to the activity of God but to the Kingdom as a house, by
which he means an experience of deliverance and blessing: 'Kingdom of God means
also here deliverance, salvation' (p. 231). The difference is one of emphasis rather
than substance, for, if we recognize that Kingdom can refer to both the activity of
God and the blessings secured for man by that activity, and the present writer
would insist that this is the case, then we can read the saying either with the
emphasis upon the activity of God (Perrin) or upon the experience of deliverance
thereby secured (Aalen). It would be going too far to strike out the possibility of
either emphasis.

[4] Or, imminence of the Kingdom, see further immediately below.

[5] N. Perrin, *Kingdom, passim*. (See refs. to Matt. 12.28 in Index.)

We would argue, then, that Luke 11.20 represents a saying attributed to Jesus in the tradition, the authenticity of which may be regarded as established beyond reasonable doubt. Since there are very few such sayings in the tradition, it behoves us to derive as much as we reasonably can from this one with regard to the content and emphases of the teaching of Jesus.

But if it is by the finger of God that I cast out demons, then the Kingdom of God has come upon you.

The saying clearly implies a *Sitz im Leben Jesu*; it implies a practice of exorcism in the ministry of Jesus to which it refers. The evidence for exorcism as a feature of the ministry of Jesus is very strong indeed: exorcisms are to be found in every strata of the synoptic tradition, and the ancient Jewish texts regard Jesus as a miracle worker, i.e. an exorcist.[1] The present writer vividly remembers a conversation with Ernst Käsemann, at that time in Göttingen, in which that leading member of the 'Bultmann school' exclaimed that he had no choice, if he wished to remain a historian, but to accept the historicity of the tradition that Jesus was an exorcist. Today this would be a widely accepted consensus of critical opinion. This does not mean that we can diagnose the condition of the suffering people of ancient Galilee and Judea with whom Jesus dealt, nor does it guarantee the authenticity of any single account of an exorcism in the tradition, but it does mean that we can accept a ministry of exorcism as a *Sitz im Leben Jesu* for our saying.

If we accept the fact of Jesus' exorcisms and this saying as relating to them, then it follows that the saying *interprets* the exorcisms. The Beelzebul controversy which Mark (3.19–22) supplies as the context for his version of the tradition with which we are concerned may or may not be historical, but it is certainly evidence for the fact that in the first century exorcisms as such were comparatively meaningless until they were interpreted. So far as the historical circumstances of the ministry of Jesus are concerned, the exorcisms could only have

[1] J. Klausner, *Jesus of Nazareth* (New York: Macmillan, and London: Allen and Unwin, 1925), pp. 17–47. J. Jeremias, *The Eucharistic Words of Jesus* (ET by N. Perrin of *Abendmahlsworte Jesu* [³1960]; London: SCM Press, and New York: Scribner's, 1966), p. 19, n. 7, follows G. Dalman in regarding the most often quoted passage, b.Sanh.43a, as referring to someone other than Jesus, but even if this should be the case the cumulative effect of the other passages quoted by Klausner and the testimony of the Christian fathers (e.g. Justin Martyr, *Dial. cum Tryphone Judaeo* lxix; Origen, *Contra Celsum* I, 28) are sufficient to establish the point.

become significant to his purpose if they were accepted as manifestations of the Kingdom of God. As evidence that Jesus possessed magical powers, knew the right incantations or was on good terms with the prince of demons, they would be of most dubious worth! Hence, our saying is a saying designed to interpret something that happened in the ministry of Jesus so that it might become a challenging event to those who were confronted by it.

Treating this saying as an interpretation of the exorcisms, we should note that it interprets them in terms of an Old Testament text, for the reference to 'finger of God' is an allusion to Ex. 8.15,[1] as T. W. Manson pointed out.[2]

In recent times a flood of light has been thrown on this practice of interpreting experienced events in terms of Old Testament texts by the discoveries at Qumran, where it is a regular feature of the literature, especially in the *pesharim*. That a similar practice was a feature of early Christian theologizing is also clear,[3] and this raises the question of whether or not this instance should also be ascribed to the early Church. Against this, however, there are the strong reasons noted earlier for accounting this saying as authentic, and the consideration that no similar use of Ex. 8.15 is to be found elsewhere in the New Testament.[4] So we are justified in recognizing that Jesus has availed himself of an Old Testament text in this interpretation of the exorcisms, and that, in addition, he has also probably alluded to an existing Jewish interpretation of that text. In Ex. 8.15 the Egyptian magicians confess to Pharaoh that the third plague (lice) is beyond their power to duplicate and therefore: 'This is the finger of God.' Midrash Exodus Rabbah 10.7 interprets this by saying: 'When the magicians saw that they could not produce the lice, they recognized immediately that the happenings (the plagues) were the work of God and not the work of demons.' This is strikingly apposite to the thought of Jesus' saying, and the fact that it is in the Midrash Rabbah cer-

---

[1] To understand it simply as an idiom used in exorcism narratives in the ancient world would be wrong. It is true that 'finger of God' has been found in magical texts, but there it is part of an oath ('I adjure . . . by the finger of God that he open not his mouth', in A. Deissmann, *Light from the Ancient East* [ET by Lionel R. M. Strachan of *Licht vom Osten*; London: Hodder & Stoughton, 1927], p. 306), not an exorcism formula.

[2] T. W. Manson, *Teaching of Jesus*, pp. 82f.

[3] See, above all, B. Lindars, *New Testament Apologetic*, 1961. We mentioned this work in our first chapter, above, pp. 23f.

[4] We shall have occasion to note below that the case is very different in connection with the use of Dan. 7.13.

tainly does not preclude the possibility that the tradition goes back to the first century. Certainly the thought of the saying is: 'This is not the work of demons, but of God, and if God is at work in this manner, then you are even now experiencing the New Exodus: the Kingdom of God has come upon you.'

The suggestion that the use of an Exodus text implies an allusion to the New Exodus may or may not be justified, but there can be no doubt that the saying does refer to the exorcisms as an experience of the eschatological activity of God. The hotly debated question as to whether this implies that the Kingdom is to be regarded as present, inbreaking, dawning, casting its shadows before it, or whatever, becomes academic when we realize that the claim of the saying is that certain events in the ministry of Jesus are nothing less than *an experience* of the Kingdom of God. As the present writer claimed in his previous work,[1] we are here moving in the world of a holy-war theology such as we find at Qumran, where references to God and his Kingdom are to be found in the context of the eschatological conflict of the 'War of the Sons of Light against the Sons of Darkness'. When an exorcism is a manifestation of the Kingdom of God, then that Kingdom is manifested in terms of a conflict between good and evil, between God and Satan, between the Sons of Light and the Sons of Darkness. The Kingdom is not only God acting; it is God acting in a situation of conflict.[2]

The parallel here between the teaching of Jesus and the eschatological-conflict expectations of the Qumran community should not blind us to an all-important difference: an exorcism may be a manifestation of a victory of God in an eschatological-conflict situation, but it is also the experience of an individual. The victory of God is resulting not in the restoration to a state of purity of the land Israel and its people, but in the restoration to wholeness of a single disordered individual. The experience of the individual, rather than that of the people as a whole, has become the focal point of the eschatological activity of God. As we shall see, this concentration upon the individual and his experience is a striking feature of the teaching of Jesus, historically considered, and full justice must be done to it in any interpretation of that teaching.

[1] N. Perrin, *Kingdom*, p. 171.
[2] For a detailed study of the proclamation of Jesus from this perspective, set in the context of a thorough study of the Qumran material, see Jürgen Becker, *Das Heil Gottes* (Studien zur Umwelt des Neuen Testaments 3 [Göttingen: Vandenhoeck & Ruprecht, 1964]), esp. pp. 197–217.

The next saying we must discuss is Luke 17.20f., the discussion of which has produced a literature in its own right.[1]

Luke 17.20f.

[20]Being asked by the Pharisees when the Kingdom of God was coming he answered them, 'The Kingdom of God is not coming with signs to be observed; [21]nor will they say, "Lo, here it is!" or "There" for behold, the Kingdom of God is in the midst of you.'[2]

The saying as it stands in Luke serves a function in terms of the evangelist's theology, and especially in terms of his eschatology.[3] It is the first of four places where teaching is given in response to a question about the End: Luke 17.20; 19.11; 21.7; Acts 1.6. In 17.20f. the general apocalyptic-type expectation is denied, but this is followed by a reiteration of the traditional Christian hope in the form of waiting for an End, the coming of which cannot be prognosticated, vv. 22–37. The parable following 19.11 develops this theme in that it instructs the Christians to settle down to the long haul of history in the general context of an ultimate parousia, a parousia which, however, is clearly receding both in time, so far as the Lukan hope is concerned, and in importance for the Lukan theology. The teaching following 21.7 is designed to combat false hopes that the End is to be expected in connection with the fall of Jerusalem, and is here preserved by Luke because it is in agreement with his general anti-apocalyptic thrust. Acts 1.6 introduces teaching from the risen Lord in which Luke's own particular conception of the Kingdom is presented.

The fact that Luke 17.20f. serves a function in terms of the Lukan theology does not, of course, mean that it is a Lukan construction; the next question to ask is whether it existed in the tradition before Luke. Clearly, it is a saying without direct parallels in the other gospels; yet there are parallels to various parts of it: Mark 13.21 (par. Matt. 24.23): 'And then if any one says to you, "Look, here is the Christ!" or "Look, there he is!" do not believe it.' This is parallel to Luke 17.21a, and Luke omits this Markan verse at that point in his own narrative, presumably because he recognizes that he already has it in 17.21a, and he wishes to avoid duplication. It would be quite in

---

[1] See Annotated Bibliography No. 5: Literature on Luke 17.20f.

[2] In what follows we assume the previous discussion of the saying in N. Perrin, *Kingdom*, pp. 174–8. What is said here is to be regarded as supplementing that previous discussion.

[3] In what follows we are indebted in part to H. Conzelmann, *Theology of St Luke*, pp. 120–5.

keeping with the Lukan practice to prefer a version of a saying he found in another source to that of Mark, as, for example, he prefers the Q version of the teaching about divorce (Luke 16.18//Matt. 5.32) to that of Mark (10.1–12), which he omits. So the saying may come from a Lukan special source, which he has preferred to Mark in so far as there is duplication. But it could also be that Luke himself has created the saying, a hypothesis recently presented very vigorously by A. Strobel.

Strobel's argument is that the saying has been created by Luke to serve as an introduction to the following eschatological instruction to the disciples. As in 19.11 he introduces such instruction by a narrative verse reporting the disciples' supposition about the coming of the Kingdom, so here he creates a question and answer story to serve the same purpose. The answer is designed to refute the expectation, particularly held among the Pharisees (hence the Pharisaic interrogators) that the Messiah would come on the 'night of observation', i.e. the night of the Passover (Ex. 12.42). Indeed, Aquila uses the very word for observation in Luke 17.20 (*paratērēsis*) in his translation of Ex. 12.42, and certainly there is a Jewish tradition that the Messiah would come on that night.[1]

This is an original and interesting hypothesis, introducing a refreshingly new note into the discussion, but there are several considerations that can be urged against it. In the first place, it is by no means certain that the messianic expectation associated with Passover night is as old as it would have to be to meet the needs of this hypothesis. M. Black suggests that the expectation must be as old as Christianity, because it would have been difficult for it to have developed among the Jews after the Christians began to associate themselves with 15 Nisan, but he quotes an eminent Jewish authority (J. Weinberg) who gives reasons for doubting that it dates from before the destruction of the Temple.[2] Further, even if this form of expectation is early enough, there is absolutely no evidence that Luke knows either it or the Pharisees as especially concerned with it. In his account of the Passion there is no evidence that he knows or is concerned with Jewish Passover traditions, and he is inclined to see the Pharisees simply as those who believe in the Resurrection and

---

[1] A. Strobel in the works listed in Annotated Bibliography No. 5, especially the first.

[2] M. Black, *An Aramaic Approach to the Gospels and Acts* (Oxford: Clarendon Press, ²1954), pp. 173f.

the 'Beyond', and, in consequence, to present them sympathetically
(Acts 23.8).[1] Perhaps more telling than this, however, is a second
point, namely, that Luke 17.20f. is a vivid Pronouncement Story of
the type absolutely characteristic of the oral tradition.[2] It would be
possible for Luke to have constructed a story in writing that would
bear all the hallmarks of oral tradition, but it is unlikely. Then there
is a third point: the very real possibility that Thomas knows this
saying in a form independent of Luke. We discussed above the general
probability that Thomas is independent of the canonical gospel
tradition,[3] and now we must return to the point with specific reference to Luke 17.20f. In Thomas, we find two logia which bear some
resemblance to it: 3 and 113.[4]

> **Thomas 3.** Jesus said: 'If those who lead you say to you: "See, the
> Kingdom is in heaven", then the birds of the heaven will precede you.
> If they say to you: "It is in the sea", then fish will precede you. But the
> Kingdom is within you and it is without you. If you (will) know your-
> selves, then you will be known and you will know that you are the sons
> of the Living Father. But if you do not know yourselves, then you are in
> poverty and you are poverty.'

> **Thomas 113.** His disciples said to Him: 'When will the Kingdom
> come? [Jesus said:] It will not come by expectation; they will not say:
> "See, here", or: "See, there". But the Kingdom of the Father is spread
> upon the earth and men do not see it.'

In this logion, 'by expectation' translates the Coptic *gōsht ebol* and
this expression turns up again in logion 51:

> **Thomas 51.** His disciples said to Him: 'When will the repose of the
> dead come about and when will the new world come?' He said to
> them: 'What you expect (*gōsht ebol*) has come, but you know it not.'

We have, therefore, three logia related to one another, and two
of them to Luke 17.20f. So far as the interrelationship of the three

---

[1] H. Conzelmann, *Die Mitte der Zeit* (Tübingen: J. C. B. Mohr [Paul Siebeck],
[3]1960), p. 114, n. 1.

[2] Using the terminology of Vincent Taylor, *Formation of the Gospel Tradition*
(London: Macmillan, 1933), pp. 63–69; cf. R. Bultmann, *History of the Synoptic
Tradition*, pp. 56ff.

[3] See Chapter I above, pp. 35–37.

[4] The logia are numbered according to the publication of the text by A. Guillaumont *et al.*, *The Gospel According to Thomas*, 1959. The translation given in that
volume is also used.

Thomas logia are concerned, it seems fairly clear that 113 is less developed than 3. It still has the simple form of the question-answer, and the three elements of the Lukan saying, the two negations and the affirmation, are still present. The affirmation has changed its form, but not in any aggressively gnosticizing manner. The reference to the Kingdom 'spread upon the earth' is perhaps a reference to the mysterious 'sign of extension' referred to in second-century literature, e.g. *Didache* 16.6 and Justin, *Apol.* i. 55 (referring to it as the shape of the cross present in nature).[1] This reference to the Kingdom being spread upon the earth has replaced the *entos hymōn* reference in the Lukan version. Logion 3 is a much more highly developed and gnosticized version of the saying; the question and the two negations have disappeared, and in their place we have, in fact, a highly developed gnostic midrash on the original affirmation, the Kingdom is *entos hymōn*. The original negations have come together and have been developed out of recognition; only the reference to 'seeing', and the fact that the reference is to seeking the Kingdom, preserves their memory. The fact that this saying has concentrated upon the *entos hymōn* and logion 113 lost it would seem to indicate that they are independent developments from the original saying. Logion 51, on the other hand, is clearly a development from logion 113: it has the same expression, *gōsht ebol*, which, indeed, has become the central theme, the original affirmation having disappeared and the Kingdom question having been replaced by that of the 'repose of the dead'.

We are concerned then with logia 3 and 113 as independent versions of the Lukan saying. But are they dependent upon the saying as it stands in Luke? Logion 3 is dependent upon a version with a negation that can be translated into Coptic by *gōsht ebol*. If that were a translation of *meta paratērēseōs*, our question would be settled, but the fact is that it is not. Neither the Sahidic nor Bohairic versions of the Coptic New Testament use it in this way; indeed, in the Coptic New Testament it translates the *apokaradokian* ('eager expectation') of Phil. 1.20, not the *paratērēseōs* of Luke 17.20. The Coptic versions of the New Testament and Thomas logion 113 lead us to look for an expression that can be translated both 'with observation' (Luke 17.20) and 'by expectation' (Thomas 113), and that search takes us not to the Greek *paratērēsis*, but to the Aramaic *ḥwr*, which can have these two

---

[1] Robert M. Grant, *The Secret Sayings of Jesus* (New York: Doubleday, and London: Fontana, 1960), p. 190.

meanings.[1] So we move behind the Greek of Luke 17.20 to an Aramaic tradition which has been variously translated, and we must necessarily conclude that Thomas 113 is not, in fact, dependent upon Luke 17.20, but upon a tradition upon which Luke also is dependent. Luke 17.20f. had, then, at one time an Aramaic form and is not, therefore, a creation by Luke, writing in Greek and drawing upon vv. 22f. Minor support for this thesis is to be found in the difficult *entos*, which can mean either 'in' or 'among'. Such an ambivalent word naturally raises the question of the possibility that we are here dealing with translation Greek. It is not that there is a word in Aramaic that expresses the same ambivalence, but rather that the phrase is very clumsy in Greek, and being clumsy in Greek is not something of which one would normally accuse Luke.

We have argued this point in detail because with our view of the nature of the synoptic tradition we must necessarily move with great care. Even now the case is not iron-clad—nothing in this area can be—but we would claim that it is reasonable to assume a basic (Aramaic) saying which belongs to the earliest strata of the tradition and is used by Luke. If this is the case, then such a presumed saying has high claims to authenticity, for it has characteristics which, as we argued above, belong to the teaching of Jesus: it speaks of the Kingdom clearly referring to God's decisive intervention in history and human experience, and it speaks of that Kingdom as 'coming'. There is, therefore, no good reason to deny its authenticity and, in fact, there is a wide consensus of critical scholarship today that it is a genuine saying of Jesus, Strobel's being the only significant voice raised against it in the recent discussion.

So far as the interpretation of the saying is concerned, there is general agreement that the 'not with observation' denies the possibility of the usual kind of apocalyptic speculation, and the present writer claimed earlier,[2] and would still claim, that this means that here there is a denial of the apocalyptic concept of history and a return to the prophetic. The apocalyptic seers regarded history as a whole running a pre-determined course to a foreordained conclusion, hence, the very possibility of 'signs', and they understood God as to be known in the totality, the whole course of events. The prophets, on the other hand, looked for the activity of God in specific events,

---

[1] Suggested by G. Quispel, 'Some Remarks on the Gospel of Thomas', *NTS* 5 (1958/9), 276–90, here p. 288.
[2] N. Perrin, *Kingdom*, pp. 176ff.

tending to regard history as an arena in which God 'acted'. Jesus here seems to be negating the first of these conceptions and modifying the second. He is negating the first by denying the very possibility of 'signs'; the Kingdom is not of such a nature that a sign visible in terms of the totality of world events or the externals of history or the cosmos will mark its presence; God is not to be seen at work in the clash of heavenly bodies or of earthly armies. He is modifying the second because the activity of God as king is to be known, not in such a way that men can say 'Lo, here!' or 'Lo, there!' but rather as *entos hymōn*.

The difficulty with these two elements in the saying is twofold: the integrity of the 'Lo, here,' 'Lo, there' reference[1] and the meaning of *entos hymōn*. The difficulty with the 'Lo, here' 'Lo, there', reference is that it has both been translated from Aramaic and also become part of the stock in trade of early Christian apocalyptic (Mark 13.21 par.), so that it is no longer possible to say with any degree of certainty what the original reference was. But in light of *entos hymōn* and Luke 11.21, it is possible to hazard a guess. Intensive discussion of the linguistic aspects of the meaning of *entos hymōn* have been inconclusive: the Greek can mean both 'within you' and 'among you',[2] and the same is true of the Hebrew equivalent *beqereb*, while in Aramaic there are two distinct prepositions, *byny* (with pronominal suffix, as in our saying), 'among', and *bgw* (with pronominal suffix), 'within'. The fact that the original translator has chosen *entos* to translate the Aramaic does not help. Although in the LXX this normally translates prepositions meaning 'within',[3] it can also translate one meaning 'among' and, indeed, Aquila twice translates *bqrbnw* ('among us') by *entos hēmōn*.[4] So we must turn to more general considerations, and here

[1] We do not find the future tense in this part of the saying ('nor will they say') in contrast to the later present ('is *entos hymōn*') a difficulty, as does, for example, C. G. Montefiore, *The Synoptic Gospels* (London: Macmillan, ²1927) II, 547. In the first place, it is impossible to know what the tense was in the original Aramaic; secondly, the tension may be Lukan, for Luke certainly believed that the Kingdom was both present in Jesus' ministry (4.21) and to come (9.27); and, thirdly, the future tense may be due to the 'then' in the parallel Mark 13.21 ('and *then* if anyone says to you . . .').

[2] W. G. Kümmel, *Promise and Fulfilment* (ET by Dorothea M. Barton of *Verheissung und Erfüllung* [³1956] [Studies in Biblical Theology 23]; London: SCM Press, 1957), p. 33, with full references.

[3] E.g. Ps. 108 (MT 109): 22 (*bqrb*); Song of Sol. 3.10 (*twk*).

[4] Ex. 17.7; 34.9. F. Field, *Origenis Hexaplorum* (Oxford: Clarendon Press, 1875) I, 111, 144. J. A. Baird, *The Justice of God in the Teaching of Jesus* (Philadelphia: Westminster Press, and London: SCM Press, 1963), p. 173, appears to have overlooked these references.

there are two that are decisive: (1) the translation 'within you' would give us a meaning and usage completely without parallel elsewhere in the teaching of Jesus concerning the Kingdom; and (2) in the Oxyrhynchus Papyrus-Gospel of Thomas tradition, where 'within you' is certainly understood, the saying has to be recast to make this meaning unambiguous.[1] We must therefore, with the great majority of contemporary exegetes, understand: 'the Kingdom is among you.' When we add to this the understanding of the teaching of Jesus reached in connection with Luke 11.20 above,[2] we may claim that the meaning is: 'the Kingdom is a matter of human experience.' It does not come in such a way that it can be found by looking at the march of armies or the movement of heavenly bodies; it is not to be seen in the coming of messianic pretenders.[3] Rather, it is to be found where-ever God is active decisively within the experience of an individual and men have faith to recognize this for what it is.[4]

Matt. 11.12

This is the third and last individual saying that we shall discuss in this context.

> From the days of John the Baptist until now, the Kingdom of heaven has suffered violence (*biazetai*), and men of violence (*biastai*) plunder it (*harpazoysin*) (RSV: take it by force; NEB: are seizing it).[5]

The parallel in Luke reads:

> **Luke 16.16.** The law and the prophets were until John; since then the good news of the Kingdom of God is preached, and every one enters it violently (*biazetai*).

This is generally regarded as secondary in comparison to the Mat-

---

[1] N. Perrin, *Kingdom*, pp. 174–6. The only two recent attempts to return to the meaning 'within you' are by R. Sneed, 'The Kingdom of God is Within You', *CBQ* 24 (1962), 381, and J. A. Baird, *The Justice of God in the Teaching of Jesus*, pp. 169–78. The former mentions it only in passing and does not discuss any evidence or arguments. The latter has an elaborate argument, but it is so full of phrases such as 'the Kingdom (is) potentially . . . an inner spiritual dimension', and 'this new dimension of soul', that it is difficult to take it seriously, and it also appears to be wrong on a crucial linguistic point (see above, p. 73 n. 4).

[2] pp. 63–67.

[3] This is only a guess at the meaning behind the 'Lo, here', 'Lo, there' reference, but in view of the actual use made of this reference in the Church, and the number of messianic revolts that took place in the half-century before AD 70, it is surely justified.

[4] We will return to 'faith' in this connection, below, pp. 130–42.

[5] The translation is by the present writer and the exegesis upon which it is based will be found in N. Perrin, *Kingdom*, pp. 171–4.

thaean version, and with good reason: the idea of one epoch ending with John and the phrase 'to preach the good news of the Kingdom of God' are both Lukan,[1] and the 'everyone enters it violently' smooths out the linguistic and theological problems of the Matthaean saying. This does not mean that Luke is here dependent upon Matthew, but only that he has edited a saying they have in common more drastically than has Matthew.

The saying itself is part of the tradition about John the Baptist and, as such, it is part of a tradition with a very special history, a history of a continuous 'playing down' of the role of the Baptist.[2] As the background to this tradition we have two hard facts: Jesus was baptized by John and he began his ministry only after John's had been brought to a violent end. These are certainly historical facts, because they both imply an element of dependence of Jesus upon the Baptist and they are inconceivable as products of a Christian community concerned to exalt its Lord and engaged in rivalry with a Baptist sect.[3] Thus, sayings which reflect a high estimate of the Baptist both stand in the earliest stratum of the tradition about him and reflect the attitude of Jesus rather than that of the early Church. There are three such sayings, all of which Dibelius regarded as authentic: Matt. 11.12f.; Matt. 21.32; Mark 11.27–30.[4]

On these grounds Matt. 11.12 has a very strong claim to authenticity: it stands in the earliest stratum of this particular tradition and it reflects the attitude of Jesus to John rather than that of the early Church, to which he was at best the Forerunner (Mark 9.11–13; Matt. 11.14). The authenticity of the saying has been disputed by Bultmann, who argues that it is a product of anti-Jewish or anti-Baptist polemics, probably the latter, since it relegates the Baptist to a bygone age.[5] But the saying does not, in fact, relegate the Baptist to a

---

[1] H. Conzelmann, *Theology of St Luke*, pp. 23ff., 40.

[2] This was convincingly demonstrated by M. Dibelius,, *Die urchristliche Überlieferung von Johannes dem Täufer*; Göttingen: Vandenhoeck & Ruprecht, 1911. On the validity of this analysis of the tradition, see James M. Robinson, *A New Quest of the Historical Jesus* (Studies in Biblical Theology 25 [London: SCM Press, 1959]), pp. 117f.

[3] For a recent judicious discussion of the evidence for the existence of a Baptist sect and its relations with the Christian community, see Charles H. H. Scobie, *John the Baptist* (London: SCM Press, and Philadelphia: Fortress Press, 1964), pp. 187–202.

[4] M. Dibelius, *Urchristliche Überlieferung von Johannes dem Täufer*, pp. 20–29.

[5] R. Bultmann, *Geschichte der synoptischen Tradition* ([5]1961), pp. 177f. The ET is here somewhat misleading, as, unfortunately, is the case only too often, in that it omits the reference to anti-Jewish polemic (p. 164).

bygone age; rather, the opposite is the case in that 'From (*apo*) the days of John the Baptist . . .' must be understood as including the Baptist in the present age, that of the Kingdom.[1] The saying, therefore, belongs to the positive sayings about the Baptist and as such would have to be rejected, on Bultmann's grounds, as having a *Sitz im Leben* in anti-Jewish polemic in the early Church.[2] But there is no evidence for this in our sources and there is, therefore, no good reason, on form-critical grounds, to dispute the authenticity of the saying.[3]

Accepting the saying as authentic, the first point to arise in connection with its interpretation is that it looks back upon the Baptist as one whose ministry marks the 'shift of the aeons'. This point has been stressed in the energetic discussion of the saying that has gone on within the 'Bultmann school'. Here the *Schüler* tend to disagree with the master (who argued that Jesus looked forward to this decisive event in the future, whereas Paul looked back upon it in the immediate past), in that they say that '. . . Jesus did in fact see in the coming of the Baptist the shift of the aeons'[4] and support this by an exegesis of Matt. 11.12. The first to do this was Ernst Käsemann in his seminal essay 'The Problem of the Historical Jesus',[5] where he argues in detail, and most convincingly, that in this saying Jesus is looking back over the completed Old Testament epoch of salvation and drawing the Baptist to his own side in presenting him 'as the initiator of the new aeon'.[6] Thus, we have again the clarion call of the

---

[1] E. Percy, *Die Botschaft Jesu* (Lunds Universitets Arsskrift, N. F. Adv. 1 Bd. 49 Nr. 5 [Lund: C. W. K. Gleerup, 1953]), p. 199. See also James M. Robinson, *New Quest of the Historical Jesus*, p. 117, n. 1.

[2] As indeed it is by E. Jüngel, the only recent contributor to the discussion to deny the authenticity of the saying, who argues that Matthew has set John on the side of Jesus 'aus antijüdischer Polemik' (*Paulus und Jesus* [Tübingen: J. C. B. Mohr (Paul Siebeck), [2]1964], p. 191). But this is '. . . a motivation for which he neither provides documentation nor explanation' (J. M. Robinson in his review of Jüngel's book, *Interpretation* 18 [1964], 357), and, moreover, the tendency in Luke to make John the end of one epoch of the *Heilsgeschichte*, and Jesus the beginning of another, is so well attested that we must assume that it is Luke and not Matthew who has made the change.

[3] J. M. Robinson, *New Quest of the Historical Jesus*, p. 117.

[4] *Ibid.*, p. 118. For a more detailed discussion of this aspect of the differences between Bultmann and the 'post-Bultmannian' see N. Perrin, *Kingdom*, pp. 112–24.

[5] E. Käsemann, *Essays on New Testament Themes*, pp. 15–47. We are concerned especially with pp. 42f., and it should be noted that on p. 42 'Matt. 11.25f.' is a misprint for 'Matt. 11.12f.'

[6] *Ibid.*, p. 43. Similarly G. Bornkamm, *Jesus of Nazareth* (ET by Irene and Fraser McLuskey with James M. Robinson; New York: Harper & Bros., 1960), p. 51: John '. . . belongs himself to the time in which the promise is being fulfilled'.

proclamation of the Kingdom of Jesus: Now is the time of God's decisive activity! Expressed in Luke 11.20 in terms of an interpretation of the exorcisms, in Luke 17.20f. in terms of a challenge to think in new ways about God manifesting himself as king, and here in terms of the concept of the history of God's activity on behalf of his people, it is always the same urgent challenge: Now is the time of fulfilment of promise.

So far as the remainder of the saying is concerned, the present writer has nothing to add to his previous discussion.[1] He is in complete agreement with E. Käsemann: the import of the logion is that 'the Kingdom of God suffers violence from the days of the Baptist until now and is hindered by men of violence'.[2] What we have here is the reverse of the situation envisaged in the interpretation of the exorcisms: there the Kingdom of Satan is being plundered, here that of God. What is envisaged is an aeon of conflict, of victory and defeat, of achievement and disappointment, of success and failure. It may be that the saying was originally inspired by the fate of the Baptist and that to this extent the present editorial setting is correct, but of this there can be no proof. One thing we may know, and it is strange and new, is that the intervention of God into human history is not only in terms of a conflict situation—this the apocalyptic seers envisaged—but it is also in terms of a conflict in which defeat as well as victory is a real, if not an ultimate, possibility.

Thus, this saying confirms what we have learned already from other sayings, namely, that the time of God's activity as king is now, and that the form of this activity can be envisaged in terms of conflict. But it also adds a strange, new note: the conflict can issue in defeat as well as victory. The outcome of the battle may be sure, but the casualties are going to be real, not sham.

EXEGESIS 2. MARK 2.18–22. ESCHATOLOGICAL SIMILES

We have seen that there are a small group of authentic sayings of Jesus which are eschatological pronouncements; they proclaim the presence of God manifesting himself as king in aspects of the ministry of Jesus. They are the very heart of the message of Jesus. Jesus understood the Kingdom of God as being manifest in his ministry; all else in his teaching takes its point of departure from this central,

[1] N. Perrin, *Kingdom*, pp. 171–4.
[2] E. Käsemann, *Essays on New Testament Themes*, p. 42.

awe-inspiring—or ridicule-inspiring, according to one's perspective—conviction. The conviction is manifest not only in the eschatological pronouncements to which we have referred, but also in a number of eschatological similes which are to be found in the teaching.

Jesus' use of metaphor, in the form of simile and analogy (the parables), is the best attested and surest documented feature of his teaching that we possess. As we pointed out in chapter I, above, it is here that the modern attempt to reconstruct his teaching has been most successful and, today, the best-known feature of that teaching is its incomparable use of simile and analogy. It is here that the clear vision of one mind, the depth of comprehension of one individual's vision and understanding, is most apparent. Nowhere else is the change from Jesus to the early Church more apparent. Having the tradition of similes and analogies of Jesus, but lacking the vision to maintain or understand them, she transformed them into allegories expressive of a post-Easter faith and reflecting a post-Easter situation. From our point of view, this was fortunate, because, if it had not happened, the tradition would have been lost to us. As it is, the pedestrian nature of the allegorizing, and the clear reflections of the post-Easter faith or situation, are easy to recognize and to remove.

The most significant of the eschatological similes are those found in Mark 2.18-22, a passage which divides naturally into two parts:

Mark 2.18-20. Now John's disciples and the Pharisees were fasting; and people came and said to him, 'Why do John's disciples and the disciples of the Pharisees fast, but your disciples do not fast?' [19]And Jesus said to them, 'Can the wedding guests fast while the bridegroom is with them? As long as they have the bridegroom with them, they cannot fast. [20]The days will come, when the bridegroom is taken away from them, and then they will fast in that day.'

Mark 2.21-22. No one sews a piece of unshrunk cloth on an old garment; if he does, the patch tears away from it, the new from the old, and a worse tear is made. [22]And no one puts new wine into old wineskins; if he does, the wine will burst the skins, and the wine is lost, and so are the skins; but new wine is for fresh skins.

The parallels in Matthew (9.14-17) and Luke (5.33-39) are dependent upon Mark. Two logia from Thomas are in some way related to this tradition: 104 and 47b.

Thomas 104. They said [to Him]: 'Come and let us pray today and let us fast.' Jesus said: 'Which then is the sin that I have committed, or in what have I been vanquished? But when the bridegroom comes out of the bridal chamber, then let them fast and let them pray.'

Thomas 47b. . . . No man drinks old wine and immediately desires to drink new wine; and they do not put new wine into old wineskins, lest they burst, and they do not put old wine into a new wineskin, lest it spoil it. They do not sew an old patch on a new garment, because there would come a rent.

Mark 2.18–20

Verse 18 is an editorial setting for the following sayings, and in itself has a somewhat complex history. The reference to the Pharisees has probably been added to make the story fit into the Markan sequence of pericopes of conflict between Jesus and the Pharisees, and the awkward 'disciples of the Pharisees' is almost certainly an imitation of the 'John's disciples'.[1] So originally the pericope circulated as a dispute between 'John's disciples' and 'your disciples', i.e. it reflected tension between Christians and members of the Baptist sect, and as such was given an appropriate introduction. But an editorial introduction tells us nothing about the age, authenticity or original context of the saying(s) to which it has been supplied, so we must consider vv. 19 and 20 independently of the introduction.

Verse 20 immediately falls under suspicion, since it seems to provide a reason for early Christian fasting, and, more importantly, it uses the allegory bridegroom = Jesus[2] and reflects upon the death of Christ. As reflection upon the cross, as using allegory, and as having a natural *Sitz im Leben der alten Kirche*, it is to be regarded as a product of the Church. But if v. 20 falls out, so does 19b, because the only reason for its existence is to serve as a transition to v. 20. Thus, we are left with the single, isolated saying: 'Jesus said (to them), "Can the wedding guests fast while the bridegroom is with them?"' or, as J. Jeremias[3] prefers to translate it, probably rightly: 'Can the wedding guests fast during the wedding?'

In this form the saying has high claims to authenticity. In the first place, the evidence of the New Testament as a whole is very

[1] So already J. Wellhausen, *Das Evangelium Marcus* (Berlin: Georg Reimer, 1903), p. 20. It should be noted that the RSV here given has smoothed over the awkwardness; the Greek reads: 'the disciples of John and the disciples of the Pharisees'.

[2] This allegory is itself a product of early Christian piety, arising out of the concept of the Church as the bride of Christ (II Cor. 11.2). In Judaism, the bridegroom is not a figure used of the Messiah (J. Jeremias, *Parables of Jesus* [rev. ed., 1963], p. 52).

[3] *Ibid.*, p. 52, n. 14.

strongly in favour of the assumption that Jesus and his disciples did not, in fact, fast during his ministry. The gospel traditions are unanimous on this point; the early Church has to give reasons for the practice of fasting (Mark 2.20; *Didache* 1.3), itself something demanding explanation, since fasting is such a normal feature of ancient piety; and the parables reflect a note of joyousness in which fasting would be quite out of place. Further, the allusion to the practice of not fasting during a wedding is an allusion to a well-documented ancient Jewish practice of freeing wedding participants, including the guests, from religious obligations during the seven days of the wedding celebrations.[1] Lastly, a joyous table-fellowship was a key element in the common life of Jesus and his followers, as will be argued below, and this gives the saying a natural *Sitz im Leben Jesu*.

As an authentic saying, this simile tells us a good deal about the ministry of Jesus. It tells us that Jesus regarded it as a time of release from normal religious obligations, a time of rejoicing, and since 'in the symbolic language of the East the wedding is the symbol of the day of salvation',[2] a time of the enjoyment of the fruits of God's decisive activity on man's behalf.

Mark 2.21–22

The various versions of this simile illustrate the characteristic developments of tradition where no particular theological motivation is at work. Luke, for example, adds a proverbial saying 'No one after drinking old wine desires new: for he says, "The old is good." '[3] In Thomas this sentiment has become the introduction to the simile and the simile itself has been 'completed', i.e. a new 'old wine/new wineskin' antithesis has been added to the original 'new wine/old wineskin', and this replaces the original comment, itself probably an addition in the tradition, of '. . . but new wine is for fresh skins'. The fact that tradition tends to grow by addition, and to 'complete' antitheses, puts the stamp of originality—and knowledge of the pitfalls facing the amateur Palestinian wine-maker—upon the simple 'new/old' of the Markan version. The 'patch/cloth' simile also has an element of homeliness in the Markan form which stamps it as original.

---

[1] References in Billerbeck, *Kommentar* I, 506.

[2] J. Jeremias, *Parables of Jesus* (rev. ed., 1963), p. 117.

[3] Luke 5.39. The verse is omitted by some 'western' authorities (D, Old Latin) and by Marcion, Irenaeus and Eusebius, which makes it possible that the addition was made in the textual tradition and complicates the problems of the relationship of Thomas to the canonical gospels.

One can readily imagine that in the days before Sanforization it was the height of housewifely folly to patch a garment that had been worn, wetted and shrunk with a piece of unshrunken cloth. The original simile, therefore, represents the kind of acute observation of Palestinian peasant life that is characteristic of the parables of Jesus. As the tradition developed, this acute observation is lost, because the tradition is no longer regarded as arising naturally from observation of life but as existing as a mysterious and powerful entity in its own right. So Luke loses the point altogether, thinking it has something to do with the incompatibility of new and old, and Thomas simply summarizes the simile without concern for the original point of departure in observation of life.

It is this quality of freshness and of acute and sympathetic observation of Palestinian peasant life which we may claim is characteristic of Jesus, since we have demonstrated that it is lost in the transmission of the tradition by the Church, and it marks these two similes as dominical. But if these similes are dominical, they tell us something quite startling about Jesus' understanding of his ministry: they tell us that Jesus regarded his ministry as marking a new point of departure quite incompatible with the existing categories of Judaism. The Jewish scholar C. G. Montefiore saw this quite clearly and was startled by it, 'The advanced radicalism of these rules or principles is very remarkable', but then proceeded to comfort himself by claiming that Jesus did not live up to them: '. . . but practically he does not apply them . . . so far as he is concerned, he holds fast to Judaism and the Old Testament.'[1] As we hope to show, Jesus' teaching in other respects is every bit as radical, in the context of first-century Judaism, as these similes lead one to expect. In any case, there is no doubt of the force and point of these similes: something new and different in the ministry of Jesus marks that ministry as bursting the bounds of late Judaism. In the light of the eschatological pronouncements we have already discussed this can only mean: the Kingdom of God is here!

There are other eschatological similes in the recorded teaching of Jesus[2] that could be regarded as authentic by the criterion of coherence, even though some of them, e.g. that of the shepherd, are so

[1] C. G. Montefiore, *The Synoptic Gospels* I (1927), 89.

[2] J. Jeremias, *Parables of Jesus* (rev. ed., 1963), pp. 115–24, discusses the many such similes that are found in the tradition without going particularly into the question of their authenticity.

close to both Judaism and the use of the early Church as to be suspect
on the criterion of dissimilarity. But there is no need here to labour
the matter, for the similes we have discussed are to be accepted as
authentic and they are sufficient to make the point. Jesus taught the
same thing both by proclamation and by simile: the decisive activity
of God as king is now to be experienced by men confronted by his
ministry in word and deed.

Having discussed the 'Kingdom' teaching of Jesus as we find it in
sayings and similes, we now turn to the most highly developed and
distinctive element in his teaching: the parables.

THE PARABLES OF THE KINGDOM: INTRODUCTION[1]

Modern discussion of the parables has established the fact that
their *Sitz im Leben Jesu* is his eschatology; they are concerned with the
Kingdom. As we pointed out in our first chapter, the first stage in the
decisive 'breakthrough' in the modern study of the parables was taken
in 1935 when C. H. Dodd published the first edition of his book, *The
Parables of the Kingdom*. The first half of this book was taken up by a
discussion of Kingdom of God in the teaching of Jesus, and the
second with setting the parables in the context of the results of that
discussion. Today, it is a commonplace to recognize this eschatological orientation of the parables. Indeed, the most recent study of
them, by E. Jüngel in his *Paulus und Jesus*, claims that the Kingdom
of God actually becomes a reality for the hearer of the parables in
the parables themselves, which are, by their nature as parable, peculiarly well designed to manifest the reality of the Kingdom as parable.[2]
Less ambitious, and for that reason more persuasive if less dramatic,
is the statement by A. Wilder that 'true metaphor or symbol is more
than a sign; it is a bearer of the reality to which it refers' and so the
parables are to the disciples '. . . Jesus' interpretation to them of his
own vision by the powers of metaphor'.[3]

Following Wilder's altogether persuasive statement of the matter,
we might say that the parables impart to their hearers something of
Jesus' vision of the power of God at work in the experience of the
men confronted by the reality of his proclamation, and this would be

[1] See Annotated Bibliography No. 6: Modern Research on the Parables.

[2] E. Jüngel, *Paulus und Jesus* ([2]1964), pp. 135–74; cf. J. M. Robinson, *Interpretation* 18 (1964), 351–6.

[3] Amos N. Wilder, *Language of the Gospel* (New York: Harper & Row, and
London: SCM Press [as *Early Christian Rhetoric*], 1964), pp. 92f.

true if we are allowed to stress the '*in the experience of the men confronted
. . .*' It is a remarkable and little noted fact that, *pace* Jüngel, there is
only a very limited number of parables which are concerned to proclaim the Kingdom of God *per se*. The vast majority of them are
concerned with the experience and/or subsequent activity of men
confronted by the reality of God at work. We would group the major
parables as follows:

1. Concerned to emphasize the joyousness with which the activity
of God may be experienced: Hid Treasure, Pearl.

2. Concerned to express the challenge of the major aspect of this
divine activity, the forgiveness of sins: Lost Sheep, Lost Coin,
Prodigal Son.

3. Concerned with the necessity for men to decide *now*: Great
Supper, Unjust Steward.

4. Concerned to warn against the danger of preconceived ideas
blinding one to the reality of the challenge: Labourers in the Vineyard, Two Sons, Children in the Market Place, Pharisee and the Tax
Collector.

5. Concerned to depict the various aspects and true nature of the
necessary response to the challenge: Good Samaritan, Unmerciful
Servant, Tower Builder, King Going to War.

6. Concerned to stress the confidence in God which the experience
of his activity should bring: Friend at Midnight, Unjust Judge.

7. Concerned to stress the confidence in God's future which the
experience of his activity in the present should bring: Sower, Mustard
Seed, Leaven, Seed Growing of Itself, Fish Net, Weeds in the Field.

It can be seen that only the parables in 1 and 2 may be said to be
concerned with proclaiming the Kingdom in the same sense that the
eschatological similes proclaim it. Groups 3 to 6 are concerned with
men's recognition of the challenge of this proclamation and response
to it; and group 7 is concerned with the future both as promise and as
threat. We will discuss groups 1 and 2 here, 3 to 6 in our next chapter,
and 7 in chapter IV. At the end of our discussion of 2 we will turn to
the acted parable of the 'table-fellowship of the Kingdom of God'.

Before we go on to discuss and interpret the parables, we must say
a word about the way in which they are to be interpreted. This we
propose to do by giving two examples which illustrate what we would

argue is the correct methodology. The first is a Jewish parable taken from the Mekilta, and typical, we would claim, of the form taken up and developed by Jesus himself. The second is from the synoptic tradition, and it is probably the only instance we have where we may be reasonably sure that the parable and that to which it originally referred are given in the same context in our tradition, and that the tradition at this point is authentic.

Mekilta on Ex. 20.2 (Lauterbach, II, 229f.)

I am the Lord thy God

Why are the Ten Commandments not said at the beginning of the Torah? They give a parable. To what may this be compared? To the following: A king who entered a province said to the people: 'May I be your king?' But the people said to him: 'Have you done anything good for us that you should rule over us?' What did he do then? He built the city wall for them, he brought in the water supply for them, and he fought their battles. Then when he said to them: 'May I be your king?' They said to him: 'Yes, yes.' Likewise, God. He brought the Israelites out of Egypt, divided the sea for them, sent down the manna for them, brought up the well for them, brought the quails for them, he fought for them the battle with Amalek. Then he said to them: 'I am to be your king.' And they said to him: 'Yes, yes.'

The crux of the matter here is that we have two parallel, analogous situations: a king in his dealings with the people of the province, and God in his dealings with the Israelites. It should be noted that the king is not God, and the people of the province are not the Israelites. If this were the case, then we would have allegory; but it is not the case and what we have is a comparison ('To what may this be compared?'), the hallmark of a parable, not hidden identity, the hallmark of an allegory. The story of the king is in itself natural. Kings did build city walls, bring in water supplies and fight battles for their people. In this way they demonstrated and maintained their power and right to rule. Similarly, God had done things for Israel in which he had demonstrated his kingship: as with the king, so with God. The secret in interpreting a parable, then, is to find the analogous situation and so come to understand the point of the comparison. Usually in the teaching of Jesus the analogous situation is implied but not stated, and the problem of interpretation is, therefore, the problem we would have with this Mekilta parable if it began: 'To what may we compare the Kingdom of God? It is a like king who entered a province . . .,' and ended '. . . May I be your king? They said to him: Yes, yes,' i.e. the problem of finding the analogous situation to which the parable refers.

Matt. 11.16–19

16But to what shall I compare this generation? It is like children sitting in the market places and calling to their playmates. 17'We piped to you, and you did not dance; we wailed, and you did not mourn.' 18For John came neither eating nor drinking, and they say, 'He has a demon'; 19the Son of man came eating and drinking, and they say, 'Behold, a glutton and a drunkard, a friend of tax collectors and sinners!' Yet wisdom is justified by her deeds.

The authenticity and unity of this parable and its application will be argued later, and at that point the significance of these for our understanding of the message of Jesus will be discussed.[1] At the moment our only concern is with the way in which the application, supplied by Jesus himself, gives us an insight into his parabolic method.

The first thing we have to do in this connection is to determine the situation referred to in the depiction of the children at play, for if we cannot do that, we cannot grasp the point on which the analogy turns. As is so often the case in matters of understanding references to Palestinian customs and circumstances, the expert witnesses here are Bishop and Jeremias.[2] According to their investigations, the reference is to part of a group of children who are sitting, wishing to play only a passive part in the games the whole group is playing. So they are prepared to pipe but not to dance (as the boys would when playing 'Weddings'), to wail but not to mourn (i.e. to beat their breasts, etc., as the girls would when playing 'Funerals'). The laziness of those who insist on sitting and 'leaving the more strenuous exercises for the others' (Bishop) has led to a quarrel, and in the course of this quarrel the lazy children try to blame the others for spoiling the play-time: 'We piped to you, and you did not dance; we wailed, and you did not mourn.'[3] It should be noted in passing that this is an exegesis of the

[1] See below, pp. 119–21.
[2] E. F. F. Bishop was for many years principal of the Newman School of Missions in Jerusalem. J. Jeremias lived in Jerusalem as a boy and has devoted a large part of his academic life and work to research into Palestinian Judaism at the time of Jesus.
[3] E. F. F. Bishop, *Jesus of Palestine* (London: Lutterworth Press, 1955), p. 104; J. Jeremias, *Parables of Jesus* (rev. ed., 1963), pp. 160ff.

Matthaean version of the parable. It is he, more knowledgeable than Luke in matters Palestinian, who has the more correct version of the parable.

The parable, then, turns on the behaviour of some of the members of a group of children who, characteristically, if not very admirably, blame others for something which is really their own fault. The parabolic method is such that there should be an analogous situation or group among those to whom Jesus is speaking and, if we had no application in the text, we would have to seek this group or situation for ourselves. But in this one instance, and probably in this one instance only, we do have a dominical application. The group who are like these children are those who find offence in John because he is an ascetic and rigorist, and in Jesus because he is not. Like the children who would pipe but not dance, wail but not mourn, they want everything to be in accordance with their wishes, desires and expectations, and when this does not work out, it is always someone else's fault.

This is the parabolic method of Jesus: to tell a story which turns upon a point which has its parallel or analogy within the experience of some of those to whom it is addressed. Once this central point of the parable is grasped, and the parallel or analogy found, then, and only then, does the message of the parable become clear. An interpretation of a parable is, therefore, essentially a search for this crucial point in it, and for its parallel or analogy in the situation of the ministry of Jesus or that of his hearers confronted by that ministry.

Again, we must stress the fact that a parable is a parable and not an allegory. The essence of a parable is that its story and situation should be realistic and natural; if this were not the case, then the central point could not be grasped and the parallel or analogy could never be found. The essence of an allegory, on the other hand, is that it can be as unnatural and complex as the allegorist cares to make it, since it has no central point and is intended to refer to no parallel or analogy, but always needs a key to be understood.

The parables of Jesus are almost never provided with an application in the tradition; the one we have just discussed is an exception to the rule and the esoteric explanations of the parables in the tradition make the parables allegories and are certainly not from Jesus.[1]

---

[1] See J. Jeremias, *Parables of Jesus* (rev. ed., 1963), *passim*. The three arguments against the authenticity of the allegorizing explanations are: (1) they use the language and concepts of the early Church, not of the historical Jesus; (2) they

This is so very noticeably the case that it can scarcely be accidental; indeed, the extent of the Church's search for an application for the parables—the provision of generalizing conclusions, the addition of allegorizing explanations, etc.—is an indication that there never were original applications for them. It may well be the case, therefore, that the normal practice of Jesus was deliberately to end the parable and to leave his hearers to grasp the point and to find the parallel or analogy for themselves. This would certainly be more challenging than to give the application himself. But if this were the case, then the point of the parable must have been comparatively obvious and simple to grasp, that is, to and for men who stood in the situation of the hearers of Jesus. The primary task of the exegete of the parables, then, is to set the parable in its original context in the ministry of Jesus so that, by an effort of historical imagination, he may grasp the crucial point of the parable itself and then find the parallel or analogy to which it is directed.[1]

EXEGESIS 3. THE HID TREASURE AND THE PEARL. THE JOYOUSNESS OF THE EXPERIENCE OF GOD'S KINGLY ACTIVITY

Matt. 13.44–46; Thomas 109; 76

[44]The kingdom of heaven is like a treasure hidden in a field, which a man found and covered up; then in his joy he goes and sells all that he has and buys that field. [45]Again, the kingdom of heaven is like a merchant in search of fine pearls, [46]who, on finding one pearl of great value, went and sold all that he had and bought it.

---

belong to late strata of the tradition; (3) in their allegorizing, they are parallel to the allegorizing touches demonstrably added to the parables in the course of their transmission by the Church.

[1] We should note in passing that we are not going to pay attention to the German division of the parables into three groups: *Gleichnisse* (similes), *Parabeln* (parables) and *Beispielerzählungen* (exemplary stories). The distinction is that the *Gleichnis* refers to a natural and inevitable sequence of events (e.g. the action of leaven), the *Parabel* to a freely created, one-of-a-kind story (e.g. the Prodigal Son), and the *Beispielerzählung* is a story teaching by example. Quite apart from the fact that the distinction is not always easy to observe, it remains the case that the parables all have in common the element of comparison, and they all demand the finding of the point to which reference is being made and the parallel or analogy to which it is directed. We shall note from time to time that a given parable is a simile or exemplary story, if we find this helpful, but we shall make no attempt to carry through the distinction regularly or systematically.

Thomas 109. Jesus said: 'The Kingdom is like a man who had a treasure [hidden] in his field, without knowing it. And [after] he died, he left it to his [son. The] son did not know (about it), he accepted that field, he sold [it]. And he who bought it, he went, while he was plowing [he found] the treasure. He began to lend money to whomever he wished.'

Thomas 76. Jesus said: 'The Kingdom of the Father is like a man, a merchant, who possessed merchandise (and) found a pearl. That merchant was prudent. He sold the merchandise, he bought the one pearl for himself. Do you also seek for the treasure which fails not, which endures, there where no moth comes near to devour and (where) no worm destroys.'

These twin parables originally circulated separately, as can be seen from the difference in tenses used in Matthew, i.e. present in v. 44 and past in v. 46, and also from the fact that Thomas has them independently of one another. In Thomas the characteristic vivid quality of the dominical parables has been lost, and, indeed, both have been reinterpreted. The Hid Treasure has been very considerably modified under the influence of a popular folk tale about a man who inherited a field he deemed worthless, sold it and then, to his chagrin, saw the purchaser find a treasure in it and enjoy the fruits thereof.[1] The Thomas version seems to have been inherited by Thomas rather than created by him, since enjoying the fruits of the discovery by becoming a money-lender is contrary to logion 95 ('If you have money, do not lend at interest . . .'). In the rabbinical version the finder builds a palace and purchases many slaves. As it stands in Thomas, the parable teaches the gnostic conception '. . . that most men have no idea what treasure they have within themselves and so not everyone finds the treasure hid in his field = discovers the divine self within.'[2]

The Pearl has also been considerably modified in Thomas. The motive of joy has been replaced by prudence[3] and a saying reminiscent of Matt. 6.20 has been added as a 'generalizing conclusion',

[1] R. M. Grant, *Secret Sayings of Jesus*, p. 188, calls attention to versions of this story in Aesop's Fables and in the Jewish rabbinical literature (Billerbeck, *Kommentar* I, 674).

[2] E. Haenchen, *Die Botschaft des Thomas-Evangeliums* (Berlin: Verlag Alfred Töpelmann, 1961), p. 47. Similar interpretations are offered by R. McL. Wilson, *Studies in the Gospel of Thomas* (London: Mowbray, 1960), p. 93; B. Gärtner, *The Theology of the Gospel According to Thomas* (New York: Harper & Bros., and London: Collins, 1961), p. 237.

[3] As in the reminiscence of the parable in the Clementine *Recognitions* iii, 62.

such additions being a feature of the development of parabolic tradition.[1] In two respects, however, the Thomas version may be more
original than the Matthaean, for, as Jeremias points out, the fact that
the merchant is a general merchant and not a dealer in pearls, preserves the element of surprise, and that the merchant sold his
merchandise is more likely to be original than that he sold all that he
had.[2] Both changes are easy to account for in the tradition; the first
under the influence of the fact that the merchant found a pearl, and
the second under the influence of v. 44 when the two parables were
brought together by Matthew.

The original form of these parables, then, has a double element:
surprise and joy. They both speak of a man going about his ordinary
business who is surprised by the discovery of a great treasure, and, in
this respect, they reflect the sympathetic observation of the men of
first-century Palestine that we claim is so strong a feature of Jesus'
parables. In a land as frequently fought over as ancient Palestine the
chance discovery of valuables hidden for safe keeping in some past
emergency was by no means unusual, and every peasant ploughing
his field must have had some such secret dream. Similarly, pearls
could be of fabled worth, and every merchant whose business took
him to far places must have speculated upon the chance of stumbling
across one such pearl. So we have the secret dream suddenly and
surprisingly fulfilled, and the overwhelming joy that then seizes the
man[3] and determines and dominates his future activity. The analogy
is clear: so it is with the Kingdom of God. A man can suddenly be
confronted by the experience of God and find the subsequent joy
overwhelming and all-determinative.

There is another parable in Thomas which has exactly the same
point and which may, therefore, be accepted on the criterion of
coherence: logion 8.

Thomas 8. And He said: 'The Man is like a wise fisherman who
cast his net into the sea, he drew it up from the sea full of small fish;
among them he found a large (and) good fish, that wise fisherman, he
threw all the small fish down into the sea, he chose the large fish without
regret. Whoever has ears to hear let him hear.'

[1] J. Jeremias, *Parables of Jesus* (rev. ed., 1963), pp. 110–14.
[2] *Ibid.*, p. 199.
[3] There is general agreement today that Jeremias is right to claim (*ibid.*, pp.
200f.) that 'in his joy' are the key words and that they apply to both the peasant
and the merchant.

Claus-Hunno Hunzinger, who first called attention to this parable,[1] points out that 'The Man' in the introduction is readily understandable as a gnosticizing substitute for an original Kingdom of
Heaven, and, further, that it is a simple matter to conceive of a form
of the parable in which a Galilean fisherman, using a hand net from
the shore, suddenly and unexpectedly has a chance to catch an un-
usually large fish and to do this gladly sacrifices the remainder of
the catch. Several commentators see this as the Thomas version of the
Dragnet,[2] Matt. 13.47f., but the point is completely different and the
similarity of language could be explained as due to the influence of
the Dragnet parable on the tradition. We prefer to join Hunzinger
and Jeremias[3] in viewing it as a hitherto unknown parable making
the same point as the Hid Treasure and the Pearl.

EXEGESIS 4. THE LOST SHEEP, THE LOST COIN, THE
PRODIGAL SON. THE CHALLENGE OF THE FORGIVENESS
OF SINS

If one asks the natural question: In what way is the kingly activity
of God primarily known? then the answer of the teaching of Jesus is
abundantly clear: In the forgiveness of sins. According to the gospel
tradition, this is the central, specific aspect of Jesus' proclamation of
the Kingdom, and we have every reason to accept the impression
created by the tradition at this point. This is particularly the case since
the tradition is here supported by the central petition in the Lord's
Prayer[4] and by a major group of parables. But before we discuss these
parables, we must say something about the understanding of the
forgiveness of sins among the Jews at the time of Jesus, and especially
about the frequently recurring 'tax collectors and sinners' in the
gospel tradition.

The Jews had, of course, a very highly developed sense of sin, and a
whole system of means for dealing with it. Any transgression of the
law of God was sin and any suffering endured in the world a con-

---

[1] C.-H. Hunzinger, 'Unbekannte Gleichnisse Jesu aus dem Thomas-Evangelium', *Judentum, Urchristentum, Kirche* (Festschrift für Joachim Jeremias), ed. W.
Eltester (Beihefte zur *ZNW* 26 [Berlin: Verlag Alfred Töpelmann, 1960]), pp.
209–20.

[2] E.g. R. M. Grant, *Secret Sayings of Jesus*, p. 124; R. McL. Wilson, *Studies in the
Gospel of Thomas*, p. 54; E. Haenchen, *Die Botschaft des Thomas-Evangeliums*, p. 48
(explicitly rejecting Hunzinger's suggestion).

[3] J. Jeremias, *Parables of Jesus* (rev. ed., 1963), p. 201.

[4] See N. Perrin, *Kingdom*, pp. 194–6, and, further, below, pp. 151–3.

sequence of sin (John 9.2!). A man owed God full obedience, and any failure to achieve this meant that the man was in debt to God. So, in Aramaic the word for sin and the word for debt are the same word, witness the word play in the Lord's Prayer. This debt could be paid in several different ways: Temple sacrifice, the Day of Atonement ritual, ritual cleansing, works of supererogation, especially alms-giving, repentance, suffering, and, under certain circumstances, death. But all of these ways were of limited effectiveness, as was evidenced by the fact that Jews still suffered and the godless Gentiles ruled in the Holy City itself, things which must be due to the sin of Israel. So, God himself must ultimately forgive sin, and it is in the expression of this hope for ultimate forgiveness that ancient Judaism reached its height. Since we shall be concerned with the finest ex-pressions of the concept of forgiveness in the teaching of Jesus, let us give some examples of the best of ancient Judaism.

The Parable of Rabbi Meir

Rabbi Meir was famous for his parables ('When R. Meir died there were no more makers of parables' [Sota 9.15]), and this one is to be compared with the Prodigal Son. It is quite probably older than R. Meir himself (second century AD), having been attributed to him because of his reputation for parables:

> A King's son went out into evil courses, and the King sent his guardian (*paidagōgos*) after him. 'Return, my son,' said he. But the son sent him back, saying to his father: 'How can I return, I am ashamed.' His father sent again saying: 'My son, art thou indeed ashamed to re-turn? Is it not to thy father that thou returnest?'[1]

Here we have the characteristic Jewish hope: the Lord God of Heaven and Earth is their father; he will accept his penitent son.

The Pharisees strove to maintain a balance between man's duty to strive to earn pardon and his inability to attain it except as a gracious gift from God. This comes out in the famous saying of Anti-gonos of Socho: 'Be not like slaves that minister to the master for the sake of receiving a bounty, but be like slaves that minister to the master not for the sake of receiving a bounty' (Aboth 1.3). The Jew must serve: God will give.

The idea of the Father giving undeservedly is also found in a Talmudic legend:

[1] Deut. R. 2.24 quoted from I. Abrahams, *Studies in Pharisaism and the Gospels: First Series* (Cambridge: University Press, 1917), p. 142.

A legend tells, that when the Almighty Lord
Proclaimed to Moses his eternal word,
He in a vision showed to him likewise
The treasures that lie stored in Paradise.
And at each one in turn the heavenly voice
Spake: 'This the treasure is, that shall rejoice
His soul who freely giveth alms, and here
His portion is who dries the orphan's tear.'
Thus one by one were all to him made known,
Until unnamed remained but one alone.
Then Moses said: 'I pray thee, what is this?'
And answer made the Lord most High: 'It is
The treasure of my mercy, freely given
To those who else were treasureless in heaven.'[1]

Thus far, we have been concerned with Jewish thought about Jews who sinned and fell short of their obligations to their God and Father. When we consider the Gentiles the situation changes somewhat, for a Gentile was a sinner, as it were, 'by definition': he lived apart from the Law and necessarily defiled God with every breath that he drew. There is evidence of this in the New Testament, for Paul betrays it unconsciously in his passionate altercation with Peter at Antioch: 'We ourselves, who are Jews by birth and not Gentile sinners . . .' (Gal. 2.15). 'Sinner' and 'Gentile sinner' were by no means the same thing; a Jew who sinned could hope for mercy from his heavenly Father, but a Gentile could not count God as his Father in the same way. The ancient Jews did at times reach a universalism that recognized the possibility of a righteous Gentile, but this attitude was by no means general. It is reported that one of the points in dispute between the Shammaites and the Hillelites was whether non-Jews had any share in the 'age to come', the Shammaites denying it, the Hillelites allowing the possibility.[2] Certainly for the time of Jesus, when anti-Gentile feeling was running high, the following apocalyptic passage would be typical:

And there shall be forgiveness of sins,
And every mercy and peace and forbearance:
There shall be salvation unto them, a goodly light.
And for all of you sinners there shall be no salvation,

---

[1] I. Abrahams, *Studies in Pharisaism and the Gospels: First Series*, p. 148.
[2] Asher Finkel, *The Pharisees and the Teacher of Nazareth* (Arbeiten zur Geschichte des Spätjudentums und Urchristentums IV [Leiden: E. J. Brill, 1964]), p. 136.

But on you shall abide a curse.
But for the elect there shall be light and joy and peace,
And they shall inherit the earth.

(*I Enoch 5.6f.* [*Charles*])

It is clear that we have here two different groups of 'sinners'; one of which can hope for forgiveness and one which cannot. The previous verse identifies the second group as 'the sinners and godless'; they are the Gentiles.

This passage is typical of apocalyptic in that it identifies the forgiveness of sins as a major aspect of the apocalyptic hope. Naturally enough, with the rise of apocalyptic, the hope for God's ultimate forgiveness becomes the hope for God's eschatological forgiveness, and with the rise of Messianism, it becomes the hope for messianic forgiveness: In Pesiḳta 149a, the Messiah comes 'with grace and pardon (*slyḥh*) on his lips.' This passage is also typical of apocalyptic in that it denies any hope to the 'godless sinners', and in apocalyptic this designation would include both the Gentiles and also those Jews of whom the particular seer disapproved, or who disapproved of the particular seer!

But it is not only in apocalyptic fanaticism that we find a group of *Jews* who are regarded as beyond hope, regarded, in fact, as Gentiles. In Palestinian Judaism there were a number of professions or activities which made the Jews who practised them 'Gentile sinners' in the eyes of their fellow Jews. Of these the worst were: dice player, usurer, pigeon flyer, trafficker in seventh-year produce (Sanh. 3.3), to which a Baraitha adds: shepherd, tax collector, and revenue farmer[1] (b. Sanh. 25b; b. B.K. 94b). These were all notoriously robbers and in the first century the last two would also be especially hated as 'Quislings', because they collected taxes from their fellow Jews on behalf of hated Gentiles. They were all denied their normal citizenship rights; for example, so far as bearing witness was concerned, they had the same lack of standing as Gentile slaves (R.H. 1.8). 'In other

---

[1] We shall make no attempt to distinguish between the various kinds of tax collectors, tax farmers and excise men. In Jewish eyes they were all tarred with the same brush and our sources do not distinguish them systematically from one another. In what follows, therefore, we are using 'tax collector' in a collective sense to include them all. Soncino B. T. Sanhedrin I, 148, n. 6, defines 'tax collectors and publicans': 'Government lessees who collected customs duties, market tolls and similar special imposts, thus helping the Romans to exact the heavy taxes imposed upon the Jews.'

words: they were denied even those civil rights which every other Israelite, even the illegitimately born, could claim.'[1]

So we have to think in terms of three groups of 'sinners': Jews who could turn to their heavenly Father in penitence and hope; Gentile sinners for whom hope was dubious, most Jews regarding them as beyond the pale of God's mercy; and Jews who had made themselves as Gentiles, for whom penitence was, if not impossible, certainly almost insurmountably difficult. The language usage of our sources, both Jewish and Christian, bears this out, for we find the following combinations: tax collectors and thieves (Toh. 7.6, the passage concerns defilement: a tax collector defiles everything within the house by entering, *as does a Gentile*; B.K. 10.2); tax collectors and harlots (Matt. 21.32); extortioner, swindler, adulterer *or even* tax collector (Luke 18.11); murderers, robbers, tax collectors (Ned. 3.4); and, most important of all: tax collector and sinner (Mark 2.15f., and frequently), compare: tax collector and Gentile (Matt. 18.17). We are entitled to claim that the 'tax collectors and sinners' frequently found in the New Testament may be understood as 'tax collectors and other Jews who have made themselves as Gentiles'. Such Jews were widely regarded as beyond hope of penitence or forgiveness, and their very presence in a house defiled all that was in it (Toh. 7.6, noted immediately above).

Against this background, we may appreciate the startling nature of Jesus' proclamation of the forgiveness of sins, and understand the point at dispute between himself and those of his contemporaries who took offence at this proclamation. We may come to it by considering the parable of the Prodigal Son.

Luke 15.11–32. And he said, 'There was a man who had two sons; [12]and the younger of them said to his father, "Father, give me the share of the property which falls to me." And he divided his living between them. [13]Not many days later, the younger son gathered all he had and took his journey into a far country, and there he squandered his property in loose living. [14]And when he had spent everything, a great famine arose in that country, and he began to be in want. [15]So he went and joined himself to one of the citizens of that country, who sent him into his fields to feed swine. [16]And he would gladly have fed on the pods that the swine ate; and no one gave him anything. [18]But when he

---

[1] J. Jeremias, *Jerusalem zur Zeit Jesu* (Göttingen: Vandenhoeck & Ruprecht, [3]1962), pp. 346f. (ET in preparation). We are indebted to this work all through this section of our discussion.

came to himself he said, "How many of my father's hired servants have bread enough and to spare, but I perish here with hunger! [18]I will arise and go to my father, and I will say to him, 'Father, I have sinned against heaven and before you; [19]I am no longer worthy to be called your son; treat me as one of your hired servants.' " [20]And he arose and came to his father. But while he was yet at a distance, his father saw him and had compassion, and ran and embraced him and kissed him. [21]And the son said to him, "Father, I have sinned against heaven and before you; I am no longer worthy to be called your son." [22]But the father said to his servants, "Bring quickly the best robe and put it on him; and put a ring on his hand, and shoes on his feet; [23]and bring the fatted calf and kill it, and let us eat and make merry; [24]for this my son was dead, and is alive again; he was lost, and is found." And they began to make merry.

'[25]Now his elder son was in the field; and as he came and drew near to the house, he heard music and dancing. [26]And he called one of the servants and asked him what this meant. [27]And he said to him, "Your brother has come, and your father has killed the fatted calf, because he has received him safe and sound." [28]But he was angry and refused to go in. His father came out and entreated him, [29]but he answered his father, "Lo, these many years I have served you, and I never disobeyed your command; yet you never gave me a kid, that I might make merry with my friends. [30]But when this son of yours came, who has devoured your living with harlots, you killed for him the fatted calf!" [31]And he said to him, "Son, you are always with me, and all that is mine is yours. [32]It was fitting to make merry and be glad, for this your brother was dead, and is alive; he was lost, and is found." '

The details at the beginning of the story are vividly drawn from life. In first-century Judaism the cities of the Levant offered far more opportunities for energetically inclined younger sons than did Palestine itself, and the procedure of dividing the property during the father's lifetime, so that the younger son might have some capital for his venture, was both legal and feasible. In fact, the situation must have arisen many times as Jewish younger sons ventured into the Dispersion, in the way that, later, British younger sons 'emigrated to the colonies' or American younger sons responded to the challenge: 'Go west, young man.' The hopes and fears surrounding such a venture would have been well known to Jesus' hearers, and the fate of the son one with which they were familiar from known instances in their own family or district. The parable of Rabbi Meir, above, assumes exactly the same circumstance. It is at this point, however, that the two parables diverge, and the climax to this part of Jesus' story is the fact that the boy became a swineherd. We saw above that the professional shepherd was one regarded as beyond the pale of Judaism, and this was doubly the case when the animals were swine, for they were unclean. Indeed, in the Tosephta we are told that Jewish swineherds are to be treated in the same way as Gentiles: they are not to be thrown into a pit, but neither are they to be helped out of one![1] A Jew who became a swineherd became a Gentile; he could no longer count the king as his father as could the son in Rabbi Meir's parable. This, then, is the crux of the parable as Jesus told it. So far as many of his hearers were concerned, and certainly so far as the ones to whom the parable was particularly addressed were concerned, at this point the son becomes dead in his father's eyes and any self-respecting Jewish father would have spurned him had he returned in such disgrace.

In the remainder of the first part of the parable, Jesus goes out of his way to contradict this viewpoint. The father is depicted as recognizing the gravity of the son's offence (v. 24: '. . . was dead . . . was lost . . .'), but as forgiving it in a way that can only be described as extravagant; and no doubt the extravagance is deliberate. The father runs out to welcome the son, 'a most unusual and undignified procedure for an aged oriental' (Jeremias), freely forgives him, treats him as an honoured guest and restores him to a position of dignity and authority in his household.[2] Every touch of which a creative mind could conceive, and still stay within the limits of a realistic story, has been used to depict the free and absolute nature of the father's forgiveness, all in deliberate contrast to the expectation of those to whom the parable was addressed. But their viewpoint is not ignored. Far from it! It is introduced on the lips of the elder son.

The second part of the parable is integral to the whole, and the characters in it are every bit as realistically conceived and presented as those in the first part. There is, therefore, no reason to regard it as a later addition, as Bultmann suggests is possible.[3] The first part depicts the father as acting completely contrary to the expectations of the hearers; the second part brings their (from their point of view)

---

[1] Reference taken from Billerbeck, *Kommentar* IV, 359.

[2] The kiss is (as in II Sam. 14.33) a sign of forgiveness; the feast is a sign of rejoicing; the robe marks him as an honoured guest; the ring is a signet ring and a symbol of authority; the shoes mark him as a free man, not a slave. J. Jeremias, *Parables of Jesus* (rev. ed., 1963), p. 130.

[3] R. Bultmann, *History of the Synoptic Tradition*, p. 196.

legitimate protest to expression through the elder son. Completely realistically and, indeed, sympathetically conceived and presented, he protests, in the name of a regular and quite proper Jewish concept of justice, against the unfairness, to him, of the whole proceedings. We fail to appreciate the significance of this part of the parable if we think of the elder son as being presented as an unsympathetic and ill-natured character. His attitude was proper, granted his presuppositions, and, without the kind of legalism his presuppositions represent, the conduct of human affairs and the regular business of living in family or community would rapidly become impossible. The whole point of the father's reply is that this is an extraordinary situation, a once-in-a-lifetime situation, wherein the ordinarily proper rules do not apply, a situation through which the family can attain a quite new and hitherto impossible quality of life and relationship.

We must here stress the point that the story is a parable and not an allegory. The father is not God, the elder son is not a Pharisee; the whole story concerns a real family in a familiar situation. The characters in it do and express things that were live options in first-century Palestine. If the father behaves in an unorthodox fashion, well, it is not the first time that paternal love has overstepped the bounds of conventional religious behaviour. The reality of the story is its power, and the point that makes it a parable is the analogy between the situation of the family and that of Palestinian Judaism at the time of Jesus' ministry. The family was confronted by the crisis of the fall and return of the prodigal, and in this crisis the quality of the father's love made possible a new and deeper reality of family life and relationships. Palestinian Judaism was confronted by a crisis when Jesus proclaimed the eschatological forgiveness of sins, and 'tax collectors and other Jews who had made themselves as Gentiles' responded in glad acceptance. Here was a situation in which the reality of God and his love was being revealed in a new and decisive way, and in which, therefore, the joys of the salvation time were suddenly available to those who had longed for them so long and so earnestly. The tragedy was that the new situation demanded a willingness to sacrifice principles and attitudes previously regarded as essential to the life of the community and its relationship with God, and for this many were unprepared. The new wine was bursting the old wineskins.

It has recently been said, in the context of a discussion of this parable, that '. . . *Jesus' conduct* was itself a real framework of his proclamation',[1] and there is no doubt of the validity of this claim. The parable clearly reflects the situation of the ministry of Jesus, and is equally clearly designed to open men's eyes to the reality of that situation, *as Jesus himself saw it.* It expresses Jesus' understanding and reflects his vision. It challenges men to join him in the joyous celebration of the new relationship with God and one another which the realization that the time of the eschatological forgiveness of sins is *now* makes possible.

The same point is made in the twin parables of the Lost Sheep and the Lost Coin, Luke 15.3–8 par., Matt. 18.12–14, and Luke 15.8–10, to a discussion of which we now turn.

The Lost Sheep

Luke 15.3. So he told them this parable: 4'What man of you, having a hundred sheep, if he has lost one of them, does not leave the ninety-nine in the wilderness, and go after the one which is lost, until he finds it? 5And when he has found it, he lays it on his shoulders, rejoicing. 6And when he comes home, he calls together his friends and his neighbours, saying to them, "Rejoice with me, for I have found my sheep which was lost." 7Just so, I tell you, there will be more joy in heaven over one sinner who repents than over ninety-nine righteous persons who need no repentance.'

Matt. 18.12. What do you think? If a man has a hundred sheep, and one of them has gone astray, does he not leave the ninety-nine on the hills and go in search of the one that went astray? 13And if he finds it, truly, I say to you, he rejoices over it more than over the ninety-nine that never went astray. 14So it is not the will of my Father who is in heaven that one of these little ones should perish.

There is a version of this parable in Thomas.

Thomas 107. Jesus said: 'The Kingdom is like a shepherd who had a hundred sheep. One of them went astray, which was the largest. He left behind ninety-nine, he sought for the one until he found it. Having tired himself out, he said to the sheep: "I love thee more than ninety-nine." '

The Thomas version does not help us very much. We know from the Fathers, e.g. Irenaeus *Adv. haer.* II 24.6, that this parable was

---

[1] Ernst Fuchs, 'The Quest of the Historical Jesus', in his collected essays *Studies of the Historical Jesus* (Studies in Biblical Theology 42 [London: SCM Press, 1964]), ET by Andrew Scobie of *Zur Frage nach dem historischen Jesus* (Gesammelte Aufsätze II [1960]), p. 21.

much used by Gnostics, and, both in Thomas and in the Gospel of Truth where a version of it is also to be found, it has become so much a vehicle for expressing gnostic teaching that the versions do not help us to reconstruct the teaching of Jesus.[1] Turning to the canonical versions, it is immediately apparent that the conclusion in each instance represents the evangelist's understanding and use of the parable—Matthew in connection with the Christian zeal for an apostate brother and Luke with divine concern for the outcast in Israel. Of these two, only the latter could be dominical, but it was pointed out by Cadoux that the verse appears to have been composed on the basis of the closing verse of the Lost Coin with the help of a sentence that the Matthaean version has in the parable itself.[2] Further, it is clearly inappropriate to the parable itself, for the question immediately arises: Where did the shepherd take his sheep? Are we to assume that he took it back home to his village, leaving the other ninety-nine in the wilderness? The most probable assumption is that the ending was added to this parable in the tradition at a time when it was brought together with that of the Lost Coin.[3] Of the two versions, Matthew's seems nearer to the original, since it is less developed than Luke's: 'until he finds it' in Luke 15.4 reflects the assurance that God has sought out the outcast as over against the more realistic 'If he finds it' in Matt. 18.13, and the vivid touch about the shepherd carrying the sheep, while completely realistic, is the kind of thing that is more readily accounted for as an addition than as an omission.

The most original form of the parable available to us still presents a problem: Where did the shepherd leave the ninety-nine sheep? To those who know the conditions in Palestine, then and now, it is inconceivable that he should have left them to fend for themselves 'on the hills' or 'in the wilderness',[4] and a scholar who lived there for many years suggests that it would be very nice if we could understand the reference to the hills/wilderness as indicating where the shepherd went to look for the lost sheep, assuming that he had left the flock

---

[1] For a good discussion of the meaning and use of this parable in its gnostic setting, see B. Gärtner, *Theology of the Gospel According to Thomas*, pp. 234ff.

[2] A. T. Cadoux, *Parables of Jesus* (London: James Clarke, 1931), p. 231.

[3] E. Linnemann, *Parables of Jesus* (ET by John Sturdy of *Gleichnisse Jesu* [1961]; London, SPCK, and New York, Harper and Row, 1966), pp. 67f.

[4] These two phrases are certainly synonyms, the hill country of Judea being wilderness country and the Aramaic *ṭura* having both meanings. J. Jeremias, *Parables of Jesus* (rev. ed., 1963), p. 133; M. Black, *Aramaic Approach to the Gospels and Acts* (^{2}1957), pp. 254f.

safely in the fold.[1] But although this is the reading of the *Textus Receptus*, and of the AV and RV translations, it is certainly not the original reading, but one introduced in the textual tradition precisely to remove this difficulty. Luke has no such rendering, and all modern critical texts reject it in Matthew. Unimpressed by the reading, but impressed by the problem, Jeremias appeals to the normal Palestinian practice of counting the sheep as they enter the fold at night and argues that the story implies that this is when the loss was discovered. So we are to assume that the shepherd left the flock in the care of other shepherds who shared the fold with him and went off to look for the missing animal.[2] Both Bishop and Jeremias quote the story of the young goatherd Muhammed ed-Deeb, who discovered the first Qumran cave. Having omitted to count his flock, according to custom, for two consecutive evenings, he counted them in mid-morning, found one missing and went off to look for it, leaving the remainder of his flock (fifty-five head) in the charge of two companions. But although this is reasonable and in accord with Palestinian shepherd life, it is still only an assumption and not in accordance with the text as we have it. There is no reason here to give up the text-critical principle of preferring the more difficult reading. We cannot even argue that it is possible that the story changed as the tradition lost contact with the Palestinian countryside, because the T.R. reading in Matthew is evidence that the difficulty was felt in the tradition.

Our discussion of this parable leaves us to interpret a version very much like that now found in Matt. 18.12, 13, and the moment we turn to those verses, deliberately forgetting the other versions and interpretations, we find we have a story of panic and pleasure, of a sudden crisis that changes all values and of a new situation of joy and gladness. A man suffers a loss and panics, and we must remember that in first-century Palestine, constantly on the edge of famine, the loss of one sheep from a flock was a most serious loss. In his consternation, the shepherd leaves the ninety-nine and goes after the one, the crisis having made him forget the normal principles of caution and reasonable behaviour. In his searching, the dangers inherent in what he had done would dawn on him and he has, therefore, a double reason for rejoicing when he not only recovers the one but finds the ninety-nine safely awaiting him on his return.

[1] E. F. F. Bishop, 'Parable of the Lost or Wandering Sheep', *ATR* 44 (1962), 44–57.
[2] J. Jeremias, *Parables of Jesus* (rev. ed., 1963), p. 133.

One reason for accepting a version of the story such as this as the original is that the shepherd comes out of it as all too human, and as 'dead lucky', to use a modern idiom. The difficulty with accepting the Lukan interpretation as essentially correct and seeing the shepherd as Jesus' 'image of God's activity of love', as does Jeremias,[1] is that the shepherd was a 'Jew who had made himself a Gentile' in ancient Judaism. While this does not mean that Jesus could not have used the figure in this way, it does lend weight to an interpretation in which the shepherd is not a symbol for God, but rather the whole situation of the story is analogous to the situation of the ministry of Jesus. In the story a crisis led to a seemingly obtuse forgetfulness of normal and normally good practices, but the end result was a new kind of joy. The same was true of the crisis of the ministry of Jesus: for those who would accept the challenge and realize the need for 'new wineskins' the possibility of a wholly new kind of joy was very real.

The Lost Coin

> **Luke 15.8.** Or what woman, having ten silver coins, if she loses one coin, does not light a lamp and sweep the house and seek diligently until she finds it? [9]And when she has found it, she calls together her friends and neighbours, saying, 'Rejoice with me, for I have found the coin which I had lost.' [10]Just so, I tell you, there is joy before the angels of God over one sinner who repents.

Here again, the conclusion in v. 10 is to be disregarded as editorial. We have a simple and vivid story of a peasant woman who loses either a significant part of her small hoard of money or a part of her wedding head-dress,[2] carries out a desperate search for it and is so overjoyed to find it again that she calls in friends and neighbours to celebrate with her. One is tempted to see the lighting of the lamp in daylight as a measure of forgetfulness induced by the crisis, but it probably is simply a vivid touch reflecting the lack of light in a peasant's cottage even in daytime. As compared to the other parables, Prodigal Son and Lost Sheep, there is here less emphasis upon the 'need for new wineskins' and proportionately more upon the crisis and the ultimate rejoicing; indeed, in this respect, the parable is nearer to the Hid Treasure and Pearl than to its companion parables in Luke 15.

---

[1] J. Jeremias, *Parables of Jesus* (rev. ed., 1963), p. 133.
[2] So Jeremias, *Parables of Jesus* (rev. ed., 1963), p. 134, with the support of E. F. F. Bishop, *Jesus of Palestine*, p. 191.

It may be that originally its purpose was nearer to that of the Hid Treasure and Pearl, i.e. it was concerned to stress the joyful response to the finding of a hid treasure, a pearl or a lost valuable, and that it is the element of something lost in it which brought it together with the Lost Sheep in the tradition. There is, however, no need to force a decision on this point. Clearly, the parable belongs to one or other of these two groups in which Jesus challenges his hearers to recognize the crisis of the Now of the proclamation, the proclamation of God reaching out to men in the challenge of the forgiveness of sins and offering them thereby the real possibility of a new kind of relationship with himself and with one another.

THE TABLE-FELLOWSHIP OF THE KINGDOM OF GOD

This brings us to the last aspect of Jesus' proclamation of the Kingdom of God with which we shall be concerned: his table-fellowship with 'tax collectors and sinners'. This is not a proclamation in words at all, but an acted parable. But it is more, indeed, than an acted parable; it is the aspect of Jesus' ministry which must have been most meaningful to his followers and most offensive to his critics. That it has all but disappeared from the gospel tradition is an indication of how far removed from historical reminiscence of the ministry of Jesus that tradition is, in its present form.

At this juncture we should note the point made recently by N. A. Dahl, namely, that any historical understanding of the ministry and message of Jesus must make sense of the fact that that ministry ended on the cross.[1] There must have been something about it that gave very grave offence indeed to his contemporaries. It is difficult to believe that this would be an interpretation of the Law, however radical. Rabbis threatened one another with all kinds of things in their disputes with one another, as their literature testifies. But this was mostly hyperbole, and to bring in the Romans to settle a dispute about the Law, however vehement that dispute might be, is really beyond the bounds of reasonable possibility. The cleansing of the Temple itself hardly suffices. The Romans would certainly have taken very stern notice of any uproar in the Temple at a festival, since they feared, and rightly, the constant possibility of an uprising beginning

[1] N. A. Dahl, 'The Problem of the Historical Jesus', *Kerygma and History*, ed. Carl E. Braaten and Roy A. Harrisville (New York: Abingdon Press, 1962), pp. 138–71, esp. 158f.

there at such a time. But to hand a fellow Jew over to the Romans was a desperate step for the Jewish authorities to take, and the Temple incident itself is sufficient neither to explain how they came to determine among themselves to do it nor why they were prepared to risk their control over the Jewish populace—in the case that Jesus' action should have been popular—by taking such a step. There must have been a factor in the situation which both drove the authorities themselves to desperate measures and also gave them a defence against popular accusation. We suggest that a regular table-fellowship, in the name of the Kingdom of God, between Jesus and his followers, when those followers included 'Jews who had made themselves as Gentiles', would have been just such a factor.

We must always remember that the Jews were under the pressure of being a people living under the occupation of their country by a foreign power. This pressure was such that it led to the hopeless, but none the less inevitable revolt against Rome of AD 66–70. Under these circumstances, the overwhelming tendency would be to close ranks against the enemy, and Jews who served him, like the Quislings of occupied Europe during the Second World War, would be especially hated. Moreover, the religious hope was the mainspring of the Jewish morale; the conviction that God was on their side was what upheld them and gave them hope. Then came Jesus, claiming that they were wrong in their understanding of God and his attitude to these outcasts and so striking a blow at the fundamental convictions which upheld the Jewish people. But more than that, Jesus welcomed these outcasts into table-fellowship with himself in the name of the Kingdom of God, in the name of the Jews' ultimate hope, and so both prostituted that hope and also shattered the closed ranks of the community against their enemy. It is hard to imagine anything more offensive to Jewish sensibilities. To have become such an outcast himself would have been much less of an outrage than to welcome those people back into the community in the name of the ultimate hope of that community. Intense conviction, indeed, is necessary to explain such an act on the part of Jesus, and such an act on the part of Jesus is necessary, we would claim, to make sense of the fact of the cross. Now the Jewish authorities could act in face of the necessity to keep the community whole and its hope pure; now they could face a popular resentment with the overwhelming retort that the fellow, for all his personal attractiveness and superficial popularity, was worse than a Quisling!

Further evidence for the existence of table-fellowship with 'tax collectors and sinners' as a feature of the ministry of Jesus is the role played by communal meals in earliest Christianity.[1] We have every reason to believe that these were very important indeed: the testimony of Acts (i.e. 2.46) is to this effect, and the epistles of the New Testament, and the *Didache*, bear witness to it. Further, it is evident that the meals themselves were the important thing and not a theological purpose which they might be said to serve. The existence of such different theological emphases as those connected with the 'Lord's Supper' in the New Testament (I Cor. 11) is an indication that the occasion has called forth the theologies, not the theologies the occasion. The practice of early Christian communal meals existed before there was a specifically Christian theology to give it meaning. We may not argue that the meals are an echo of a 'last supper' held by Jesus with his disciples during the Passion, because, even if such an occasion as is reported in the gospels is historical, it has not, in itself, given rise to the early Christian practice. It cannot have done so, because all of our evidence indicates that the kind of theological emphasis associated with the 'last supper' in the gospels was by no means the major emphasis in early Christian communal meals from the very beginning, as it would have to have been if this had been the occasion for them. Nor is it easy to see what religious practice of ancient Judaism could have occasioned early Christian communal meals, if we want to argue that they are derived from Judaism. Not the Passover meal; that was a yearly affair. Not the *ḥaburah* fellowship meal celebrated by a group of Pharisees; no such meal existed.[2] Not the Qumran communal meal anticipating the 'messianic banquet', for all that this may have influenced the Christian practice, because that is simply a special meaning given to the regular communal meal at Qumran, whereas our evidence indicates that the Christian practice was something out of the ordinary which the early Christians did and which helped to give them a special identity. They were not, after all, a monastic community to whom regular communal meals were part of a way of life. No, the most reasonable explanation of the

[1] E. Lohmeyer, *Lord of the Temple* (ET by Stewart Todd of *Kultus und Evangelium* [1942]; Edinburgh: Oliver and Boyd, 1961), pp. 79ff., discusses the central role of table-fellowship in the ministry of Jesus, but he is particularly concerned with the development towards the Last Supper, which he sees as historical, rather than with the relationship between this table-fellowship and the cross, on the one hand, and the communal meals of early Christianity on the other.

[2] J. Jeremias, *Eucharistic Words of Jesus* (1965), pp. 30f.

fact of early Christian communal meals is that they are a continuation
of a regular practice of the ministry of Jesus.

The nature and meaning of this practice in the ministry of Jesus
has to be reconstructed from its reflection in the few authentic sayings
of Jesus we have and in the parables. In particular, there are two
sayings of great significance in this context: Matt. 11.16–19 and
Matt. 8.11, both indubitably authentic.[1]

Matthew 11.16–19

16But to what shall I compare this generation? It is like children
sitting in the market places and calling to their playmates, 17'We piped
to you, and you did not dance: we wailed, and you did not mourn.'
18For John came neither eating nor drinking, and they say, 'He has a
demon'; 19the Son of man came eating and drinking, and they say,
'Behold, a glutton and a drunkard, a friend of tax collectors and sinners!' Yet wisdom is justified by her deeds.

From the invective against Jesus in v. 19, we can see that there are
two things giving offence: his eating habits and the fact that he is a
'friend' of 'tax collectors and sinners'. With regard to the former, the
question must be: What would be serious enough in such a matter to
give rise to this kind of invective? That he was not punctilious in his
observance of prescribed fasts? This might be the case, and certainly
the evidence is that Jesus and his disciples did not, in fact, fast in the
prescribed manner, as we saw earlier in this chapter. But it is hard to
think that failure to observe the prescribed fasts would attract the
same kind of attention as John's marked asceticism (clothing, manner
of speech, burden of his message, etc.) and so cause a similarly vehement response. It would surely have to be something much more
noticeable and something inherently much more offensive. Further,
in Hebrew or Aramaic, two parallel phrases of the type

> . . . a glutton and a drunkard,
> a friend of tax collectors and sinners!

would normally express some kind of parallelism, and they would
certainly imply a close relationship between the two things. Laxness
in observance of fasts and friendship with religious and social outcasts

---

[1] See the detailed argumentation on this point in our further discussion and
interpretation of these sayings below, pp. 119–21 (Matt. 11.16–19), and pp. 161–
64 (Matt. 8.11).

could certainly be regarded as related to one another, but only in a quite general way.

If, however, we understand the phrase 'a glutton and a drunkard' to refer to Jesus' habit of holding table-fellowship, and the 'friend of tax collectors and sinners' to refer to the people with whom he was prepared to hold that fellowship, then we have at one and the same time a matter of notable and noticeable offensiveness. We have also two parallel phrases supplementing one another in reference to the same matter, an altogether regular Semitic idiom. Finally, the tone of the whole ('glutton', 'drunkard', 'friend') could be an allusion to the joyousness which characterized this table-fellowship. We are prepared to argue that this is a reasonable understanding of the invective: it refers to the practice of Jesus in holding table-fellowship with 'tax collectors and other Jews who had made themselves as Gentiles', and it characterizes that table-fellowship as joyous.

Matthew 8.11

I tell you, many will come from east and west and sit at table with Abraham, Isaac and Jacob in the kingdom of heaven.

This saying demands a context such as the table-fellowship we are discussing. It clearly refers to the expected messianic banquet of the time of salvation,[1] and it emphasizes the universalism that will be a feature of it. In view of the emphasis upon 'tax collectors and sinners' that is so widespread in the tradition, it is natural to see this emphasis upon universalism as arising out of that concern. Teaching relating to a messianic banquet is a commonplace of Jewish apocalyptic, but, in view of the pointed reference normally to be detected in sayings and parables of Jesus, we would not expect his saying to be either general or commonplace. That it should have its point of departure in the table-fellowship with tax collectors and sinners is so natural in itself and so fitting to the concern of the saying that we are surely justified in setting the saying in this context. But in that case, this saying tells us a great deal about the table-fellowship; it tells us that the fellowship was an anticipation of that to be expected in the Kingdom.[2] The parallel between the situation envisaged in the saying and that providing its point of departure in the ministry of Jesus is

[1] On this see our discussion below, pp. 161–64.
[2] On the future aspect of the fellowship, see our discussion of this saying below.

such that we must see the table-fellowship of that ministry as a table-fellowship 'of the Kingdom' and as anticipating a table-fellowship 'in the Kingdom'.

Finally, there are the parables that reflect the offence created by Jesus' relationship to, and acceptance of, 'tax collectors and sinners', above all, the Prodigal Son, Lost Sheep and Lost Coin, discussed above. The situation to which these are directed is clearly one of grave offence; any cause less than table-fellowship with the outcasts in the name of the Kingdom of God is scarcely adequate to the result. The table-fellowship of the ministry of Jesus was not, of course, restricted to the penitent tax collectors and sinners. These are the extreme examples of the acceptance of the challenge of the forgiveness offered in the proclamation of Jesus, and they are the occasion for the greatest offence of Jesus in the eyes of his opponents; but in the group of his disciples and followers they could only have been a small minority, however spectacularly noticeable their presence in the group might be. The 'table-fellowship of the Kingdom', as we have called it, was a feature of the common life of Jesus and his followers altogether, and a symbol of the new kind of relationship made possible by the common acceptance of the challenge. Scribe, tax collector, fisherman and Zealot came together around the table at which they celebrated the joy of the present experience and anticipated its consummation in the future.

The central feature of the message of Jesus is, then, the challenge of the forgiveness of sins and the offer of the possibility of a new kind of relationship with God and with one's fellow man. This was symbolized by a table-fellowship which celebrated the present joy and anticipated the future consummation; a table-fellowship of such joy and gladness that it survived the crucifixion and provided the focal point for the community life of the earliest Christians, and was the most direct link between that community life and the pre-Easter fellowship of Jesus and his disciples. In all probability, it was the vividness of the memory of that pre-Easter fellowship between the disciples and the earthly Jesus that provided the pattern for the development of that remarkable sense of fellowship between the early Christians and the risen Lord which is such a feature of primitive Christianity—and which has had such an effect on the Jesus tradition. At all events, we are justified in seeing this table-fellowship as the central feature of the ministry of Jesus; an anticipatory sitting at table in the Kingdom of God and a very real celebration of present joy and challenge. Here a great deal of the private teaching of Jesus to his disciples must have had its *Sitz im Leben*—especially the Lord's Prayer must belong here—and here the disciples must have come to know the special way that Jesus had of 'breaking bread' which gave rise to the legend of the Emmaus road (Luke 24.35).

III

RECOGNITION AND RESPONSE

ANY DIVISION OF the teaching of Jesus into various parts by subjects is an act of violence against that teaching, which is a constantly interrelating and interlocking whole. We have therefore sought to approach it on the basis of differing emphases rather than different subjects, although even this is an artificial procedure. In the previous chapter we discussed the proclamation of the Kingdom of God, i.e. those aspects of the teaching where the emphasis is upon God and his activity, and even there we had occasion to note emphases upon the experience of men confronted by the proclamation. Now we turn to aspects of the teaching where the emphasis is more directly upon man and his experience, and upon what he must do in terms of recognition of the meaning of this experience and response to it.

In speaking in the way of recognition and response, we are intending to cover ground that might be considered under such a rubric as 'ethics'. But 'ethics' is a misleading word, because it carries with it the assumption that there is a Christian ethic as there is a Socratic or humanistic ethic. So far as the teaching of Jesus is concerned, this latter is simply not true. There is nothing in that teaching about standards of conduct or moral judgements, there is only the urgent call to recognize the challenge of the proclamation and to respond to it. To talk about the 'ethical teaching of Jesus' is to talk about something that can only be found by a process of abstraction and deduction from the teaching as a whole. While we may sometimes wish to carry out such a process, let us recognize that it is always a process which does violence, to a greater or lesser degree, to the intent of the historical Jesus.

We begin this chapter by continuing the discussion of the parables, and here the artificial nature of our division of the parables becomes immediately apparent. For convenience of presentation, we have made a break between the second and third of the seven groups into which we divided the parables, but this difference is not, in fact, any greater than that between any other two of those groups. But it is the point at which attention is focused more sharply upon man than it has been before, which is the only justification we can offer for our procedure.

EXEGESIS I. THE GREAT SUPPER, THE UNJUST STEWARD. THE NECESSITY FOR DECISION NOW

The Great Supper: Matt. 22.1–14; Luke 14.16–24; Thomas 64

Matt. 22.1. And again Jesus spoke to them in parables, saying, ²'The kingdom of heaven may be compared to a king who gave a marriage feast for his son, ³and sent his servants to call those who were invited to the marriage feast; but they would not come. ⁴Again he sent other servants, saying, "Tell those who are invited, Behold, I have made ready my dinner, my oxen and my fat calves are killed, and everything is ready; come to the marriage feast." ⁵But they made light of it and went off, one to his farm, another to his business, ⁶while the rest seized his servants, treated them shamefully and killed them. ⁷The king was angry, and he sent his troops and destroyed those murderers and burned their city. ⁸Then he said to his servants, "The wedding is ready, but those invited were not worthy. ⁹Go therefore to the thoroughfares, and invite to the marriage feast as many as you find." ¹⁰And those servants went out into the streets and gathered all whom they found, both bad and good; so the wedding hall was filled with guests.

¹¹'But when the king came in to look at the guests, he saw there a man who had no wedding garment; ¹²and he said to him, "Friend, how did you get in here without a wedding garment?" And he was speechless. ¹³Then the king said to the attendants, "Bind him hand and foot, and cast him into the outer darkness; there men will weep and gnash their teeth." ¹⁴For many are called, but few are chosen.'

Luke 14.16. But he said to him, 'A man once gave a great banquet, and invited many; ¹⁷and at the time for the banquet he sent his servant to say to those who had been invited, "Come; for all is now ready." ¹⁸But they all alike began to make excuses. The first said to him, "I have bought a field, and I must go out and see it; I pray you, have me excused." ¹⁹And another said, "I have bought five yoke of oxen, and I go to examine them; I pray you, have me excused." ²⁰And another said, "I have married a wife, and therefore I cannot come." ²¹So the servant came and reported this to his master. Then the householder in anger said to his servant, "Go out quickly to the streets and lanes of the city, and bring in the poor and maimed and blind and lame." [22]And the servant said, "Sir, what you commanded has been done, and still there is room." [23]And the master said to the servant, "Go out to the highways and hedges, and compel people to come in, that my house may be filled. [24]For I tell you, none of those men who were invited shall taste my banquet." '

Thomas 64. Jesus said: A man had guest-friends, and when he had prepared the dinner, he sent his servant to invite the guest-friends. He went to the first, he said to him: 'My master invites thee.' He said: 'I have some claims against some merchants; they will come to me in the evening; I will go and give them my orders. I pray to be excused from the dinner.' He went to another, he said to him: 'My master has invited thee.' He said to him: 'I have bought a house and they request me for a day. I will have no time.' He came to another, he said to him: 'My master invites thee.' He said to him: 'My friend is to be married and I am to arrange a dinner; I shall not be able to come. I pray to be excused from the dinner.' He went to another, he said to him: 'My master invites thee.' He said to him: 'I have bought a farm, I go to collect the rent. I shall not be able to come. I pray to be excused.' The servant came, he said to his master: 'Those whom thou hast invited to the dinner have excused themselves.' The master said to his servant: 'Go out to the roads, bring those whom thou shalt find, so that they may dine. Tradesmen and merchants [shall] not [enter] the places of my Father.'

As background to this parable, the rabbinical story of the tax collector and the pious student is to be noted, j. Sanh. 6, 23c.[1]

Two pious men lived together in Ashkelon, devoting themselves to the study of the Law. One of them died and no honour was paid to him at his funeral. Bar Ma'yon, a tax collector, died and the whole town honoured his funeral. The remaining pious man was deeply disturbed and cried out that the wicked in Israel did not get their deserts. But his dead companion appeared to him in a dream and told him not to despise the ways of God in Israel. He himself had committed one evil deed and hence had suffered dishonour at his funeral, whereas Bar Ma'yon had committed one good deed and for that had been honoured

[1] We give a free rendering of the text as printed by G. Dalman, *Grammatik des jüdisch-palästinischen Aramäisch und Aramäische Dialektproben* (Darmstadt: Wissenschaftliche Buchgesellschaft, 1960), pp. 33f. Cf. T. W. Manson, *Sayings of Jesus*, p. 297; J. Jeremias, *Parables of Jesus* (rev. ed., 1963), pp. 178f., 183.

at his. What evil deed had the pious man committed? On one occasion
he had put on his phylacteries in the wrong order. What good deed had
the tax collector committed? Once he had given a breakfast for the
leading men of the town and they had not come. So he gave orders that
the poor were to be invited to eat it, that it should not go to waste. After
some days the pious man saw his dead companion walking in the gar-
den of paradise beside fountains of water; and he saw Bar Ma'yon the
tax collector lying on the bank of a river, he was striving to reach the
water and he could not.

This story probably originated in Egypt and there are numerous
versions of it to be found in the ancient world, including the one in the
synoptic tradition: the story of the Rich Man and Lazarus, Luke
16.19–31. The rabbinical version is interesting as illustrating the
doctrine of exact retribution: the one evil deed and the one good deed
are cancelled out by the funerals, and then the two inherit their
respective rewards. Neither this version nor the one in the synoptic
tradition tells us anything about the views of the afterlife held by
the rabbis and Jesus respectively; those details are supplied from
(? Egyptian) folk material and are simply used to make a point. The
further point of interest, and the one with which we are immediately
concerned, is the illustration of the act of charity involved in inviting
the poor to eat a meal when the invited guests do not turn up.

One last piece of background material to this parable is the saying
in Midrash Lamentations Rabbah 4.2: 'None of them (men of
Jerusalem) would attend a banquet unless he was invited twice.' We
are to imagine a situation in which guests are invited to the banquet,
signify their acceptance, and then await a second invitation con-
firming the first one, perhaps giving the specific time. Such custom is
implied in a parable of Rabban Johanan ben Zakkai[1] about a king
who invited men to a banquet, but did not specify the hour, and later
sent messengers to summon them to the feast. Those who were wise
had dressed for the occasion and awaited the summons. The foolish
were found unready and not admitted to the feast.

When we turn to the three versions of the parable we can see that
each evangelist has adapted the basic tradition to make it a vehicle
for his particular message. Matthew and Luke have both understood
the story as having reference to the missionary situation of the
Church, and in particular to the situation created by the success of
the Gentile mission. Matthew has heavily allegorized the story,

[1] b. Shab. 153a. J. Jeremias, *Parables of Jesus* (rev. ed., 1963), p. 188.

making the feast giver a king (= God) and the feast a marriage feast (= the life of the age to come), in accordance with the regular Jewish use of these symbols. He has also made the servants and their fate represent the servants of God and the Jewish treatment of them, and the destruction of the city is certainly a reference to the destruction of Jerusalem by the Romans interpreted as the judgement of God upon the Jews, all in accordance with early Christian apologetic. Finally, he has added a version of the rabbinical parable of the unprepared guests, referred to above, to make the whole an allegory of the mixed state of the Church and the sorting-out process of the future judgement of God, a theme characteristic of his gospel (allegories of weeds of the field, 13.24–30, 36–43, dragnet, 13.47–50, sheep and goats, 25.31–33). Luke has introduced allegory in connection with the servant who is sent out three times, to the original guests (= Jews), to the poor, etc., within the city (= outcasts among the Jews) and to travellers on the highways outside the city (= Gentiles). Thus, the story becomes an allegory of the ministry of Jesus to Jews and outcasts among the Jews, the theme of Luke's gospel, and of the ministry of the Church first to Jews and then to Gentiles, the theme of Acts.

The version of the parable in Thomas is of extraordinary interest in that it seems to be both completely independent of either of the canonical versions and also more primitive than they are, except in one single respect: the excuses. The feast giver is a man (= Luke; Matthew: king) and the feast is a supper (*deipnon*; Luke: great supper, *deipnon mega*; Matthew: marriage feast, *gamos*). Only one servant is sent out to the guests (= Luke; Matthew: servants) and he only once (= Luke; Matthew allegorizes heavily). The guests give four excuses (Luke three; Matthew has no specific excuses); this part of the story is more elaborate than the canonical versions and the excuses are different. There is no allegory at all in the Thomas version, and the point is made by a generalizing conclusion which reflects gnostic contempt for the material world and those engaged in its business. It is hard to resist the conclusion that this version is nearer to the teaching of Jesus than either of the others. It does not reflect the situation of the Church, nor, except for the generalizing conclusion, is it at all concerned with anything specifically gnostic. Except for the excuses, it is in all respects the simplest and least developed version, and stories grow and develop in the telling and retelling.

We are to imagine, then, a story about a man who gave a supper and invited his guests. As the time drew near he sent out his servant the second time to the guests, who had previously signified their willingness to attend, but now all begin to make excuses; for one reason or another not one of them can come. What will the host do? Mindful of the merit and charity of almsgiving, he will send his servant out to invite the poor of that place to his supper, as did the tax collector, Bar Ma'yon.

The point of this story lies in the relationship between the guests and the host, which is analogous to that between the Jews and God. The Jew cannot simply assume, on the strength of this relationship, that he will automatically 'sit at table with Abraham, Isaac and Jacob in the Kingdom of God'; to this end he must also respond to the challenge of the hour, the Now of the ministry of Jesus and his proclamation. If he fails to respond to this challenge, then he may find that others have taken the place he had assumed was his. But the emphasis is not upon these others, despite the interpretation of the story in the tradition, it is upon the original guests and their ultimate failure to accept the invitation.

The Unjust Steward: Luke 16.1–9

[1]He also said to the disciples, 'There was a rich man who had a steward, and charges were brought to him that this man was wasting his goods. [2]And he called him and said to him, "What is this that I hear about you? Turn in the account of your stewardship, for you can no longer be steward." [3]And the steward said to himself, "What shall I do, since my master is taking the stewardship away from me? I am not strong enough to dig, and I am ashamed to beg. [4]I have decided what to do, so that people may receive me into their houses when I am put out of the stewardship." [5]So, summoning his master's debtors one by one, he said to the first, "How much do you owe my master?" [6]He said "A hundred measures of oil." And he said to him, "Take your bill, and sit down quickly and write fifty." [7]Then he said to another, "And how much do you owe?" He said, "A hundred measures of wheat." He said to him, "Take your bill, and write eighty." [8]The master commended the dishonest steward for his prudence; for the sons of this world are wiser in their own generation than the sons of light. [9]And I tell you, make friends for yourselves by means of unrighteous mammon, so that when it fails they may receive you into the eternal habitations.'

Here we have no other version to help us reconstruct the original form of the parable, but the task is not difficult, since the tradition has sought to make the parable edifying by means of additions at the conclusion rather than by allegorizing the story itself. Probably it was felt that no touching up of the story itself could make such a wholly disreputable character edifying!

The concluding verses, 8 and 9, reflect a series of attempts to use the parable in Christian teaching or exhortation. Verse 8a, 'The master commended the dishonest servant for his prudence', is the first, and the 'master' here must be Jesus; it cannot be the rich man of the story. We have here the words of some early Christian teacher, and they are next expanded by the addition of the reference to the sons of this world and the sons of light, the latter term now abundantly illustrated from the Qumran texts. Verse 9 offers a quite different attempt to make sense of the story. Following Jeremias,[1] we understand the subject of the verb 'to receive' to be God and the saying as an attempt to use the steward as an example of prudence: he used the money to help others and for this reason God will accept him, almsgiving being a strong intercessor. This, we would argue, is a further attempt to use the story in Christian exhortation.

Leaving vv. 8 and 9 out of consideration, we have a parable, the force and vigour of which can best be appreciated by translating it into a modern idiom. We suggest: the parable of the Labour Racketeer.

'There was a certain labour racketeer who had grown rich on sweetheart contracts and illegal use of the union pension fund. One day he found that the FBI was tailing him and he began to suspect that there was no escape for him. So what did he do? Carefully, he put a large sum of money away where no one could touch it and then faced trial. He was duly convicted and after he had exhausted all his rights to appeal, he finally served a sentence in the Atlanta Federal penitentiary. Having served his time, he took his money and moved to Miami Beach, where he lived happily ever after.'

The point of the story is that we have here a man in crisis. True, he is a peculiarly disreputable man (was there an actual case known by Jesus and his hearers or were unjust stewards as well known in that society as labour racketeers are in our own?), but he is a man of decision: faced with a crisis, he acted decisively. Again, we are back to the point of the crisis of the men confronted by Jesus, his ministry and proclamation, and the necessity for decision *now*.

---

[1] J. Jeremias, *Parables of Jesus* (rev. ed., 1963), p. 46.

EXEGESIS 2. THE LABOURERS IN THE VINEYARD, THE TWO
SONS, THE CHILDREN IN THE MARKET PLACE, THE PHARISEE
AND THE TAX COLLECTOR. THE DANGER OF PRECONCEIVED
IDEAS BLINDING ONE TO THE REALITY OF THE CHALLENGE

The Labourers in the Vineyard: Matt. 20.1–16

¹For the kingdom of heaven is like a householder who went out early
in the morning to hire labourers for his vineyard. ²After agreeing with
the labourers for a denarius a day, he sent them into his vineyard.
³And going out about the third hour he saw others standing idle in the
market place; ⁴and to them he said, 'You go into the vineyard too,
and whatever is right I will give you.' So they went. ⁵Going out again
about the sixth hour and the ninth hour, he did the same. ⁶And about
the eleventh hour he went out and found others standing; and he said
to them, 'Why do you stand here idle all day?' ⁷They said to him,
'Because no one has hired us.' He said to them, 'You go into the vineyard too.' ⁸And when evening came, the owner of the vineyard said to
his steward, 'Call the labourers and pay them their wages, beginning
with the last up to the first.' ⁹And when those hired about the eleventh
hour came, each of them received a denarius. ¹⁰Now when the first
came, they thought they would receive more; but each of them also
received a denarius. ¹¹And on receiving it they grumbled at the householder, ¹²saying 'These last worked only one hour, and you have made
them equal to us who have borne the burden of the day and the scorching heat.' ¹³But he replied to one of them, 'Friend, I am doing you no
wrong; did you not agree with me for a denarius? ¹⁴Take what belongs
to you, and go; I choose to give to this last as I give to you. ¹⁵Am I not
allowed to do what I choose with what belongs to me? Or do you
begrudge my generosity?' ¹⁶So the last will be first, and the first last.

Verse 16 is an independent saying which is found in various forms
in the synoptic tradition (Mark 10.31 = Matt. 19.30; Luke 13.30)
and in a gnosticized form ('For many who are first shall become last
and they shall become a single one') in Thomas, logion 4. The
parable itself has been well preserved in the tradition, probably because the story itself is so natural, consistent and coherent, and it has
a natural *Sitz im Leben Jesu*—the offence caused by his acceptance of
the 'tax collectors and sinners' who responded to the challenge of the
forgiveness of sins.

To understand the point of the story we must compare with it the
rabbinical saying: 'Some obtain and enter the Kingdom in an hour,

while others hardly reach it after a lifetime'[1] and the parable that is
the funeral oration for Rabbi Bun:

> To whom was R. Bun like? To a king who had a vineyard and hired
> many labourers to work it. Among them was one far more skilful in his
> work than the rest, so what did the king do? He took him by the hand
> and walked with him up and down. At evening the labourers came to
> receive their wages and this one came with them and he gave him the
> full amount. The others began to grumble, saying, 'We toiled all day,
> whereas this man toiled only two hours, and yet the king has given him
> the full wage.' The king said to them, 'What cause have you for grumb-
> ling? This man did more in the two hours than you in a whole day.'[2]

The point of the saying and parable is that a Jew might earn his
place in the Kingdom in a comparatively short time if his work were
of a superlative quality.

The story Jesus told reflects the conditions of first-century Palestine
and we are to assume, as his hearers certainly would have assumed,
that the labourers hired later in the day expected to receive a part of a
denarius, a *denarius* being a regular payment for one day's labour. So
we share the surprise that this was not done, but rather each group
was paid the same. Naturally, the workers hired first grumbled, and
we would stress the *naturally*; there never was a group of workmen
who would not have grumbled under the same conditions. The whole
point is that we should enter into their situation: How would we have
reacted in this situation? If we enter into their situation, then we are
confronted by the dilemma which confronted them: the householder's undeniable right to be generous. If he wishes to treat his
workmen according to their need, rather than according to the letter
of an implied contract, that is entirely his business. Despite this fact,
however, it is undeniably true that the situation is an intolerable
situation from the workmen's viewpoint. It is an intolerable situation
precisely because the employer has chosen arbitrarily to treat one
group according to their rights and another group according to his
generosity. If he is to be generous to one, let him be generous to all;
if he is to be legalistic with one, let him be legalistic with all. Incidentally, the employer is cutting his own throat; the next time he wanted

---

[1] b. Abodah Zarah 17a. C. G. Montefiore, *The Synoptic Gospels* II (1927), 274.
[2] j. Ber. 2.3c. Parallels: Eccles. R. 5.11; Song of Sol. R. 6.2. Cf. J. Jeremias,
Parables of Jesus (rev. ed., 1963), p. 138, where it is suggested that this is secondary
to the gospel parable.

to employ workmen his reputation would have preceded him and a very interesting situation would have arisen!

But is not the intolerable nature of this situation from the workmen's viewpoint the point on which the analogy turns? If the employer acts both legalistically and generously, then the situation becomes intolerable. By analogy, if God accepts some on the basis of merit and others on the basis of forgiveness, the situation is similarly intolerable. Either all must work out their own salvation in fear and trembling, or all must rejoice in the goodness and mercy of the Lord; there is no third possibility. With this parable, therefore, Jesus throws down the gauntlet in challenge to an attitude to God that seeks to hold together both merit and mercy. Since in his own proclamation and ministry he has so clearly stressed the latter, he must of necessity challenge the former.

Two things become evident at this point. In the first place, we see a further aspect of the challenge of Jesus to his contemporaries not to allow a preconceived idea, however good it might have seemed in its own place, to blind them to the realities of the new situation created by his proclamation and ministry. That the workman is worthy of his hire is a good idea, but not in the context of the eschatological activity of God and the challenge of the forgiveness of sins. Then we see, further, as Ernst Fuchs and his pupils Eta Linnemann and Eberhard Jüngel rightly stress, that a tremendous personal claim is implied by Jesus in that he explicates and defends the situation of his ministry by means of a parable which has reference, by analogy, to the activity and attitude of God. Matthew regards the parable as an illustration of the 'last, first: first, last' principle, but we must assume that it was originally spoken in a context in which Jesus was being attacked for his attitude to 'tax collectors and sinners', with all that this implied to many of his contemporaries. But if this is the case, then, as Miss Linnemann has put it: 'There is a tremendous personal claim involved in the fact that Jesus answered an attack upon his conduct with a parable concerned with what *God* does!'[1]

The Two Sons: Matt. 21.28–32

28'What do you think? A man had two sons; and he went to the first and said, "Son, go and work in the vineyard today." 29And he answered, "I will not"; but afterward he repented and went. 30And he went to the second and said the same; and he answered, "I go, sir," but

---

[1] E. Linnemann, *Die Gleichnisse Jesu*, p. 93; cf. *Parables of Jesus*, p. 87. Cf. E. Fuchs, *Studies of the Historical Jesus*, p. 36; E. Jüngel, *Paulus und Jesus*, pp. 168f.

did not go. [31]Which of the two did the will of his father?' They said, 'The first.' Jesus said to them, 'Truly, I say to you, the tax collectors and the harlots go into the kingdom of God before you. [32]For John came to you in the way of righteousness, and you did not believe him, but the tax collectors and the harlots believed him; and even when you saw it, you did not afterward repent and believe him.'

The history of this particular bit of tradition has been established by Jeremias, who points out[1] that v. 32 is a variant of Luke 7.29f. and has probably been added to this parable because of the verbal association, 'tax collectors and harlots'. It was probably added at a pre-Matthaean stage of the tradition, since Matthew seems already to have found it and to have used it as the reason for inserting it in its present context, i.e. in close connection with another reference to the baptism of John (v. 25). We have to consider the parable without reference either to its Matthaean context or to its present conclusion, v. 32.

Interesting as background to the parable is a rabbinical simile about the giving of the Torah to Israel:

> It can be compared to a man who has a field which he wishes to entrust to peasants. Calling the first of them he asked: 'Will you take over this field?' He replied: 'I have no strength; the work is too hard for me.' In the same way the second, third and fourth declined to undertake the work. He called a fifth and asked him: 'Will you take over this field?' He replied, 'Yes.' 'On the condition that you will till it?' The reply was again: 'Yes.' But as soon as he took possession of it, he let it lie fallow. With whom is the king angry . . .? Surely with him who undertook it (*Exod. R. 27.9*).

The simile that Jesus uses is similar to this, except that it reduces the number to two and strengthens the contrast by making the first man 'afterward repent and go'. It is certainly possible that here we have a deliberate allusion to the rabbinical simile; in any case, the point is clear: to refuse and then to repent is better than to accept and then to disobey. The allusion again is to a situation in which outcasts are accepting forgiveness and other Jews are finding offence in this, and thereby blinding themselves to the reality of their own situation.

Children in the Market Place: Matt. 11.16–19 (par. Luke 7.31–35)

[16]But to what shall I compare this generation? It is like children sitting in the market places and calling to their playmates, [17]'We piped

[1] J. Jeremias, *Parables of Jesus* (rev. ed., 1963), pp. 8of.

to you, and you did not dance; we wailed, and you did not mourn.' [18]For John came neither eating nor drinking, and they say, 'He has a demon'; [19]The Son of man came eating and drinking, and they say, 'Behold, a glutton and a drunkard, a friend of tax collectors and sinners!' Yet wisdom is justified by her deeds.

The arguments for the authenticity of both this simile and its application are very strong indeed. The tradition is markedly Semitic and retranslates readily into Aramaic; hence it is early. The reference to the children reflects a sharp and sympathetic observation of Palestinian life which we have found to be characteristic of Jesus rather than of the early Church. The parable's application reflects a high estimate of the Baptist, since it puts his ministry and that of Jesus on the same level. We have already seen that this, too, is characteristic of Jesus and not of the early Church. The reference to the Son of man is certainly, as it stands, a confessional reference to Jesus, and so the product of the early Church. But in Aramaic *bar nash* could be used in such a context as an indirect reference to the speaker himself, as in the Aramaic of Genesis Rabbah.[1] It is only when it is translated into Greek, given the definite article and set in the context of early Christian tradition that it becomes confessional. Further, the designation of Jesus as 'a glutton and a drunkard' belongs to the polemics of the controversy surrounding Jesus' earthly ministry during his lifetime, rather than to the circumstances of the controversies between the early Church and Judaism. The other epithet, 'friend of tax collectors and sinners', should be understood as 'holder of table-fellowship with tax collectors and other Jews who have made themselves as Gentiles', and, together with the first epithet, it is an unmistakable reference to the major aspect of the ministry of Jesus we discussed at the end of

---

[1] E.g. Gen. R. 7.2, 3: 'When R. Haggai heard of this [a ruling by R. Jacob that fish must be ritually slaughtered] he said to him, "Come and be beaten." He replied, "A son of man who gives a ruling from the law is to be beaten!" . . . When R. Haggai heard of this [a ruling by the same R. Jacob that the infant son of a gentile woman, born to a Jew, could be circumcised on the sabbath] he sent to him, "Come and be beaten." He replied, "A son of man who gives a legal ruling to be beaten!" ' (Cf. M. Black, *ExpT* 60 (1948/9), p. 35.) Here 'son of man' is being used in reference to the speaker himself, although this use seems to be no more than could be the case in English with 'one'. It would perhaps be going too far to describe 'son of man' here as a circumlocution for the first personal pronoun. It is reported that the third edition of M. Black, *The Aramaic Approach to the Gospels and Acts*, not published at the time of writing, will contain an important discussion of the problem of the idiomatic and titular use of 'son of man' in Aramaic (by G. Vermès).

our last chapter: the table-fellowship 'of the Kingdom of God'.[1] The first epithet reflects the joyousness of that fellowship, and the second its radical nature. Finally, there is also no doubt but that the parable and its application have belonged together in the tradition from the very beginning. On the basis of the arguments just given, we may claim that both are certainly from Jesus, and the comparison between them is so apt and striking that it is impossible to imagine that they ever belonged, separately, to other bits of tradition now lost, or that they were originally independent units which were brought together only in the tradition.

The parable has reference to a situation in the ministry of Jesus with which we have become familiar: the relationship of that ministry to, and Jesus' personal association with, 'tax collectors and sinners'. In this particular instance the point of maximum offence is that Jesus enters into table-fellowship with these people, and we must compare with this the Pharisaic opinion that a tax collector defiled any house he entered and all within it.[2] We can appreciate that to many the offence would have been real, and that the challenge to change deep-rooted convictions about the basic conditions governing relations of men with God and of men with men very difficult to meet. But we can see from this parable that there were also those who were unprepared for any real challenge, and who could be offended equally by John the Baptist, to them an unreasonable ascetic, and Jesus, to them a libertine.

This parable has significance beyond that of revealing the challenge of the message of Jesus to the presuppositions of his hearers, for it offers evidence for the fact that table-fellowship with those who responded to the proclamation was a well-known aspect of the ministry of Jesus, and it brings out the fact that joyousness was the keynote of this fellowship. As we argued in chapter II, above, this is a strong indication that a table-fellowship which anticipated the joys of the age to come was a feature of the ministry of Jesus.

The Pharisee and the Tax Collector: Luke 18.9–14

[9]He also told this parable to some who trusted in themselves that they were righteous and despised others: [10]'Two men went up into the temple to pray, one a Pharisee and the other a tax collector. [11]The Pharisee stood and prayed thus with himself, "God, I thank thee that

---

[1] On this see our discussion of the saying in that context, above, pp. 105f.
[2] Quoted above, p. 94.

I am not like other men, extortioners, unjust, adulterers, or even like this tax collector. [12]I fast twice a week, I give tithes of all that I get." [13]But the tax collector, standing far off, would not even lift up his eyes to heaven, but beat his breast, saying, "God, be merciful to me a sinner!" [14]I tell you, this man went down to his house justified rather than the other; for every one who exalts himself will be humbled, but he who humbles himself will be exalted.'

The generalizing conclusion in v. 14b is certainly foreign to the parable itself. It is an independent saying found elsewhere in the tradition (e.g. Matt. 23.12; Luke 14.11) which refers to the future, the age to come, rather than the present. Apart from this, however, the tradition seems to have preserved the parable well. It is marked by numerous Semitisms, much more so than any other Lukan parable, and it reflects exactly the religious situation, customs and prayers of Palestine at the time of the second Temple. For this reason, it is particularly suited to the exegetical methodology of J. Jeremias, and his exegesis of this parable[1] is beyond all praise, and certainly beyond our power to imitate.

The crux of the matter, for our purposes, is the fact that we are here again confronted by the distinction between righteous Jew, here exemplified by the Pharisee with his characteristic[2] prayer and attitude, and the 'Jew who had made himself a Gentile', here shown as penitent before God. In this story these characters and their situation are not depicted by analogy but directly, and, in consequence, the hearers are not left to draw their own conclusions, but rather are challenged by the direct statement: 'I tell you . . .' The challenge is the one we have seen throughout this group of parables, the fundamental challenge of Jesus to his hostile contemporaries. We should note in passing that 'I tell you . . .' with its direct challenge to dearly held preconceptions of the period is an indirect personal claim of great magnitude.

EXEGESIS 3. THE GOOD SAMARITAN, THE UNMERCIFUL SERVANT, THE TOWER BUILDER, THE KING GOING TO WAR. THE NECESSARY RESPONSE TO THE CHALLENGE

The Good Samaritan: Luke 10.29–37

[29]But he, desiring to justify himself, said to Jesus, 'And who is my

---

[1] J. Jeremias, *Parables of Jesus* (rev. ed., 1963), pp. 139–44.
[2] *Ibid.*, p. 142, we find two parallels to the Pharisee's prayer: b. Ber. 28b and 1QH vii. 34.

neighbour?' [30]Jesus replied, 'A man was going down from Jerusalem to Jericho, and he fell among robbers, who stripped him and beat him, and departed, leaving him half-dead. [31]Now by chance a priest was going down the road; and when he saw him he passed by on the other side. [32]So likewise a Levite, when he came to the place and saw him, passed by on the other side. [33]But a Samaritan, as he journeyed, came to where he was; and when he saw him, he had compassion, [34]and went to him and bound up his wounds, pouring on oil and wine; then he set him on his own beast and brought him to an inn, and took care of him. [35]And the next day he took out two denarii and gave them to the inn-keeper, saying, "Take care of him; and whatever more you spend, I will repay you when I come back." [36]Which of these three, do you think, proved neighbour to the man who fell among the robbers?' [37]He said, 'The one who showed mercy on him.' And Jesus said to him, 'Go and do likewise.'

As it stands in the tradition, this parable has been attached to the Lukan equivalent of the lawyer's question about the greatest commandment (Mark 12.28–31), probably because of the catchword 'neighbour', but this is an editorial connection and we must disregard it.[1] Treated as an independently circulating parable, it still has reference to the question 'Who is my neighbour?' a question of great concern to both first-century Judaism and the early Christian Church, and so it has a natural *Sitz im Leben* in both the ministry of Jesus and the life and work of the Church. Since the vividness and power of the story itself is adequate testimony to its authenticity, we may assume that it was a parable told by Jesus in answer to such a question, although the circumstances of the questioner and the questioning are now lost to us.

The parable itself is an 'exemplary story' and as such is concerned to teach by example, in this instance the example of true neighbourliness. Of the three characters involved, only one is motivated by the recognition of overwhelming need. The others allow other concerns to override the challenge of the stranger's need, and no doubt the original hearers of the parable would have supplied these concerns in their own minds as they listened, each according to his own estimate of 'priest and Levite': fear of involvement, possibility of ceremonial defilement if the man were dead, ecclesiastical hypocrisy, and so on. Actually, the original hearers would have expected an Israelite lay-man to appear as the third character, and it is hard for us today to

[1] Miss Linnemann has convinced the present writer of this point; E. Linnemann, *Parables of Jesus*, p. 138.

recapture the sense of shock that the words 'But a Samaritan . . .', must have occasioned. Jews and Samaritans hated one another passionately at this period, on both religious and racial grounds, and lost no opportunity to express that hatred. The fact that the true neighbour turned out to be a Samaritan is as important as that the Prodigal Son became a swineherd, and, as in that parable the father is made to go through every realistically possible act of welcoming the son, so in this one the Samaritan is made to take every possible step to care for the stranger. Jesus leaves no stone unturned in his effort to make the point: Be prepared to abandon presuppositions.

The purpose of the parable is to give an example of neighbourliness, to teach that the crucial aspect of human relationships is response to the neighbour's need. There is no need for us to labour this point, since the parable speaks far more effectively for itself than any modern author could speak for it. But a point we would make is that this teaching has to be set in the context of Jesus' proclamation of the forgiveness of sins and his table-fellowship with 'tax collectors and sinners'. All the various aspects of the teaching of Jesus are closely interrelated, and to speak of Jesus as teaching the necessity of response to the neighbour's need as the crucial aspect of human relationships is misleading, unless it is clearly understood that this is an imitation of God's response to one's own need. Because one knows God as responding to human needs in terms of the eschatological forgiveness of sins, one must respond to the needs of a neighbour in terms of whatever may be appropriate to the immediate situation.

This point is not made in the parable by direct reference to the forgiveness of sins, but rather becomes apparent only when the parable is set in its context in the ministry of Jesus. At first sight the parable teaches a radically new concept of neighbourliness—in terms of need as over against mutual membership in a racial or religious group—and that it does this is, of course, true enough. But the full force of its message is felt only when it is realized that this lesson is being taught by one who proclaimed a radically new concept of the forgiveness of God: it extended even to the 'Jew who had made himself a Gentile'. The two belong together as obverse and reverse of the same coin; the showing mercy is a response to being shown mercy. This point is somewhat obscured in the tradition by v. 37b, where the 'Go and do likewise' transforms the parable into a general exhortation, but this was most probably added in the tradition.[1]

[1] R. Bultmann, *History of the Synoptic Tradition*, p. 178.

The Unmerciful Servant: Matt. 18.23–35

²³Therefore the kingdom of heaven may be compared to a king who wished to settle accounts with his servants. ²⁴When he began the reckoning, one was brought to him who owed him ten thousand talents; ²⁵and as he could not pay, his lord ordered him to be sold, with his wife, and children and all that he had, and payment to be made. ²⁶So the servant fell on his knees, imploring him, 'Lord, have patience with me, and I will pay you everything.' ²⁷And out of pity for him the lord of that servant released him and forgave him the debt. ²⁸But that same servant, as he went out, came upon one of his fellow servants who owed him a hundred denarii; and seizing him by the throat he said, 'Pay what you owe.' ²⁹So his fellow servant fell down and besought him, 'Have patience with me, and I will pay you.' ³⁰He refused and went and put him in prison till he should pay the debt. ³¹When his fellow servants saw what had taken place, they were greatly distressed, and they went and reported to their lord all that had taken place. ³²Then his lord summoned him and said to him, 'You wicked servant! I forgave you all that debt because you besought me; ³³and should not you have had mercy on your fellow servant, as I had mercy on you?' ³⁴And in anger his lord delivered him to the jailers, till he should pay his debt. ³⁵So also my heavenly Father will do to every one of you, if you do not forgive your brother from your heart.

Verses 34 and 35 are to be regarded as additions to the story, made perhaps by Matthew himself; they convert the original challenge of the parable into a warning, and v. 35 is entirely Matthaean in phraseology and sentiment. The fact that such a simple addition made it suitable for Matthew's purpose, and its own natural balance, has preserved the story in what must be very much the form in which Jesus taught it. The present connection with Peter's question is, of course, editorial; we must, as always, treat the story as an isolated piece of tradition.

The story itself is unusual among the parables of Jesus in that it does not reflect Palestinian conditions. The Jewish monarchy had never been absolute as this one is pictured as being; in Jewish law the wife could not be sold into slavery; and in Palestine torture would not have been inflicted on a man imprisoned for debt (the word translated 'jailers' in v. 34 also means 'torturers'). Only in one respect does it accord with Jewish practice, and that is in v. 30, where the servant is imprisoned and not sold into slavery. According to Jewish law, a man could not be sold into slavery because of a sum less than the sum for which he would be sold,[1] and he could not be sold for debt, only for theft. Indeed, almost the only really Palestinian touch is in v. 28: 'seizing him by the throat'. The Mishnah begins a discussion of a hypothetical case, 'If a man seized a debtor by the throat in the street . . .', assuming this to be the normal practice (B. B. 10.8)! The story, in fact, reflects the kind of hearsay knowledge of the absolute monarchies of the East and the practices of their courts that a Palestinian might have been expected to have. In this respect, it has its own kind of verisimilitude; it corresponds to the Palestinian's picture of foreign kings and their courts and so would be meaningful to him.

The point of the story is clear: as you have been forgiven, so must you forgive. The Kingdom of God is known in terms of the experience of the forgiveness of sins; the only proper response to that experience is a preparedness in turn to forgive. The story is told in terms of kings, servants and debts large and small, and as such it is an exemplary story, as is that of the Good Samaritan, except that it makes the point in reverse. The servant of this story is held up to the judgement of the hearers as an example of what should not have been done. In passing judgement on him, the hearers are affirming the principle upon which this aspect of the teaching of Jesus turns: the experience of God demands a response in terms of imitation of that experience in relationship to one's fellow men.

The Tower Builder and the King Going to War: Luke 14.28–32

[28]For which of you, desiring to build a tower, does not first sit down and count the cost, whether he has enough to complete it? [29]Otherwise, when he has laid a foundation, and is not able to finish, all who see it begin to mock him, [30]saying, 'This man began to build, and was not able to finish.' [31]Or what king, going to encounter another king in war, will not sit down first and take counsel whether he is able with ten thousand to meet him who comes against him with twenty thousand? [32]And if not, while the other is yet a great way off, he sends an embassy and asks terms of peace.

To these parables we must add one from Thomas: the Assassin.

Thomas 98. Jesus said: 'The Kingdom of the Father is like a man who wishes to kill a powerful man. He drew the sword in his house, he

---

[1] Mekilta Ex. 22.2 (Lauterbach III, p. 104). We are indebted to J. Jeremias, *Parables of Jesus* (rev. ed., 1963), pp. 211f., for the information about the Jewish law and practices.

stuck it into the wall, in order to know whether his hand would carry through; then he slew the powerful (man).'

Here we have three vivid pictures of men from very different walks of life who have one thing in common: a willingness to prepare themselves realistically for the responsibility they assume. The man building the 'tower' is probably a farmer contemplating building farm buildings; the emphasis upon the cost of the foundation makes it probable that a large building is in question, and the word translated 'tower' (*pyrgos*) can also mean 'farm buildings'.[1] The king going to war would be a familiar enough figure in embattled Palestine, and the assassin 'draws upon the stern reality of the Zealot movement'.[2] There is every reason to accept them as authentic; their very vividness, the fact that the tradition has misunderstood the first two (v. 33 makes them examples of self-denial) and the extreme unlikelihood of anyone but Jesus using a Zealot assassin as an example (cf. the Labour Racketeer!), are overwhelming arguments in their favour.

As far as the interpretation of these pictures is concerned, C.–H. Hunzinger has recently pointed out[3] that the canonical ones begin with the rhetorical question, 'Which of you . . .?' and in this respect they belong to a whole group of parables (e.g. Luke 11.11 par.; 11.5; 15.4) which draws a conclusion about God from the conduct of man. This being the case, these three should also be understood in this way; they challenge men to consider: What God has begun, he will carry through. But, as Jeremias points out,[4] the pictures are not of successfully concluding something half begun, but of preparing oneself for a task. The farmer calculates his resources, the king estimates his strength over against his enemy's, the assassin assures himself that his hand has not lost its skill; the natural point of comparison here is not God, but man. We are justified, therefore, in claiming that Luke is, so to speak, half right: these parables are parables of discipleship, although their point is not self-denial. Set in the context of the eschatological challenge of Jesus' proclamation, these parables challenge men to sober judgement. The Hid Treasure and the Pearl challenge to a recognition of the joy of fulfilment of long-held hopes, these to a recognition that, as the present writer heard T. W. Manson

[1] B. T. D. Smith, *Parables of the Synoptic Gospels* (Cambridge: University Press, 1937), p. 220.

[2] J. Jeremias, *Parables of Jesus* (rev. ed., 1963), p. 196.

[3] 'Unbekannte Gleichnisse Jesu aus dem Thomas-Evangelium', *Judentum, Urchristentum, Kirche* (Festschrift für Joachim Jeremias), ed. W. Eltester, pp. 209–20.

[4] J. Jeremias, *Parables of Jesus* (rev. ed., 1963), p. 197, n. 23.

put it, 'Salvation may be free, but it is not cheap.' These parables emphasize the earnestness and self-preparedness that must character-ize the response to the challenge of Jesus' proclamation.

EXEGESIS 4. THE FRIEND AT MIDNIGHT, THE UNJUST JUDGE. CONFIDENCE IN GOD

The Friend at Midnight: Luke 11.5–8 (The Importuned Friend)

5Which of you who has a friend will go to him at midnight and say to him, 'Friend, lend me three loaves; 6for a friend of mine has arrived on a long journey, and I have nothing to set before him'; 7and he will answer from within, 'Do not bother me; the door is now shut, and my children are with me in bed; I cannot get up and give you anything'? 8I tell you, though he will not get up and give him anything because he is his friend, yet because of his importunity he will rise and give him whatever he needs.

In this parable we find again the sympathetic observation of Palestinian peasant life so characteristic of Jesus. The Palestinian peasant wife baked bread for the day before sunrise, normally there would be none left after dark. The responsibilities of hospitality were sacred in the ancient East and three loaves are a meal for one person. The importuned friend is living in a one-room cottage, the whole family sleeping on a mat on a raised platform, and getting up and un-bolting the door, itself a cumbersome business, would necessarily disturb the whole household.

The one difficulty in the story is the phrase translated 'because of his importunity' (*anaideian*). This can be referred either to the impor-tuner, as in the translation above, or it can be referred to the impor-tuned, in which case it must be understood in the sense of 'so as not to be shamed', i.e. not to lose face.[1] There can be no certainty as to which of these is correct, but the fact that the parable is so strongly Palestinian in atmosphere lends weight to the latter, the more oriental of the two possibilities. If we accept this as the correct rendering, then the whole weight of the story falls not upon the importuner, but upon the importuned, for it is his conduct that is singled out for explanation and comment. We would, therefore, call it the 'Impor-tuned Friend', and, with Jeremias,[2] read it as one long rhetorical question followed by a pungent comment. 'Is it conceivable that one

[1] J. Jeremias, *Parables of Jesus* (rev. ed., 1963), p. 158.
[2] *Ibid.*

of you could have a friend who would come to you at midnight . . . could you answer from within . . .? No, you could not. Even if his friendship did not get you up, the shame of refusing to accept responsibility for the needs of hospitality would be more than sufficient to do so!'

The parable argues from the lesser to the greater, and the natural interpretation is: If the importuned has to answer his friend, how much more must God hear you. We must remember that the context of the parable is the total proclamation of Jesus and that its message is, therefore, a supplement to that proclamation. Those who hear the proclamation may have full confidence in the God of which it speaks: If . . . how much more must . . . Luke, concerned with the ongoing life of the Church and experience of the Christian 'way', understands the reference to be to confidence in prayer; but it seems more probable that the original reference was to the totality of the proclamation as it challenged the hearer.

The Unjust Judge: Luke 18.1–8 (The Importuned Judge)

¹And he told them a parable, to the effect that they ought always to pray and not lose heart. ²He said, 'In a certain city there was a judge who neither feared God nor regarded man; ³and there was a widow in that city who kept coming to him and saying, "Vindicate me against my adversary." ⁴For a while he refused; but afterward he said to himself, "Though I neither fear God nor regard man, ⁵yet because this widow bothers me, I will vindicate her, or she will wear me out by her continual coming." ' ⁶And the Lord said, 'Hear what the unrighteous judge says. ⁷And will not God vindicate his elect, who cry to him day and night? Will he delay long over them? ⁸I tell you, he will vindicate them speedily. Nevertheless, when the Son of man comes, will he find faith on earth?'

Verse 1 is the Lukan introduction; as in the case of the Importuned Friend he understands the reference to be to God as the answerer of prayer, and vv. 6, 7 and 8 are a series of comments accruing to the story in the tradition. Restricting ourselves to vv. 2–5, we have a vivid picture, of which an exact modern parallel has been reported,[1] of an Eastern judge whose judgements are responsive to bribery and a poor widow whose persistence in importunity wins the day for her. Again, it is an argument from the lesser to the greater, and the probable reference is the total proclamation of Jesus as it challenged the

[1] By H. B. Tristram, quoted in B. T. D. Smith, *Parables of the Synoptic Gospels*, p. 150, and summarized by J. Jeremias, *Parables of Jesus* (rev. ed., 1963), p. 154, n. 7.

individual hearer. If an unjust judge can be importuned into responding to a poor widow, how much more can you trust the God who
reaches out to you in the word of forgiveness.

The application of these twin parables to prayer is natural and
proper. Certainly trust extended to the God known in the experience
of forgiveness would lead naturally to the practice of prayer, and the
existence of the Lord's Prayer itself is evidence enough that Jesus did,
in fact, lead his followers from the general attitude of trust to the
particular expression of it in prayer.

Thus far we have discussed the challenge of Jesus to recognition
and response in terms of the parabolic teaching; now we must turn to
another aspect of the matter: the challenge of Jesus to *faith*. 'Faith'
is a dangerous word to use in connection with the teaching of Jesus,
because its constant theological, ecclesiastical and evangelical use
among Christians inevitably leads to a tendency to associate ideas
with the word in the teaching of Jesus which really have no place
there. Despite this danger, however, we have no choice in the matter,
because Jesus did, in fact, challenge men to 'faith'. The most we can
do is to stay as close to the text as we can, mindful that the real issue
is the way the word is being used, not what ideas we may associate
with it.

'FAITH' IN THE TEACHING OF JESUS[1]

The discussion of this aspect of the teaching of Jesus has only very
recently come alive in English language research. For a long time it
did not get very far and for this there are a number of reasons. One
difficulty has been that scholars tending to a conservative view of the
tradition have, as a consequence, also tended to regard the various
claims and challenges of the Christ of the gospels as constituting the
situation of the ministry of the historical Jesus. Since there is no point
at which the gospel tradition is more influenced by the post-Easter
situation than it is in this aspect of the depiction of the risen Lord of
Christian experience in terms of Jesus of Nazareth, this has not proven
a fruitful approach to the problem. On the other hand, scholars who
were sensitive to the differences between the historical Jesus and the

---

[1] See on this subject: R. Bultmann, *Faith* (Bible Key Words from Gerhard
Kittel's *Theologisches Wörterbuch zum Neuen Testament*), London: A. & C. Black
(No. 10), and New York: Harper and Row (Vol. III with *Spirit of God*), 1961.
G. Ebeling, 'Jesus and Faith', in his collected essays *Word and Faith* (ET by J. W.
Leitch of *Wort und Glaube* [1960]. London: SCM Press, and Philadelphia: Fortress
Press, 1963), pp. 201–46.

Christ of the gospel tradition tended to see their task as depicting the historical Jesus in such a way that they and their readers might enter into his experience and so share his confidence in God,[1] which is what they understood faith to be. There has recently been a return to a view similar to this, although very differently expressed, in the work of Ernst Fuchs, who speaks of Jesus' faith, of Jesus' decision, and of the need to repeat Jesus' decision, and who speaks also of Jesus' personal prayer as 'the most eminent part of his own obedience in faith', and of the disciples as being let 'take part in his prayer'.[2] But the difficulty with this is always that it assumes two things: that faith is concerned with one's attitude to God, which is true enough, but much too broadly conceived; and that the crux of the challenge of Jesus is that men should share his faith,[3] which is a sweeping assumption, indeed. A further problem is that many of the most characteristic sayings about faith in the gospels are associated with miracles, especially healing miracles, and critical scholarship has found this aspect of the tradition very difficult. Liberal scholars tended either to rationalize the stories, or to speak movingly of 'the supreme meaning of Jesus' wonders: God's will of mercy and salvation was expressing itself through him,'[4] and then move quickly to a more congenial subject! Form criticism, building on the foundations of the immense comparative studies of the *religionsgeschichtliche Schule*, dismissed the stories as typical products of the legend-making propensities of ancient religious movements, to be paralleled in both Jewish and Hellenistic religious literature.[5] In either case, there was no desire to discuss the concept of faith involved in these stories as an aspect of the teaching of Jesus. A further factor at work in the situation was the feeling that a discussion of 'faith' in the teaching of Jesus would lead to a discussion of *Jesus*' faith and this would be an illegitimate psychologizing about Jesus.[6] It can readily be seen that there are strong reasons for

---

[1] For example, B. Harvie Branscomb, *The Teachings of Jesus* (New York: Abingdon Press, 1931), p. 209: 'This is the source and ground of Jesus' confidence and courage. . . . We usually call this Jesus' teaching of faith in God. He constantly urged greater faith on his disciples. . . .'

[2] E. Fuchs, *Studies of the Historical Jesus*, pp. 11–31 ('The Quest of the Historical Jesus') and 48–64 ('Jesus and Faith'). Quotations are from p. 62.

[3] Fuchs would want to express the matter in words very different from these.

[4] E. J. Goodspeed, *Life of Jesus* (New York: Harper & Bros., 1956), pp. 55f.

[5] E.g. R. Bultmann, *History of the Synoptic Tradition*, pp. 209–44.

[6] Cf. Bultmann's comments on the work of Fuchs, in *The Historical Jesus and the Kerygmatic Christ*, ed. C. E. Braaten and R. A. Harrisville (New York: Abingdon Press, 1964), pp. 32f.

the fact that Bultmann's article on Faith, in Kittel's *TWNT*, in many ways a classic, did not include a discussion of the teaching of Jesus.

Today, however, it is being increasingly recognized that the tradition of miracle stories in the gospels deserves much more serious attention than either the older liberal or the earlier form-critical scholarship gave it. Further, a closer study of this tradition throws into sharp relief the role played in it by references to 'faith'.

The view of the miracles held by critical scholarship has, then, changed, and for this there are a number of reasons. One is that parallels quoted from Jewish and Hellenistic literature have been more carefully examined, and they turn out to be not completely convincing as sources for all that we find in the synoptic accounts.

As a matter of convenience, and because these are the crux of the matter so far as the ministry of Jesus is concerned, we will restrict ourselves to exorcisms, giving two characteristic passages from the Hellenistic literature.

Philostratus, *Apollonius of Tyana* iv. 20

(Apollonius is discussing the question of libations and in his audience is a youth with 'so evil a reputation for licentiousness, that his conduct had once been the subject of coarse street-corner songs'. This youth interrupts Apollonius with loud and coarse laughter.) Then Apollonius looked up at him and said: 'It is not yourself that perpetrates this insult, but the demon, who drives you on without your knowing it.' And in fact the youth was, without knowing it, possessed by a devil; for he would laugh at things that no one else laughed at, and then he would fall to weeping for no reason at all, and he would talk and sing to himself. Now most people thought that it was the boisterous humour of youth which led him into such excesses; but he was really the mouthpiece of a devil, though it only seemed a drunken frolic in which on that occasion he was indulging. Now when Apollonius gazed on him, the ghost in him began to utter cries of fear and rage, such as one hears from people who are being branded or racked; and the ghost swore that he would leave the young man alone and never take possession of any man again. But Apollonius addressed him with anger, as a master might a shifty, rascally, and shameless slave and so on, and he ordered him to quit the young man and show by a visible sign that he had done so. 'I will throw down yonder statue,' said the devil, and pointed to one of the images which were in the king's portico, for there it was that the scene took place. But when the statue began by moving gently, and then fell down, it would defy anyone to describe the hubbub which arose thereat and the way they clapped their hands with wonder. But the young man rubbed his eyes as if he had just woke up, and he looked towards the rays of the sun, and won the consideration of all who now had turned their attention to him; for he no longer showed himself licentious, nor did he stare madly about, but he had returned to his own self, as thoroughly as if he had been treated with drugs; and he gave up his dainty dress and summery garments and the rest of his sybaritic way of life, and he fell in love with the austerity of the philosophers, and donned their cloak, and stripping off his old self modelled his life in future upon that of Apollonius.[1]

Lucian, *Philopseudes* 16

'You act ridiculously,' said Ion, 'to doubt everything. For my part, I should like to ask you what you say to those who free possessed men from their terrors by exorcising the spirits so manifestly. I need not discuss this: everyone knows about the Syrian from Palestine, the adept in it, how many he takes in hand who fall down in the light of the moon and roll their eyes and fill their mouths with foam; nevertheless, he restores them to health and sends them away normal in mind, delivering them from their straits for a large fee. When he stands beside them as they lie there and asks: "Whence came you into his body?" the patient himself is silent, but the spirit answers in Greek or in the language of whatever foreign country he comes from, telling how and whence he entered into the man; whereupon, by adjuring the spirit and if he does not obey, threatening him, he drives him out. Indeed, I actually saw one coming out, black and smoky in colour.'[2]

It becomes apparent that many of the details in the synoptic accounts are paralleled in the Hellenistic literature; that Christian writers did use Hellenistic models can be seen quite clearly in the apocryphal Acts of Peter, where the author improves on a version of a story similar to that told by Philostratus.

Acts of Peter XI

And as Peter spake thus and embraced Marcellus, Peter turned himself to the multitude that stood by him and saw there one that laughed (smiled), in whom was a very evil spirit. And Peter said unto him: 'Whosoever thou art that didst laugh, show thyself openly unto all that are present.' And hearing this the young man ran into the court of the house and cried out with a loud voice and dashed himself against

[1] Quoted from the translation by F. C. Conybeare in the Loeb Classical Library.
[2] Quoted from the translation by A. M. Harmon in the Loeb Classical Library.

the wall and said: 'Peter, there is a great contention between Simon and the dog whom thou sentest; for Simon saith to the dog: "Say that I am not here." Unto whom the dog saith more than thou didst charge him; and when he hath accomplished the mystery which thou didst command him, he shall die at thy feet.' But Peter said: 'And thou also, devil, whosoever thou art, in the name of our Lord Jesus Christ, go out of that young man and hurt him not at all; show thyself to all that stand here.' When the young man heard it, he ran forth and caught hold on a great statue of marble which was set in the court of the house, and broke it in pieces with his feet. Now it was a statue of Caesar. Which Marcellus beholding smote his forehead and said unto Peter: 'A great crime hath been committed; for if this be made known unto Caesar by some busybody, he will afflict us with sore punishments.' And Peter said to him: 'I see thee not the same that thou wast a little while ago, for thou saidst that thou wast ready to spend all thy substance to save thy soul. But if thou indeed repentest, believing in Christ with thy whole heart, take in thine hands of the water that runneth down, and pray to the Lord, and in his name sprinkle it upon the broken pieces of the statue and it shall be whole as it was before.' And Marcellus, nothing doubting, but believing with his whole heart, before he took the water lifted up his hands and said: 'I believe in thee, O Lord Jesus Christ: for I am now proved by thine apostle Peter, whether I believe aright in thy holy name. Therefore I take water in my hands, and in thy name do I sprinkle these stones that the statue may become whole as it was before. If, therefore, Lord, it be thy will that I continue in the body and suffer nothing at Caesar's hand, let this stone be whole as it was before.' And he sprinkled the water upon the stones, and the statue became whole, whereat Peter exulted that Marcellus had not doubted in asking of the Lord, and Marcellus was exalted in spirit for that such a sign was first wrought by his hands; and he therefore believed with his whole heart in the name of Jesus Christ the Son of God, by whom all things impossible are made possible.[1]

None the less, there is one thing conspicuous by its absence from these Hellenistic stories and that is the use of 'faith' in such a saying as 'Your faith has saved you'. Such a use of 'faith' is not only completely absent from these stories, it is also without parallel anywhere in the Hellenistic literature.

We might expect that the Jewish literature would provide a closer parallel to the gospel narratives, and, indeed, exorcism stories are more common here than they are in the Hellenistic literature. We

[1] Quoted from M. R. James, *The Apocryphal New Testament* (Oxford: Clarendon Press, 1953), pp. 314f.

give three examples from the Babylonian Talmud, quoting the Soncino edition.

b. Me'ilah 17b

(R. Simeon and R. Eleazar are going to Rome to work for the annulment of anti-Jewish decrees.) Then Ben Temalion [a demon] came to meet them. He said: 'Is it your wish that I accompany you?' Thereupon R. Simeon wept and said: 'The handmaid of my ancestor's house was found worthy of meeting an angel thrice [Hagar: Gen. 16], and I not even to meet him once. However, let the miracle be performed, no matter how.' Thereupon he [the demon] advanced and entered into the Emperor's daughter. When R. Simeon arrived there he called out: 'Ben Temalion leave her, Ben Temalion leave her', and as he proclaimed this he left her. He [the emperor] said to them: 'Request whatever you desire.'

b. Kiddushim 29b

Now a certain demon haunted Abaye's schoolhouse, so that when [only] two entered, even by day, they were injured. [R. Aha b. Jacob is on his way to visit Abaye] He [Abaye] ordered, 'Let no man afford him hospitality [so that he would be forced to sleep in the schoolhouse]; perhaps a miracle will happen [in his merit].' So he entered and spent the night in that schoolhouse, during which it [the demon] appeared to him in the guise of a seven-headed dragon. Every time he [the Rabbi] fell on his knees [in prayer] one head fell off. The next day he reproached them: 'Had not a miracle occurred, you would have endangered my life.'

b. Kiddushim 39b–40a

As in the case of R. Hanina b. Pappi, whom a certain matron urged [to immorality]. He pronounced a certain [magical] formula, whereupon his body was covered with boils and scabs [so as to protect him from temptation]; but she did something and he was healed. So he fled and hid himself in a bathhouse in which when [even] two entered, even in daytime, they would suffer harm [from demons]. The next morning [seeing he was unharmed] the Rabbis asked him. 'Who guarded you?' Said he to them, 'Two Imperial [armour] bearers guarded me all night.' Said they to him, 'Perhaps you were tempted with immorality and successfully resisted?' For it is taught, He who is tempted with immorality and successfully resists, a miracle is performed for him.

It can be seen at once that here again the emphasis upon faith so characteristic of the synoptic stories is completely missing. There is no equivalent to 'Your faith has saved you'; rather, power over the demons is an attribute of a particular rabbi, or it is granted in answer to prayer or as a reward for a meritorious act. We have restricted ourselves to exorcisms, but the same thing is true if all types of miracle stories are considered. After considering twenty-one miracle stories of all kinds as a representative cross-section of the rabbinic tradition, L. J. McGinley points out that 'faith is never demanded from the patient'.[1] As in the case of the Hellenistic stories, so also here the characteristic 'Your faith has saved you' of the gospel narratives is conspicuous by its absence.

Set in the context of their Hellenistic and Jewish parallels, then, the synoptic narratives offer many features that are reminiscent of features present in those parallels—in this respect the work of Bultmann mentioned above[2] is justified—but they also offer one strikingly different feature: the emphasis upon the faith of the patient, or his friends.

Another factor entering into the discussion at this point is the increasing willingness of critical scholars to accept the premise that Jesus did, in fact, 'cast out demons' in a way considered remarkable by his contemporaries. The evidence for this is strong. We have the testimony of the Jewish sources;[3] the fact that such stories occur in all strata of the tradition, including the two earliest, Mark and Q (criterion of multiple attestation); and the authentic Kingdom-sayings related to exorcisms, especially Matt. 12.28 par. Today, the pupils of the original form critics are prepared to accept elements of the tradition their teachers rejected.[4] We cannot, of course, diagnose the diseases and their cures over the gulf of two thousand years and radically different *Weltanschauungen*. Nor can we accept the necessary authenticity of any single story as it stands at present in the synoptic tradition; the 'legendary overlay' (Käsemann) and the influence of parallel stories from Hellenism and Judaism on the tradition are too strong for that. But we can say that behind that tradition there must lie a hard core of authenticity, even though its details are unrecoverable today. But if there is a hard core of authenticity, and if the process of transmission has been largely an expansion of this tradition by, and its accommodation to, the influence of parallel stories in other

[1] L. J. McGinley, 'The Synoptic Healing Narrative and Rabbinic Analogies', *Theological Studies* 4 (1943), p. 95.

[2] Note 2 : See above, p. 131 n. 5.

[3] Referred to above, p. 65.

[4] Most important in this context is E. Käsemann's article, 'Wunder IV. Im NT', *RGG*³ VI (1962), 1835–7, especially the opening paragraph.

traditions, then the unique element in the tradition in comparison with its parallels is that which has the highest claim to authenticity. Although we cannot, today, reconstruct a single authentic healing or exorcism narrative from the tradition we have, we are none the less entitled to claim that the emphasis upon the faith of the patient, or his friends, in that tradition is authentic.

We are concerned with the frequently occurring 'Your faith has saved you' or its equivalent: Mark 5.34 par. (woman with the flow of blood); Mark 10.52 par. (blind Bartimaeus); Luke 7.50 (woman who was a sinner); Luke 17.19 (Samaritan leper); Mark 2.5 (the paralytic's friends). Although we are not prepared to argue for the authenticity of any of the narratives concerned, we are arguing for the authenticity of such an element in the historical ministry of Jesus: he did help those who confronted him in their need in a way his contemporaries regarded as remarkable, and he did link this with the 'faith' of the people concerned.

In order to investigate the meaning to be attributed to 'faith' as Jesus used it, we have to consider, in addition, the complex of sayings about faith 'moving mountains' or 'uprooting trees'. The two fundamental sayings here are Matt. 17.20 and Luke 17.6.

> **Matt. 17.20.** He said to them, 'Because of your little faith. For truly, I say to you, if you will have faith as a grain of mustard seed, you will say to this mountain, "Move hence to yonder place", and it will move; and nothing will be impossible to you.'

> **Luke 17.6.** And the Lord said, 'If you had faith as a grain of mustard seed, you could say to this sycamine tree, "Be rooted up, and be planted in the sea; and it would obey you." '

In addition, Mark 11.23 has a saying, 'Whoever says to this mountain "Be taken up and cast into the sea", and does not doubt . . . but believes . . . it will be done for him', set in the context of the dialogue about the meaning of the withered fig tree, and in this he is followed by Matthew (21.21). Then Paul appears to allude to the saying in I Cor. 13.2, '. . . if I have all faith, so as to remove mountains . . .' and gnosticized versions of it occur twice in Thomas, where the gnostic 'unity' which is expressive of the state of salvation is such that 'they shall say to the mountain: "Be moved", and it shall be moved' (logion 48, cf. 106).

The most reasonable explanation of this complicated complex of sayings would appear to be (1) that there is widespread tradition that triumphant Christian (or gnostic) faith is such as to be able to 'move mountains' (I Cor. 13.2; Thomas 106; 48). Then (2) Mark 11.23 (= Matt. 21.21) should be recognized as a mixed saying in that it has parts of the two originally separate metaphors: the mountain from a version such as is now in Matt. 17.20 and the sea from a version such as is now in Luke 17.6. (3) Matt. 17.20 and Luke 17.6 should be recognized as two distinct sayings making exactly the same point: the inconceivable power of faith. They have different but equally vivid metaphors of contrast: the proverbially small mustard seed with the power to move mountains, and the same seed and the power to uproot a sycamine (sycamore: Heb. *shiḳmāh*) tree. The latter metaphor comes alive for us when we recognize that the Palestinian sycamine tree was notably deep rooted; the Mishnah says: 'A tree may not be grown within twenty-five cubits of a cistern, or within fifty cubits if it is . . . a sycamore (*shiḳmāh*) tree' (B. B. 2.11).[1] Since a developing tradition does not sharpen and isolate metaphors but rather mixes and blunts them, we may assume that these two sayings have given rise to the tradition of faith 'moving mountains' in the Church rather than *vice versa*, and there is good reason to accept their authenticity. Their vividness is a characteristic of the teaching of Jesus in metaphor; there are no parallels in Judaism to this form of a concept of faith,[2] and they are entirely coherent with the emphasis on faith in the exorcism-healing tradition. Nor may it be supposed that an early Christian emphasis upon faith has been read back into the tradition. The concept involved is different from that to be found in the early Church in that it is absolute and not directed towards Jesus (criterion of dissimilarity), and it is consistent in both miracle stories and sayings (criterion of multiple attestation).

The data we have to interpret, then, is that Jesus did help certain people in their need in a way his contemporaries regarded as remarkable, but he insisted that 'Your faith has saved you'; and that he taught that the veriest particle of faith could 'move mountains' or 'uproot even sycamine trees'. What does 'faith' mean in these contexts? Well, it is clearly being used absolutely; there is no *direct* relationship to God or Jesus himself, men are not being asked to believe *in* God, to believe *on* Jesus. They are not even being asked to count themselves, in the moment of faith, a part of a regular religious

---

[1] Cf. T. W. Manson, *Sayings of Jesus* (London: SCM Press, 1949), p. 141.
[2] G. Ebeling, *Word and Faith*, p. 229, with references.

community. Faith is imputed to the Samaritan leper, the Syro-phoenician woman and the Gentile nobleman irrespective of any confessional standing in regard to a specific religious faith. Whatever may be our critical estimate of the authenticity of the individual stories, this is all so startlingly unlike anything that we could parallel in Judaism (the disregard of the community of faith) or the early Church (faith not directed to Jesus)[1] that it must be the usage of Jesus himself.

To come closer to an interpretation of the data we should note another factor in this tradition: faith is used both in connection with the forgiveness of sins (Luke 7.50) and with healing (Mark 5.34 etc.); indeed, the two are linked as being one and the same thing in the context of faith (Mark 2.5ff.). Now, this is not only fully in accordance with the relationship between sin and suffering as understood by the Jews at the time of Jesus (John 9.2), but it is also the reason for the very existence of an exorcism-healing element in the ministry of Jesus. We argued in chapter II, above, that Jesus was, above all, the Proclaimer of the Kingdom of God and that a major specific aspect of that proclamation was the eschatological forgiveness of sins. But if Jesus proclaimed the forgiveness of sins as a reality for those who accepted the challenge of his proclamation, then this proclamation must be accompanied by a ministry of exorcism and healing. So deep-rooted was the connection between sin and suffering to a Palestinian Jew of the first century that if there had been no such aspect of the ministry of Jesus, the proclamation of the Kingdom of God and the forgiveness of sins must have been regarded as a vain and empty sham. The present state of the tradition testifies to the reality of this connection in the ministry of Jesus in the way in which it equates the two in the context of faith. Recognition of this brings us closer to an understanding of the absolute use of faith by Jesus, in that it calls our attention to the fact that both the offer of the forgive-ness of sins and the exorcisms were the subject of controversy between Jesus and some of his contemporaries. The synagogue scene at Capernaum pictures Jesus being accused of blasphemy in connection with the forgiveness of sins (Mark 2.7), and, although this is, no doubt, an 'ideal' or 'typical' scene, we have no reason to doubt its essential correspondence to an aspect of the historical ministry of

[1] Except in Matt. 18.6, the only place where the specifically Christian Greek construction *pisteuein eis* is found in the synoptics and where the *eis eme* is clearly secondary, being absent in the source, Mark 9.42.

Jesus. Similarly, the Beelzebul controversy (Mark 3.22–27), again certainly corresponding to an aspect of the ministry of the historical Jesus, pictures Jesus as being accused of collusion with the prince of demons in his exorcisms. In both contexts, therefore, faith must necessarily begin as recognition: recognition that Jesus does, in fact, have the authority to forgive sins, and recognition that the exorcisms are, indeed, a manifestation of the Kingdom of God, all possible arguments to the contrary notwithstanding. In this respect, faith is essentially an assent to a particular interpretation of an event, an interpretation not necessarily self-evident in the event itself. Jesus *could* have been blaspheming, his exorcisms *could* be collusion with evil forces, and what his opponents, no doubt, regarded as the indiscriminate nature of both the forgiveness (including tax collectors and sinners) and the healings (Samaritan leper) could be an argument against these aspects of his ministry, but for faith both are a manifestation of the kingly activity of God.

Faith, then, includes this vital element of recognition; it is in no small part trust in the fact that God is, indeed, active in the ministry of Jesus and that Jesus is what he implicitly claims to be. But although this faith has thus an ultimate reference both to God and to Jesus, it is by no means confidence in God or faith in Jesus. It could *become* this, on reflection, but the fact is that faith is used absolutely in the characteristic 'Your faith has saved you', or 'faith as a grain of mustard seed. . . .' It is not there further defined as faith in God, in Jesus, in the good news, as it is in the characteristic reformulations in the tradition, for example Mark 1.15: '. . . believe in the gospel'. The force of this absolute use is to concentrate attention upon the concrete nature of faith. 'Faith is concrete faith in its being related to a concrete situation.'[1] It is faith in relation to a specific occurrence, a given event, an immediate challenge. Faith means to recognize the concrete situation for what it is and to respond in the only appropriate manner to its challenge.

The appropriate response is implicit in the concept of faith itself as it was understood in ancient Judaism, for there the primary meaning of faith is certainly trust. A traditional saying, attributed in the Babylonian Talmud (b. Sot. 48b) to Rabbi Eliezer b. Hyrcanus and hence certainly coming from New Testament times, runs: 'Whoever has a piece of bread in his basket and says "What shall I eat tomorrow?" belongs only to them who are little in faith.' Faith here is

---

[1] G. Ebeling, *Word and Faith*, p. 244.

clearly trust, in this instance in God's provisioning, and the 'faith as a grain of mustard seed' in the teaching of Jesus would seem to be an allusion to some such saying as this one. Although to do so is to lose the pungency of the original, we may certainly understand it as 'even the smallest particle of trust, if it is real trust . . .' So the appropriate response to the challenge is trust; trust in God, but trust in God in the concrete situation and in the particular instance, trust in relation to the specific challenge. But to the Jews trust must of necessity issue in obedience, faith becoming faithfulness,[1] and so here we must understand the response of faith as including both trust and obedience, absolute trust and complete obedience.

One is entitled to use words such as absolute or complete in connection with trust and obedience in the teaching of Jesus. In the first place, both the absolute use of 'faith' and the imagery of the mustard seed are evidence that faith either is or is not; so far as the teaching of Jesus is concerned, there is no less or more to faith. The point of the mustard seed image in this instance is not that a mustard seed grows into a large bush, but that there is no such thing as a large mustard seed! Again, we have the vivid saying, Luke 14.26: 'If any-one comes to me and does not hate his own father and mother and wife and children and brothers and sisters, yes, and even his own life, he cannot be my disciple.' This may be regarded as authentic because of the vividness of the imagery and because the variant in Matt. 10.37 ('is not worthy of me' for 'cannot be my disciple') goes back to an original Aramaic in which we have the unusual word *shwly*[2] for disciple. As an authentic saying, it vividly illustrates the nature of the obedience required as part of the faith response to the challenge of Jesus and his proclamation. Luke 9.62: 'No one who puts his hand to the plough and looks back is fit for the Kingdom of God' has equal claim to authenticity (the imagery is vivid and without parallel in Judaism, Billerbeck, *Kommentar ad loc.*; the use of Kingdom of God is dominical) and makes the same point in a different way. Involved in faith is absolute trust and complete obedience. We may summarize: Jesus challenged men to faith as recognition and response to the chal-lenge of his proclamation—recognition that God was, indeed, active as king in his ministry, and in a specific event, occasion or incident

---

[1] Note the absolute use of faith in the sense of faithfulness in Wisd. of Sol. 3.14; IV Ezra 6.28; 7.34, and as parallel to righteousness in I Enoch 58.5; 61.4.

[2] *shwly* = apprentice. The usual word for disciple of a rabbi is *tlmyd*. T. W. Manson, *Teaching of Jesus*, p. 238.

for the individual concerned, and response in terms of absolute trust and complete obedience.

We have stressed the direct and concrete nature of the challenge to faith in the teaching of Jesus; we turn now to explore further the response-as-obedience aspect of that teaching in terms of a group of sayings which exhibit the radical and total character of the challenge of Jesus altogether. These are: Luke 9.62; Mark 10.23b, 25; Luke 9.60a; Matt. 7.13f.; Mark 10.31; Mark 7.15; Mark 10.15; Luke 14.11; 16.15; Matt. 5.39b–41; Matt. 5.44–48.

These sayings have been chosen from among the residue of logia which survives the extensive, and brilliant, investigation of 'Jesus as the teacher of wisdom' by R. Bultmann in his *History of the Synoptic Tradition* (pp. 69–105). This investigation is so thorough, the emerging history of tradition so convincing and the application of what we have called the criterion of dissimilarity so careful, that we feel no need to do more than quote Bultmann's conclusion: 'All these sayings . . . contain something characteristic, new, reaching out beyond popular wisdom and piety and yet (they) are in no sense scribal or rabbinic, nor yet Jewish apocalyptic. So here, if anywhere, we can find what is characteristic of the preaching of Jesus.'[1] No discussion of the authenticity of these sayings, therefore, will be offered here.

EXEGESIS 5. LUKE 9.62; MARK 10.23b, 25; LUKE 9.60a;
MATT. 7.13f.; MARK 10.31; LUKE 14.11, cf. 16.15. THE
CHALLENGE TO DISCIPLESHIP

Luke 9.62

No one who puts his hand to the plough and looks back is fit for the Kingdom of God.

This saying has both the vivid naturalness of imagery and the radical nature of the demand which are typical of the 'ethical' teaching of Jesus. The reference to the plough is a parable in itself ('To what shall we compare the Kingdom of God? It is like a man who puts his hand to the plough and moves steadfastly across the land, looking neither to the right nor to the left, and least of all behind him!') and characterizes the single-mindedness that is an essential aspect of the response to the challenge of Jesus' proclamation.

Some idea of the vividness of Jesus' teaching can be seen by com-

[1] R. Bultmann, *History of the Synoptic Tradition*, p. 105.

paring this saying with a rabbinical one of similar import: 'If a man was walking by the way and studying and he ceased his study and said, "How fine is this tree!" or "How fine is this ploughed field!" the Scripture reckons it to him as though he was guilty against his own soul' (Aboth 3.8).

Mark 10.23b, 25

How hard it will be (v. 24: is) to enter the Kingdom of God. . . . It is easier for a camel to go through the eye of a needle than for a rich man to enter the Kingdom of God.

The tradition here varies between the present tense and the future in vv. 24 and 23 respectively. There is no need for us to make any decision on this point, because both would be equally fitting in the teaching of Jesus, since, as we have seen and as we shall have occasion to see, there is in that teaching an absolutely characteristic tension between present and future.[1]

'To enter the Kingdom of God' is an idiom found both in Judaism and in the early Church, and it is, therefore, indefensible on the basis of the criterion of dissimilarity. But it is so widespread in the tradition (criterion of multiple attestation), and so much more used in the synoptic tradition than anywhere else in Judaism or Christianity, that we may accept it as part of the teaching of Jesus, and we may certainly accept this saying on the basis of Bultmann's analysis of the tradition. There is no need for us to blunt the hyperbole of the reference to the camel and the eye of the needle. Rabbinic Judaism knows well the imagery of an elephant going through the eye of a needle as a symbol for the impossible,[2] so Jesus' imagery was readily understandable as well as apposite.

This attitude to riches is radical. The Jews recognized the danger of riches becoming a hindrance to the observance of the Law, and they had had such an experience of the wealthier among their people succumbing to the temptation of a worldly Hellenism that the word 'poor' had become a synonym for 'pious'. None the less, the rabbis strove for a balance in this matter, and their view is well expressed in Midrash Exodus Rabbah 31 on Ex. 22.24:

You will find that there are riches that positively harm their possessors and other riches that stand them in good stead.

[1] On this see N. Perrin, *Kingdom*, pp. 185–99.
[2] Billerbeck, *Kommentar* I, 828.

When Solomon built the Temple, he said in his dedication prayer: 'Lord of the Universe! Should a man pray unto thee for money and Thou knowest that it will be harmful to him, then do not grant his request; but shouldst Thou see one that will do well with his riches, then do grant him.'

Jesus, on the other hand, sees in riches a great danger. The reason is probably that he saw in riches a hindrance to the absolute nature of the self-surrender necessary as response to the challenge of the proclamation.

Luke 9.60a

'Leave the dead to bury their own dead.' [Matthew (8.22) precedes this with 'Follow me', and Luke continues, 'but as for you, go and proclaim the Kingdom of God', a characteristically Lukan emphasis.]

This is possibly the most radical of the sayings of Jesus on response to the challenge. In Judaism the responsibility for burying the dead was one that took precedence over all other duties enjoined in the Law. 'He whose dead lies unburied before him is exempt from reciting the *Shema*, from saying the Tefillah and from wearing phylacteries' (Ber. 3.1, some texts add: 'and from all the duties enjoined in the Law'). So radical is the gospel saying that it has often been suggested that there must either be a mistranslation here (a noun participle 'burier of the dead' misunderstood as an imperatival infinitive) or the reference must be to people spiritually dead. Neither of these suggestions is convincing, and, indeed, the radical nature of the saying is the guarantee of its authenticity. The response to the challenge of the Kingdom is all-demanding; it must transcend all other responsibilities and duties, however naturally and normally important those might be.

Matt. 7.13f.

[13]Enter by the narrow gate; for the gate is wide and the way is easy, that leads to destruction, and those who enter by it are many. [14]For the gate is narrow and the way is hard, that leads to life, and those who find it are few.

Following a hint by Bultmann,[1] we may recognize in this saying and its Lukan parallel (Luke 13.24: 'Strive to enter by the narrow door; for many, I tell you, will seek to enter and will not be able') an original saying of Jesus about striving to enter (the Kingdom) by the

---

[1] R. Bultmann, *History of the Synoptic Tradition*, p. 82.

narrow gate which has been expanded in the tradition by the addition of commonplaces of Jewish exhortation. Billerbeck found that the imagery of the gate was extremely rare in Judaism, whereas that of the two ways, and the concept of ways leading to 'life' and 'destruction' respectively, occur frequently.[1] Furthermore, the terms 'destruction' and 'life' are not characteristic of Jesus; entering or failing to enter the Kingdom would be what we would expect.

A saying concerning striving to enter the Kingdom by the narrow gate would, again, stress the radical nature of Jesus' demand.

Mark 10.31

'But many that are first will be last, and the last first' (par. Matt. 19.30; cf. Matt. 20.16; Luke 13.30).

Cf. **Thomas 4.** 'For many who are first shall become last and they shall become a single one.'

With this saying we reach the climax of this particular aspect of the teaching of Jesus. The Kingdom is God's Kingdom: his activity in the present and the consummation he will establish in the future. The responsibility of man is to respond to that activity in his present —radically, thoroughly, with complete self-surrender—so that he may both deepen his experience of God in his continuing present and move towards the goal of the future. Again, the response will be God's, in the sense that it will be according to the impact which God makes upon the individual. So it will be the case, both with the activity and the response, that it will not necessarily be in accordance with man's previous expectations, nor in accordance with human values—not even human values ascribed to God! So the first will be last and the last first; the poor will be rich and the rich poor; tax collectors and sinners will be found within the Kingdom and scribes and Pharisees shut outside it.

Luke 14.11, cf. 16.15

Here this same point is made in a different way.

'For everyone who exalts himself will be humbled, and he who humbles himself will be exalted.'

Here the passives, as frequently, refer to the activity of God, and the point is that human values may well be reversed; all must be, and will be, in accordance with the values of God.

[1] Billerbeck, *Kommentar* I, 460ff.

EXEGESIS 6. MARK 10.15; MATT. 5.39B–41; MATT.
5.44–48. THE NEW ATTITUDE

Mark 10.15

Truly, I say to you, whoever does not receive the Kingdom of God
like a child shall not enter it.

This is perhaps the most memorable and pregnant of all the sayings
of Jesus, and a worthy tribute was paid to it by the Jewish scholar,
C. G. Montefiore: '. . . the beauty, the significance, the ethical
force, and the originality . . . of the great saying in (v.) 15, can
also only with injustice be overlooked, cheapened, or denied.'[1] It
sums up a whole aspect of the teaching of Jesus in one unforgettable
image: a man must bring to his response to the activity of God the
ready trust and instinctive obedience of a child. Only in this way is he
truly able to enter into the depth of the experience that has now
become a real possibility for him.

Matt. 5.39b–41

[39b]But if any one strikes you on the right cheek, turn to him the other
also; [40]and if any one would sue you and take your coat, let him have
your cloak as well; [41]and if any one forces you to go one mile, go with
him two miles.

The reference in v. 41 is to the Roman practice of impressing
civilians into temporary service, as in the case of Simon of Cyrene
being compelled to carry Jesus' cross (Mark 15.21). It was a bitterly
resented practice, but the power of Roman arms was such that the
moral philosophy of the day found a very practical reason for accepting it. 'If there is a requisition and a soldier seizes it (your ass), let it
go. Do not resist or complain, otherwise you will be first beaten, and
lose your ass after all' (Epictetus).[2] The teaching of Jesus challenges
men to an attitude radically different from the prudential morality
of an Epictetus: they are to see in the imposition a challenge to
service and to accept it gladly. 'The first mile renders to Caesar the
things that are Caesar's; the second mile, by meeting opposition with
kindness, renders to God the things that are God's.'[3]
Essentially, the same challenge is expressed in the other two ex-

---

[1] C. G. Montefiore, *The Synoptic Gospels* I (1927), 238.
[2] Quoted by T. W. Manson, *Sayings of Jesus*, p. 160.
[3] *Ibid.*

amples: the acceptance of insult and the refusal to stand on one's rights. The reference to the right cheek indicates that the act envisaged is a formal insult and not a spontaneous act of violence.[1] The 'coat' and 'cloak' in v. 40 are not particularly happy choices to translate the garments referred to, although in all fairness to the translators it must be admitted that no better could be found. The difficulty is that the modern wardrobe is vastly different from that of first-century Palestine! Then, the male attire consisted of two garments, an inner garment and an outer garment, the latter being a kind of blanket which served as clothing by day and bedding by night. Legally, no one could claim the outer garment (Ex. 22.26f.; Deut. 24.12f.), so the injunction is: 'Do not stand on your rights but rather give more than could be demanded of you!' Luke (6.29) has changed the scene from a court of law to an act of robbery, probably because his readers would not understand the allusion to a Jewish legal principle. 'In either case the issue would be nudism, a sufficient indication that it is a certain spirit that is being commended . . . not a regulation to be slavishly carried out.'[2]

This last point is particularly important and we would pause for a moment to stress it. The teaching of Jesus is spectacularly devoid of specific commandments, and nowhere is that more evident than in these three sayings. In fact, they are quite impossible to carry out except under special conditions and in very limited circumstances. True, a man could accept insult in this spirit—so long as he was living in a community which recognized the dignity of the individual and therefore could be touched by the spirit of the act. Again, a man could respond to military imposition in this spirit and it would be effective—with some armies or some soldiers. But the 'coat/cloak' saying is, literally taken, ridiculous. A man acting in that manner would soon be back before the court on a charge of indecent exposure! If we may accept the axiom that Jesus knew what he was talking about, then we must recognize that these are not specific commandments and that they were never meant to be taken literally. What we have here are illustrations of a principle. The illustrations are extreme, and in the one instance so much so as to approach the ridiculous; but that is deliberate. They are intended to be vivid

[1] Normally, a right-handed person would strike the left cheek of the victim. The reference is, then, to a back-handed slap which, according to the Mishnah (B. K. 8.6), was a grave insult. See *ibid.*, p. 51.

[2] *Ibid.*, p. 51.

examples of a radical demand, and it is as such that we must regard
them. The demand is that a man should respond to the challenge of
God in terms of a radically new approach to the business of living.
This approach is illustrated by means of vivid examples of behaviour
in crisis: in response to grave insult, to a lawsuit and to a military im-
pressment. Not natural pride, not a standing on one's own rights, not
even a prudential acceptance, are the proper response to these crises
now, however much they might have been so *before*. In light of the
challenge of God and of the new relationship with one's fellow man
one must respond in a new way, in a way appropriate to the new
situation. What the specifics of that new way are is *not* stated; these
sayings are illustrations of the necessity for a new way rather than
regulations for it. But the implication of these sayings is, surely, that
if one approaches the crisis in this spirit, and seeks the way in terms of
the reality of one's experience of God and the new relationship with
one's fellow man, then that way can be found.

Matt. 5.44–48

44But I say to you, Love your enemies and pray for those who per-
secute you, 45so that you may be sons of your Father who is in heaven;
for he makes his sun rise on the evil and on the good, and sends rain on
the just and on the unjust. 46For if you love those who love you, what
reward have you? Do not even the tax collectors do the same? 47And
if you salute only your brethren, what more are you doing than others?
Do not even the Gentiles do the same? 48You, therefore, must be perfect, as your heavenly Father is perfect.

We have no need to concern ourselves with the exact wording of
these sayings in their original form. A comparison of this passage
with its Lukan parallels (Luke 6.27–28, 32–36) shows that three
things are being said: Love your enemies; exceed the requirements of
natural love; in this, be an imitator of God. That Jesus challenged his
followers in these terms is not to be doubted and, indeed, is never
doubted. Let us, however, stress the fact with which we are concerned, namely, that this teaching is directed to those who have
experienced the love of God in terms of the forgiveness of sins. As
with all of this aspect of the teaching of Jesus, it is directed to those
who are consciously seeking to respond to the challenge of God. We
must envisage it as directed to the group gathered together in the
'table-fellowship of the Kingdom', of which we spoke at the end of
our last chapter.

Set in this context the teaching becomes explicit. The correct response to God, indeed the only response to him, is to imitate the reality one has known. Gathered around the table are those who have been 'enemies' of God, as well as those who have simply found a new means of knowing him. Whether a returned prodigal or a young man who had hitherto lacked one thing only, each rejoices in the experience which has brought him to this table, as he rejoices in the fellowship he now shares. Here he must accept the challenge to imitate what he has known, and knows. If he has enemies, then the challenge is to love them. He has neighbours and friends; the challenge is to exceed the normal and natural attitudes of love, affection, kindness and courtesy. In all things he is to strive to imitate the reality of God.

We have no need to labour the point. Once these words of Jesus can be seen in their original context, any words of ours become superfluous.

Mark 7.15

> There is nothing outside a man which by going into him can defile him; but the things which come out of a man are what defile him.

The Jewish commandments to ritual purity were born of a desire so to purify the externals of everyday human life that God might truly be known in the circumstances of that life. The basic conviction was that of a legitimate distinction between sacred and secular: between things which by nature and circumstance belonged to God and through which he might be known, on the one hand, and those which belonged to the world and tended, therefore, to separate a man from God on the other. It was believed that some of these things were so foreign to God that they must simply be avoided at all costs, a tomb, for example, or the shadow of a Gentile; but that others were of such a nature that if they were ritually purified they would cease to separate man from God, household utensils, for example, or the tools of one's trade. No Jew doubted the legitimacy of this approach to the problem of living in the world and yet not being separated from God. The characteristic response to the increasingly secular and Hellenized nature of Jewish life at the time of Jesus was to intensify the effort to attain ritual purity, e.g. by the Pharisees and, even more, by the Qumran sect. We have only one instance of a movement in the opposite direction, Johanan ben Zakkai (died about AD 80), who doubted the mechanical aspects of ritual defilement and purification by water, etc., but felt obliged none the less to maintain the commandments concerned simply because they were commandments: (he said to his disciples) 'By your life! It is not the dead that defiles nor the water that purifies! The Holy One, blessed be He, merely says: "I have laid down a statute. I have issued a decree. You are not allowed to transgress my decree." '[1] His point is that the defilement is real and the ritual effective, not because of any special properties of dead bodies or water as such, but simply because God has so ordained matters.

Mark 7.15 is, therefore, completely without parallel in either rabbinic or sectarian Judaism, and, more than this, it completely denies a fundamental presupposition of Jewish religion: the distinction between the sacred and the secular. The Jesus tradition flatly denies that there are any external circumstances in the world or of human life which can separate a man from God; a man can be separated from God only by his own attitude and behaviour. Not the world, nor life, but only man himself is the 'defiling' agent. This is perhaps the most radical statement in the whole of the Jesus tradition, and, as such, it is certainly authentic. The tradition itself (Mark 7.17–23 par.) shows how the early Church struggled to comprehend the significance of so radical a statement, and reached the mundane, although correct, conclusions that this makes all food 'clean' and human sins the means of defilement. More than this, the saying is completely coherent with the almost equally radical attitude and behaviour of Jesus in connection with 'tax collectors and sinners'; indeed, it is, so to speak, the 'theoretical' aspect of what is there exhibited in practice.

Setting the saying in the context of the Kingdom proclamation, as always, we can see at once that the experience of God acting as king requires a radically new attitude to life in the world. That experience is known precisely in terms of life in the world, and it requires, therefore, a radical reorientation toward life and the world. A man experiences God within the circumstances of his life in the world, and henceforth that world is, for him, transformed. No longer is there 'clean' and 'unclean'; no longer is there 'Jew', 'Jew who has made himself a Gentile' and 'Gentile'. There is now only the reality of God, and the life that is to be lived in terms of that reality. There are now only men who respond to the challenge of that reality and men who fail to do so.

[1] Numbers R. 19.8. The saying is also found elsewhere, refs. in Billerbeck, *Kommentar* I, 719.

THE RESPONSE TO THE CHALLENGE OF THE REALITY
OF GOD

The keynote in the 'ethical' teaching of Jesus, then, is that of response to the reality of God. Since all the teaching is set in the context of the proclamation of the Kingdom, it follows that the 'ethical' teaching is not to be considered, and indeed could not exist, apart from the challenge to recognize God eschatologically at work in the experience of men. Crucial to an understanding of the teaching of Jesus at this point is the central petition of the Lord's Prayer, Matt. 6.12 = Luke 11.4, which may be rendered: 'Forgive us our sins, as we ourselves herewith forgive everyone who has sinned against us.' We discussed this petition in some detail in our previous work[1] and have no need, therefore, to give here a further detailed exegesis of it. What we shall say below is to be regarded as supplementing our previous work.

In contrast to the Son of man sayings and Mark 9.1, further work and reflection on this petition has not led us to any change of opinion. We are more than ever convinced of its authenticity, for it is indubitably early, being a major part of the tradition from the beginning. Further, it is strongly Aramaic: the variation between the aorist (Matt.) and the present (Luke) in the second part of the petition represents the Aramaic *perfectum praesens*, and the word play debt/sin goes back to the Aramaic word *hobā'*. It satisfies the criterion of dissimilarity absolutely. In both form and content it contrasts sharply with Jewish prayers for forgiveness (in the directness, brevity and intimacy of the wording, and in the linking of the human preparedness to forgive with the reception of the divine forgiveness), as in emphasis it contrasts with the teaching of the early Church (Matt. 6.14f.[2] 'legalizes' the concept by making the forgiveness or non-forgiveness of God an exact reward or punishment for that of men, thus losing the dynamic of the petition itself). No saying in the tradition has a higher claim to authenticity than this petition, nor is any saying more important to an understanding of the teaching of Jesus.

We pointed out at the end of our second chapter that the Lord's

---

[1] N. Perrin, *Kingdom*, pp. 194–6, 201f.

[2] On this saying as a development from the petition in the 'eschatological judgement pronouncement tradition' of the early Church see chapter I, above, pp. 22f.

Prayer must be regarded as having its *Sitz im Leben* in the table-fellowship of Jesus with his followers; it is strictly a disciples' prayer. Those who are taught to pray it are men and women for whom the forgiveness of sins is already a reality. They are those who gather around the 'table of the Kingdom' with Jesus in celebration of the joy and reality of their experience, and in anticipation of its consummation in God's future. So the prayer for forgiveness is the more remarkable, and the more significant: those whose new relationship with God is made possible by an initial experience of the forgiveness of sins are taught to pray for a continuation of that experience.[1] But the Lord's Prayer does not contain a detailed listing of all possible concerns of a disciple of Jesus; it picks out only the most significant, and the most representative. It should also be noted that just as in the case of the forgiveness of sins, so also in the case of the 'coming of the Kingdom', the Lord's Prayer teaches disciples to pray for a continuation of that which they have already experienced: 'Thy Kingdom come.'[2] The Kingdom reference is certainly a reference to the experience of God acting as king; the forgiveness of sins reference is equally certainly a reference to the central aspect of that experience. But this latter reference is not all-inclusive; it does not exclude any other kind of experience of God as king, but only points to its central aspect. In other words, the disciples are taught to pray for a continuation of their experience of God as king; 'Kingdom' and 'forgiveness' are terms intended to direct attention to major aspects of that experience, but also to include the developments that will go on as the disciple's relationship with God grows and develops.

This is the first point to be recognized here: that discipleship begins and continues in the context of the experience of the activity of God as king. And the second point follows from this: '. . . as we also forgive . . .' indicates that this continuing experience is contingent upon a proper response. The Aramaic perfect that originally stood in this petition indicates an action which takes place at the same time as the action of the previous verb[3] and must be translated 'as we *herewith* forgive', as we did translate it above. The recognition of this contemporaneity of action in the petition is absolutely crucial to an understanding of the teaching of Jesus. If we lose it, then the human

---

[1] On this in more detail see, N. Perrin, *Kingdom*, pp. 190–9, esp. p. 194.

[2] On this, see further below, pp. 204–6, with the reference also there to the point made in more detail in our previous work.

[3] N. Perrin, *Kingdom*, pp. 195f., following J. Jeremias.

forgiveness becomes either an echo of the divine, and while this would be true so far as it goes it would do less than justice to the dynamic of the teaching of Jesus, or it tends to become a means whereby we earn God's forgiveness, as is happening in Matt. 6.14f. But in the teaching of Jesus the contemporaneity of the action envisages a response by man to God that is at the same time a full acceptance of the human responsibility in face of the divine mercy. In the context of God's forgiveness men learn to forgive, and in the exercise of forgiveness toward their fellow man they enter ever more deeply into an experience of the divine forgiveness.

This is not only the crux of the teaching of Jesus about forgiveness; it is also the key to understanding the 'ethical' teaching of Jesus altogether: as men learn to live their lives in the context of their experience of the divine activity, so they must learn to live them in terms of the appropriate response to that activity. In the case of forgiveness, that response is to forgive; in the case of love, it is to love. This is the keynote of the 'ethical' teaching of Jesus.

IV

JESUS AND THE FUTURE

NO PART OF THE teaching of Jesus is more difficult to reconstruct and interpret than that relating to the future. So far as
the reconstruction of this teaching is concerned, we have to face
the fact that early Christian expectation concerning the future was
many-sided, and various forms of this expectation have left their mark
on the Jesus tradition, e.g. the conventional Jewish apocalyptic view
in Mark 13 or the specifically Christian expectation of the coming of
Jesus as Son of man so often introduced into the tradition by Matthew. As regards the interpretation, we always have the almost in-
superable difficulties of transcending the gulf of two millennia and of
radically different *Weltanschauungen* which separate us from Jesus,
but nowhere are these difficulties greater than in the case of attempting to conceive what it meant in the first century to think in terms of
God acting in the future. It is no accident that nowhere do modern
exegetes vary from one another more than in their discussions of
'Jesus and the future', that, for example, unanimity with regard
to the Kingdom of God as an apocalyptic concept in the teaching of
Jesus brings with it the utmost diversity with regard to the temporal
aspects of the teaching concerning the Kingdom.[1]

In this chapter we propose to approach the problem by discussing
the following aspects of the teaching: the parables stressing confidence
in God's future, the Kingdom of God as a future expectation,
the apocalyptic Son of man sayings, and the sayings which set a

---

[1] N. Perrin, *Kingdom*, pp. 84–89; 115f.; 121–4, and, more recently, W. G.
Kümmel, 'Die Naherwartung in der Verkündigung Jesu', *Zeit und Geschichte.
Dankesgabe an Rudolf Bultmann zum 80. Geburtstag*, ed. E. Dinkler (Tübingen:
J. C. B. Mohr [Paul Siebeck], 1964), pp. 31–46 (= W. G. Kümmel, *Heilsgeschehen
und Geschichte. Gesammelte Aufsätze 1933–1964* [Marburger Theologische Studien 3
(Marburg: N. G. Elwert, 1965)], pp. 457–70), where the manifold views to be
found in contemporary exegesis are presented and discussed.

time limit to the coming of the End. We omit Mark 13 and its parallels, because this is, at best, a version of something which Jesus taught that has been so severely apocalypticized that we have no present means of recovering any authentic teaching directly from it.

EXEGESIS I. THE SOWER, MUSTARD SEED, LEAVEN, SEED GROWING OF ITSELF. CONFIDENCE IN GOD'S FUTURE

The Sower

Mark 4.3–9. 'Listen! A sower went out to sow. [4]And as he sowed, some seed fell along the path, and the birds came and devoured it. [5]Other seed fell on rocky ground, where it had not much soil, and immediately it sprang up, since it had no depth of soil; [6]and when the sun rose it was scorched, and since it had no root it withered away. [7]Other seed fell among thorns and the thorns grew up and choked it, and it yielded no grain. [8]And other seeds fell into good soil and brought forth grain, growing up and increasing and yielding thirtyfold and sixtyfold and a hundredfold.' [9]And he said, 'He who has ears to hear, let him hear.'

Thomas 9. Jesus said: 'See, the sower went out, he filled his hand, he threw. Some (seeds) fell on the road; the birds came, they gathered them. Others fell on the rock and did not strike root in the earth and did not produce ears. And others fell on the thorns; they choked the seed and the worm ate them. And others fell on the good earth; and it brought forth good fruit; it bore sixty per measure and one hundred and twenty per measure.'

In this particular instance there is no point in attempting to reconstruct the original form of the parable. It was the story of a Palestinian peasant sowing and harvesting, and the interim period of the fate of parts of the seed sown has been described, both to add vividness and verisimilitude to the story and to prepare artistically for the contrast of the successful harvest. In the process of transmission details would be added and varied in accordance with knowledge of agricultural processes and dangers, e.g. the worm eating the seed in Thomas, and the scorching sun in Mark/Matthew versus the lack of moisture in Luke. Perhaps also details were added and varied in the pre-Markan stage of the tradition in accordance with the allegorizing in the Church now to be found in Mark 4.13–20 par., but this does not seem likely. Since all of the details are natural rather than artificial, and the explanation is separate from the parable itself, it is more probable that the explanation simply uses the text already found in the stage of the development concerned. But in any case, additions and changes of detail in connection with the fate of the seed are completely unimportant, since the significant thing is simply the fact of a story of a peasant sowing and harvesting. The details, in this instance, are 'window dressing' and of no substantial significance.

There is no good reason to doubt the authenticity of the parable: it reflects the Palestinian practice of not ploughing before sowing and the Semitisms are numerous;[1] the difficulties raised by Miss Linnemann[2] concern its original meaning, not its authenticity. But the meaning of the parable is, in fact, not difficult to grasp, once we banish from our minds the varied interpretations known to us, from early Christian allegorizing to the 'parables of growth' interpretation of liberal theology. When we recognize the original point as that of the contrast between the handful of seed and the bushels of harvest, and when we set the parable finally in the context of the proclamation of God acting as king in the experience of men confronted by the message and ministry of Jesus, what *is* the significance of a story about a Palestinian peasant who sows handfuls of seed and, despite all the agricultural vicissitudes of that time and place, gathers in bushels of harvest? It is surely that of a contrast between present and future: in the present forgiveness, but also temptation; here and now table-fellowship in the name of the Kingdom of God, but only in anticipation of its richest blessings. Seed-time and harvest are well established Jewish metaphors for the work of God in the world and its consummation. With the proclamation of the Kingdom by Jesus on the one hand and this parable on the other, we are justified in arguing that Jesus, for all the claims he made and implied about the significance of his ministry and message, none the less looked forward to a consummation to which this was related as seed-time to harvest. With its original picturesque emphasis upon the vicissitudes endured by the seed, and the consequent heightening of the success aspects of the harvest, this parable was probably originally concerned to inculcate confidence in God's future; but for our purposes we must note only that it does look from the present to the future, from the seed-time to the harvest, from a beginning to its consummation. We may have all kinds of difficulties in interpreting this as an emphasis in the teaching

[1] J. Jeremias, *Parables of Jesus* (rev. ed., 1963), p. 149, n. 80.
[2] E. Linnemann, *Parables of Jesus*, pp. 117, 181–4.

of Jesus, but this should not prevent us from recognizing that the emphasis is, in fact, there.

The Mustard Seed

Mark 4.30–32. And he said, 'With what can we compare the kingdom of God, or what parable shall we use for it? [31]It is like a grain of mustard seed which, when sown upon the ground, is the smallest of all the seeds on earth; [32]yet when it is sown it grows up and becomes the greatest of all shrubs, and puts forth large branches, so that the birds of the air can make nests in its shade.'

Thomas 20. The disciples said to Jesus: 'Tell us what the Kingdom of Heaven is like.' He said to them: 'It is like a mustard seed, smaller than all seeds. But when it falls on the tilled earth, it produces a large branch and becomes shelter for the birds of heaven.'

The Thomas version has introduced gnosticizing elements into the parable, the tilled ground representing the aspect of labouring in the gnostic soteriology, and the great branch the growth of the 'heavenly man',[1] and has characteristically omitted the Old Testament allusion[2] (to Dan. 4.21 or Ezek. 17.23; 31.6) in the reference to the birds resting in the shade/branches. The parallels in Matthew (13.31–32) and Luke (13.18–19) indicate that a version of this parable was found both in Mark and Q. Matthew and Luke agree against Mark in referring (wrongly) to the mustard plant as a 'tree', and in having the birds nest in its 'branches' (although actually it is the shade which attracts them); in both instances Mark is the more correct. Matthew probably conflates Mark and Q, whereas Luke chooses Q over against Mark. But the Markan form of the parable seems superior in that it more vividly and correctly represents the Palestinian mustard plant.

The parable presents a striking contrast between a seed, proverbial for its smallness, and a bush, large and shady enough to be especially attractive to birds as a temporary roosting-place. This contrast is the point of the parable, and the reference becomes clear to us when we recognize that here again we have an allusion to a metaphor regularly used in Jewish expectation concerning the End. In the Jewish literature birds nesting in the branches of a tree could and did symbolize the nations of the world coming, penitently, to join the Jews in the blessings of the End time.[3] Jesus' parable uses this image, with the

---

[1] B. Gärtner, *Theology of the Gospel According to Thomas*, p. 232.

[2] H. Montefiore (with H. E. W. Turner), *Thomas and the Evangelists* (Studies in Biblical Theology 35 [London: SCM Press, 1962]), p. 51 and n. 2.

[3] T. W. Manson, *Teaching of Jesus*, p. 133, n. 1, with references.

change from branches to shade necessitated by the fact that the reference is to a mustard bush rather than to a cedar tree or the like. We have again, then, a parable which looks from the present beginning to the future consummation, and one, moreover, which implies a point of departure in the success of the challenge to 'tax collectors and sinners', and an expectation of this being consummated in a moment when all men come together into the Kingdom of God. The small beginning contains within itself the promise of the particular glory of God's future, precisely because both the present and the future are God's.

The Leaven

Matt. 13.33 par. He told them another parable. 'The kingdom of heaven is like leaven which a woman took and hid in three measures of meal, till it was all leavened.'

Thomas 96. Jesus [said]: 'The Kingdom of the Father is like [a] woman, (who) has taken a little leaven [(and) has hidden] it in dough (and) has made large loaves of it.'

The Thomas version of this parable has been transformed in the service of gnosticism. The picture is now that of a woman who, using leaven, is able to produce 'large loaves', and the leaven now equals the heavenly particle of light, the spiritual element within man which makes salvation possible.[1] This version, therefore, is of no value to us in our particular context. The synoptic version is a twin of the Mustard Seed, making the same point of 'Simple beginnings: great endings' by means of the homely analogy of the leaven and the dough. It would be natural to see in this the slow but sure 'leavening' of the world by the spirit of Christ, or the like, as did the older liberalism, if we did not recognize, again, that the point of departure is the activity of God as king. The beginning of the activity in the experience of men confronted by the challenge of Jesus and his ministry will reach its climax in the consummation of it, as the putting of leaven into meal reaches its climax in the batch of leavened dough. The emphasis is upon God, upon what he is doing and what he will do, and the parable, like all the parables of this group, is an expression of the supreme confidence of Jesus in God and God's future.

The Seed Growing of Itself: Mark 4.26–29

26And he said, 'The kingdom of God is as if a man should scatter seed upon the ground, 27and should sleep and rise night and day, and

---

[1] B. Gärtner, *The Theology of the Gospel According to Thomas*, p. 231.

the seed should sprout and grow, he knows not how. ²⁸The earth produces of itself, first the blade, then the ear, then the full grain in the ear.
²⁹But when the grain is ripe, at once he puts in the sickle, because the
harvest has come.'

This parable bears the stamp of authenticity, not only in that it
coheres with the others of this group, but also in that we find ourselves once again confronted by the sure and sympathetic observation
of Palestinian life so characteristic of Jesus. The Palestinian peasant
knew nothing of the process of growth as visualized by modern men;
to him this was a divine mystery. So, although he would do certain
things by rule-of-thumb experience—plough after sowing, protect
the field from birds or wandering animals, etc.—for the most part
after sowing he went his daily round with his prayers said, his fingers
crossed and a wary eye on the field. The seed grew of itself, he knew
not how; what he knew was that suddenly, from one day to the next,
the hour of harvest would come and he would be galvanized into
activity again. All of this is most vividly expressed in the parable, and
we have here once again the use of agricultural imagery to express
the reality of God at work. As the Palestinian peasant, after sowing,
trusts to God and waits for the moment of harvest, so the man who
recognizes the challenge of the activity of God in the ministry of Jesus
must learn the lesson of patient waiting, in sure confidence that what
has been sown will be reaped, that what God has begun he will
bring to a triumphant conclusion.

The message of this group of parables is clear enough: Out of the
experience of God in the present learn to have confidence in God's
future. How we may interpret this message, however, is a very
different matter, and the question as to whether it has any significance
other than that of establishing the historical fact that Jesus had
confidence in God and sought to inculcate upon others this confidence
is a very real question. But it is a question that must wait until we
have more data, for the parables are only part of the message of Jesus,
and we must include in our deliberation here what we may learn also
from other aspects of the teaching.

EXEGESIS 2. LUKE 11.2 = MATT. 6.10; MATT. 8.11
= LUKE 13.28–29. THE KINGDOM OF GOD AS A FUTURE
EXPECTATION

That the Kingdom of God is a future expectation in the teaching of Jesus is not a matter of dispute in the current discussion. The present writer has set down in detail elsewhere the course of the discussion which has led contemporary biblical scholarship to this all but unanimous conclusion,[1] and although he now finds himself more sceptical than once he was about the authenticity of some of the elements of the teaching involved, this does not change the fact that this emphasis was a part of the teaching of Jesus; there is still more than sufficient evidence to show this. In what follows we will discuss only the two most important sayings, not so much to establish the point as to determine, so far as we can, the form in which it is presented in the teaching of Jesus.

Luke 11.2 = Matt 6.10: 'Thy Kingdom Come'

There are good grounds for accepting the authenticity of this petition in the Lord's Prayer. The following 'thy will be done, on earth as in heaven' in Matthew is doubtless liturgical explication, but the petition itself differs from the Kaddish petition, 'May he establish his kingdom in your lifetime and in your days and in the lifetime of all the house of Israel, even speedily and at a near time', which it parallels in sentiment, in ways which are characteristic of Jesus, not the early Church: the brevity of formulation (cf. 'Father [abba]' versus 'Our Father who art in heaven'); the intimate 'Thy' for the formal 'his'; and the use of the verb 'to come' rather than 'to establish' (the early Church prayed for the coming of the Lord, not the Kingdom, cf. I Cor. 16.22 [Aramaic: Maranatha]; Rev. 22.20). As authentic, and as paralleling the Kaddish prayer in sentiment, it is a petition for the coming of God's Kingdom, a plea for God to manifest himself as king in the experience of his people—of this there can be no doubt. But we must remember that the Lord's Prayer is not a prayer taught to the general public, but a disciple's prayer; it is a prayer intended to be prayed by people who recognize that God has acted and is acting as king in their experience. If this were not the case for them, they would not pray this prayer at all, for they could not address God as abba. As we argued earlier,[2] the use of this extraordinary mode of address to God symbolizes the change wrought by the fact that the Kingdom had, in a real sense, 'come', so far as these people were concerned. Since this is the case, we must interpret this petition either as a prayer that others may experience the 'coming of the Kingdom',

---

[1] N. Perrin, Kingdom, passim.
[2] Ibid., p. 192.

or as a prayer from a present experience to a future consummation.[1] Of these two, the latter is much the more likely possibility, both because the highly personal nature of the Lord's Prayer altogether would make the former a jarring note and also because it coheres with the emphasis we have already detected in the parables. This petition is, then, further evidence that Jesus did look toward a future consummation of that which had begun in his ministry and in the experience of men challenged by that ministry.

Matt. 8.11 = Luke 13.28–29

> [11]I tell you, many will come from east and west and sit at table with Abraham, Isaac, and Jacob in the kingdom of heaven.

> [28]There you will weep and gnash your teeth, when you see Abraham and Isaac and Jacob and all the prophets in the kingdom of God and you yourselves thrust out. [29]And men will come from east and west, and from north and south, and sit at table in the kingdom of God.

The saying has been used differently by the two evangelists; Matthew uses it in the story of the centurion's servant, immediately following the saying about the centurion's faith (v. 10), to formulate a promise that a Gentile with such faith will share in the messianic banquet, and he follows it with another saying (v. 12) which threatens judgement on the Jews who have no such faith. Luke has no such conclusion to his version of the story (Luke 7.1–10); after the saying about the centurion's faith (v. 9), the story concludes with the report of the servant's cure. There can be no doubt but that Luke has, in this respect, the more primitive version of the story; Matthew's vv. 11 and 12 are certainly Matthaean additions. There is no parallel to Matthew's v. 12 in Luke; it is to be regarded as a Matthaean formulation using traditional phraseology, but his v. 11 turns up in a Lukan collection of sayings about the difficulties of salvation (Luke 13.22–30). This collection does seem to be Lukan rather than from Q; Klostermann has shown[2] that although some of the material in it is from Q the present arrangement and form is Lukan. Both Matthew and Luke, therefore, make different uses of an originally quite independent saying.

So far as the form of the saying is concerned, Matthew seems to

[1] We are repeating in essence our previous argument, N. Perrin, *Kingdom*, p. 193.

[2] E. Klostermann, *Das Lukasevangelium* (Handbuch zum Neuen Testament 5 [Tübingen: J. C. B. Mohr (Paul Siebeck), ²1929]), pp. 146f.

have preserved the more original wording. Luke's order is clumsy and seems designed to link the saying to the remainder of the pericope (v. 25 'stand outside', v. 28 'there'), and 'all the prophets' and 'and from north and south' seem to be Lukan additions, the former perhaps under the influence of Christian apologetic, which regularly claimed that the Jews had rejected the prophets and Jesus, and the latter under the influence of passages such as Ps. 107.3. The Matthaean version, on the other hand, is simple in construction and the movement of thought within it is natural.

The saying moves in the world of the regular Jewish symbolism of the messianic banquet. This takes its point of departure from the picture of the feast of God upon the mountains in Isa. 25.6–8, and from there spreads widely throughout the ancient Jewish literature, both apocalyptic and rabbinic.[1] A characteristic passage from apocalyptic is I Enoch 62.14:

> And the Lord of Spirits will abide over them
> And with that Son of man shall they eat
> And lie down and rise up for ever and ever.

and from the rabbinical literature, Ex. R. 25.8:

> It is written, 'For the Lord thy God bringeth thee unto a good land' (Deut. 8.7)—to see the table that is prepared in Paradise, as it says, 'I shall walk before the Lord in the land of the living' (Ps. 116.9). He (God) as it were sits above the patriarchs, and the patriarchs and all the righteous sit in His midst (*toko*) as it says, 'And they sit down (*tukku*) at thy feet' (Deut. 33.3), and he distributes portions to them. . . . He will bring them fruit from the Garden of Eden and will feed them from the tree of life.

The expectation plays a real part in the life of the Qumran sectaries, since they have a sacred meal (? their regular daily meal) which they eat in anticipation of the day when they will eat it in the presence of the Messiah: 1QSa ii. 11–22, cf. 1QS vi. 4–5.

As can be seen by simple comparison, Matt. 8.11 is concerned with the same kind of expectation as the apocalyptic and rabbinic passages, but there are some striking differences. First, there is the vividness of detail over against the apocalyptic passage, and both vividness and brevity over against the rabbinic. Although we chose

[1] Billerbeck's listing of such references occupies more than ten pages, *Kommentar* IV, 1154–65.

those passages at random, no amount of searching the literature would produce an apocalyptic or rabbinic statement on this theme with such vividness and brevity; in these respects Matt. 8.11 is reminiscent of the parables and the Lord's Prayer. Further, the saying uses the Kingdom of God to designate the End time state of blessedness, a usage characteristic of Jesus and extremely rare in Judaism. We have been unable to find any instance of a Jewish text referring to this messianic banquet which has Kingdom of God, and if one were found, it would be extremely uncharacteristic: Age to Come, Paradise, Messianic Age and the like are the characteristic Jewish phrases. Finally, the Jewish concept is concerned very much with the 'righteous', the 'elect', and so on, who enjoy this blessing; the reference to the outcast and Gentiles implied in Matt. 8.11 (and certainly understood by both Matthew and Luke), while it would not be absolutely foreign to Judaism, would certainly, again, be extremely uncharacteristic.

As far as the early Church is concerned, the saying could be a prophetic word in the context of a sacred meal anticipating the messianic banquet, at a time when the Church was concerned with the influx of the Gentiles. On the other hand, it could be a saying of Jesus addressed to the table-fellowship of the Kingdom that was a feature of his ministry, and celebrating the coming of the 'Jews who had made themselves as Gentiles' into that fellowship.[1] Of these two possibilities, the latter is overwhelmingly the more likely. Not only because of the dominical characteristics of the saying noted above, but also because it coheres so completely with undeniably genuine sayings, such as the eschatological simile of the marriage feast, Mark 2.19, and the parables discussed earlier in this chapter. We are, therefore, justified in regarding Matt 8.11 as a genuine saying of Jesus.

We have argued the authenticity of this saying with some care, not because of any need to controvert scepticism with regard to it—indeed, most critical scholars accept its authenticity—but because of its intrinsic importance. Arising directly out of the table-fellowship of the Kingdom in the ministry of Jesus, it directs attention towards a moment in the future when that fellowship will be consummated. The fellowship of the ministry of Jesus, immensely significant though it is, is still only an anticipation of the 'sitting at table with Abraham, Isaac and Jacob in the Kingdom of God'. So, again, the same theme

---

[1] On this see our previous discussion of this saying, above, pp. 106f.

is found: the fulfilment in the present, although it is truly fulfilment, still only anticipates the consummation in the future.

EXEGESIS 3. THE APOCALYPTIC SON OF MAN SAYINGS[1]

Our interest at this point is in the teaching of Jesus concerning the future, so we shall limit our discussion to the so-called 'apocalyptic' Son of man sayings, the core of which may be regarded as being found in Mark 8.38; 13.26; 14.62; Luke 12.8f. par.; 11.30; 17.24 par.; 17.26f par. The other two groups of Son of man sayings, those having a 'present' reference, e.g. Mark 2.10; 2.27f., and the 'suffering' Son of man sayings: Mark 8.31; 9.12, etc., lie outside the scope of our present enquiry. We hope to discuss them at some future date as part of a wider investigation of New Testament christological traditions. The apocalyptic sayings are sufficiently distinct from these others to warrant quite separate discussion.

Before we can discuss the apocalyptic Son of man sayings in the synoptic gospels, we must first discuss the Son of man in Jewish apocalyptic, for a great deal depends upon our assumptions in regard to this. A widespread assumption, especially in German language research, is that there existed in Jewish apocalyptic the conception of a transcendent, pre-existent heavenly being, the Son of man, whose coming to earth as judge would be a major feature of the drama of the End time. H. E. Tödt, for example, has as a heading for the first chapter of his book *The Son of Man in the Synoptic Tradition*,[2] 'The Transcendent Sovereignty of the Son of Man in Jewish apocalyptic literature', and in the subsequent discussion he assumes that there is a unified and consistent conception which reveals itself in various ways in Dan. 7, I Enoch 37–71 (the Similitudes) and IV Ezra 13, the conception of a transcendent bringer of salvation: the Son of man. He sees that there are differences between Daniel and I Enoch on the one hand and IV Ezra on the other, such as to suggest that there is not, in fact, a unified and consistent conception in Jewish apocalyptic, but he argues that in any case a conception did develop in early Christianity in which consistency was achieved and differences disappeared. This enables him to conclude his chapter with a

---

[1] See Annotated Bibliography No. 7: Jesus and the Coming Son of Man.
[2] ET by D. M. Barton of *Der Menschensohn in der synoptischen Überlieferung* ([2]1963); London: SCM Press, and Philadelphia: Westminster Press, 1965 (hereinafter = *Son of Man*).

summary of the elements which he regards as common to the different seers. Their vision is of a heavenly being, a saviour to whom are ascribed supernatural and even divine powers and functions. His sovereignty and power are not those of an earthly being, as could be the case with the Messiah, but come from the future, from the Second Aeon. The seers' conception is characterized by a strict dualism which radically distinguishes between the present and the coming Aeon, and which determines the transcendental character of the conception of the sovereignty of this redeemer figure.[1] Despite the widespread acceptance of this assumption there seems to be a number of difficulties with it.

In the first place, neither of the two cycles of tradition using Son of man subsequent to Dan. 7 in Jewish apocalyptic introduce Son of man as an independent conception with a title which is in itself a sufficient designation; rather, each cycle begins afresh with clear and careful references to Dan. 7. Whether we regard I Enoch 70, 71, as the climax of the Similitudes or as the earliest use of Son of man in the Enoch saga,[2] this remains true, for I Enoch 71 has clear references to Dan. 7 (e.g. vv. 2, 10) while I Enoch 46, where Son of man is first introduced in the Similitudes as they now stand, is virtually a midrash on Dan 7.13. IV Ezra 13.3 carefully identifies its 'as it were the form of a man' which comes from the sea as the one who flies 'with the clouds of heaven', i.e. as the Son of man from Dan. 7.13.

Further, the differences between the Son of man in I Enoch and the Man from the sea in IV Ezra are such that the reference to Dan. 7.13 is the only thing they have in common, apart from the fact that pre-existence, in the special apocalyptic sense, is ascribed to both figures, as it is to many other things. In view of the fact that IV Ezra 13 does not have a titular use of Son of man at all, we are not justified in regarding it as supplementing I Enoch in references to a Son of man concept. Having identified its Man from the sea with the figure from Dan. 7.13, it then goes on to refer to him as 'the same Man' (v. 12), 'a Man from the sea' (vv. 25, 51), 'a Man' (v. 32), but never as 'Son of man'. As for the distinction between the sovereignty and

---

[1] H. E. Tödt, *Son of Man*, pp. 22, 30f. Cf., in more summary form, F. Hahn, *Christologische Hoheitstitel*, pp. 28, 29; Ph. Vielhauer, 'Gottesreich und Menschensohn in der Verkündigung Jesu', *Festschrift für Günther Dehn* (Neukirchen: Verlag der Buchhandlung des Erziehungsvereins Neukirchen, 1957), pp. 51–79, esp. p. 52; E. Jüngel, *Paulus und Jesus*, pp. 246ff.; A. J. B. Higgins, *Jesus and the Son of Man* (London: Lutterworth Press, 1964), p. 15.

[2] On this see further below, p. 167.

powers of the (earthly) Messiah and those of the (pre-existent, heavenly) Son of man, it should be noted that although IV Ezra 13.26 has the Man from the sea being kept 'many ages' by the Most High, the description of the redemptive activity of this figure in vv. 9ff. is couched in language drawn largely from Ps. Sol. 17, a description of the activity of the (earthly) Messiah.

What we have, in fact, in Jewish apocalyptic is not a Son of man conception at all, as Tödt and others assume, but a use of Dan. 7.13 by subsequent seers, a usage which does not end with apocalyptic, but continues on into the midrashim. In so far as Dan. 7.13 exhibits a concept we may speak of a Son of man conception in Jewish apocalyptic, but it would be better to speak of an 'image', and, therefore, of the varied use of 'Son of man imagery' in Jewish apocalyptic and midrashic literature. In order to make our meaning clear, and in view of the intrinsic importance of this subject, we shall offer an analysis of the use of 'Son of man imagery' in Jewish apocalyptic and midrashic literature as we see it.

1. Dan. 7 itself takes up an existing image from ancient Canaanite mythology, the nearest parallels to which, in texts now available to us, are from Ugarit and Tyre.[1] This is to be found in Dan. 7.9, 10, 13, 14, which because of its metric structure is to be distinguished from the remainder of the chapter, and is the account of an assembly of gods at which authority is passed from one god, designated Ancient of Days, to another, younger god, designated Son of man. This existing image the author of Daniel weaves into his vision, a procedure altogether characteristic of apocalyptic literature, and then goes on to offer his interpretation of the Son of man figure (v. 27). It represents 'the people of the saints of the Most High', almost certainly the Maccabean martyrs, and his coming to dominion, glory and

---

[1] Endless possibilities from the history of religions and from Jewish speculative theology have been proposed as the origin of the Son of man figure in Jewish apocalyptic, but two recent articles have pointed strongly to Ugarit and Tyre: L. Rost, 'Zur Deutung des Menschensohnes in Daniel 7', in *Gott und die Götter: Festgabe für Erich Fascher* (Berlin: Evangelische Verlagsanstalt, 1958), pp. 41–43 (Ugarit), and J. Morgenstern, 'The "Son of Man" of Dan. 7.13f. A New Interpretation', *JBL* 80 (1961), 65–77 (Tyre). C. Colpe, himself a *Religionsgeschichtler* of real standing, has investigated thoroughly all the proposed possibilities and reached the conclusion that this 'Canaanite hypothesis' comes nearest to meeting the needs of the case, so far as our present knowledge goes, *TWNT* article, *B. Das religionsgeschichtliche Problem*, esp. BVc *Ergebnis*. This investigation is so thorough and convincing that its publication may be expected to produce a general consensus of agreement. For details of this work by Colpe, see Annotated Bibliography No. 7.

greatness is their coming to their reward for the sufferings they have endured. In other words, the use of Son of man in Daniel is a cryptic way of assuring the (Maccabean) readers of the book that their suffering will not go unrewarded. In exactly the same way the Christian apocalyptic seer uses a vision of white-robed figures 'before the throne and before the lamb' (Rev. 7) to assure the persecuted Christians that their suffering will not go unrewarded. In all probability, the author of Daniel was attracted to the mythological scene he uses because it is a cryptic reference to a giving of power and glory, and, therefore, will bear his message, and also because it has in it a mysterious figure which he can set in contrast to the beasts of his vision. That the figure is 'one like unto a Son of man' is probably a pure accident; any other cryptically designated figure would have served his purpose equally well. His purpose was to bring to his readers a message of assurance, of power and glory to be theirs as a reward for their constancy, and nothing more should be read into his use of this Son of man imagery than that. But Daniel becomes the fountain-head of a stream of apocalyptic and, like much else in his book, the Son of man scene is taken up and used by subsequent seers.

2. The first use of the imagery from Dan. 7 in subsequent apocalyptic is in I Enoch 70–71. We accept M. Black's contention that this is earlier than the remainder of the Similitudes, that it is, in fact, the third of three descriptions of the 'call' of Enoch (14.8ff., 60, 70–71), each of which is built upon the model of Ezek. 1, and describes Enoch's call to a different task.[1] These are not doublets but rather developments going on within an ever-expanding Enoch saga.

The Enoch saga is a major development in Jewish apocalyptic, inspired by the cryptic references to Enoch in the Old Testament, especially Gen. 5.22, 24: 'Enoch walked with God; and he was not, for God took him.' Indeed, the 'call' of Enoch in I Enoch 70–71 is an elaboration of the second part of this verse, i.e. the reference to Enoch's translation to heaven, with a characteristic use of existing imagery, in this instance Ezek. 1 and Dan. 7. From Ezek. 1 come the chariots of the spirit (70.2), the flaming cherubim (71.7), the fire which girdles the house (71.6; in Ezekiel fire surrounds the cherubim); and Enoch, like Ezekiel, falls to the ground when confronted by the vision (71.11; Ezek. 1.28). From Dan. 7 come the stream(s) of fire (71.2), the Head of Days (71.10) and, above all, the use of the

---

[1] M. Black, 'Eschatology of the Similitudes of Enoch', *JTS* (n.s.) 3 (1952), 1–10.

Son of man in connection with Enoch. It is easy enough to see what has happened: the seer has interpreted the translation of Enoch in terms of the call of Ezekiel and of the appearance before the Ancient of Days of the Son of man. This was no doubt the easier because in Ezek. 2.1, Ezekiel is addressed as Son of man; indeed, that use of Son of man may well have been the connecting link for the seer, that which brought together for him the two scenes he uses in connection with the translation of his hero. Because the translation of Enoch is interpreted in terms of Dan. 7.13, Enoch becomes the Son of man.

Dan. 7 and the figure of the Son of man having been introduced into the Enoch saga in this way, they come to play a major ròle in that part of the saga we call the Similitudes. In Enoch 46 the scene from Dan. 7 is taken up again and attention focused anew on the Son of man, who now for the seer is Enoch. Significantly, the first thing said about him is that he has 'righteousness' (46.3), which is surely an allusion to Gen. 5.22, 24, where Enoch 'walked with God' (MT), 'was well pleasing to God' (LXX). At this point the characteristic concerns of apocalyptic come to the fore and Enoch/Son of man reveals 'the treasures that are hidden', namely, the way in which through him the wicked shall be destroyed, and the passage moves on to concentrate upon the coming destruction of the wicked. In connection with this revealing of the hidden we must remember that the basis for the work of the apocalyptic seer is always the idea that the things which will make up the drama of the End time already exist, so to speak, in prototype, in 'the heavens', where they await the moment of their revealing. An apocalyptic seer is granted a vision of these things prior to their being revealed to all the world at the End; hence, he has a message concerning the End to bring to his audience. In this sense all the features of the End are pre-existent, including the New Jerusalem of IV Ezra and the Christian apocalypse, and these are the hidden treasures which are revealed to Enoch.

In I Enoch 48.2 the Son of man/Ancient of Days imagery is taken up again, and the Son of man is further distinguished as the one whose role had been determined (48.3). We are on the way to an assertion that he is is pre-existent in the heavens awaiting his revelation at the End. The role of the Son of man is elaborated in terms taken from the prophetic books of the Old Testament, especially Isaiah, and in the course of this elaboration of the role of the Son of man, his pre-existence, in this apocalyptic sense, is affirmed (48.6), and he is further identified with the Messiah (48.10).

The imagery from Dan. 7 is taken up for a third time in 62.5. Here the seer depicts the distress of the kings and the mighty when they see the Son of man 'sitting on the throne of his glory'. Clearly he has in mind Dan. 7.14, and he is expressing the idea of the dominion, glory and kingdom of the Son of man from that verse in these terms. With his mind set on the Son of man on his throne, the seer proceeds to elaborate the role of the Son of man as judge of the oppressors and as the one with whom the elect and righteous will dwell for ever. Both of these are, of course, common apocalyptic themes. Normally in apocalyptic, God himself is the judge, but in the Similitudes of Enoch, the Son of man assumes this function. But again, the reason is the scene from Dan. 7. In 47.3 God himself is the judge, but God designated as the Head (Ancient) of Days. Precisely because the Son of man is given the throne of the Ancient of Days in Dan. 7.14, as our seer understands it, he can assume the role of apocalyptic judge; indeed, this becomes his major role. Having assumed the role of judge, he can also assume that of leader of the redeemed community, which elsewhere is also the role of God himself (Isa. 60.19, 20; Zeph. 3.15–17).

The seer returns to Dan. 7 for the last time in 69.26–29, which is the close of the third parable and a kind of closing summary of the role of Enoch as Son of man. The name of that Son of man is revealed to the righteous, i.e. the (future) function of Enoch as Son of man is revealed, and he sits on the throne of his glory and exercises his function of judgement. It is interesting that here in this summary we should have reference only to the revealing of the name of the Son of man to the righteous, the characteristic message of hope to the readers of apocalyptic, and to the function of the Son of man as judge. This latter fact, together with the sheer extent of the references to this function in the previous Son of man passages, indicates that the seer is concerned predominantly with the Son of man as judge.

What has happened in I Enoch is, then, in our view, that in the course of the development of the Enoch saga the translation of Enoch has been interpreted in terms of Ezek. 1 and Dan. 7, and Dan. 7 has then been understood as referring to the giving of the role of eschatological judge to the one represented by the Son of man figure (a quite different interpretation from that given to this scene by the author of Daniel) which in this saga is Enoch. Then the saga goes on to elaborate on the theme of the judgement to be carried out by the Son of man, although constantly returning to the initial scene, and in the course of this elaboration, other ideas characteristic of apocalyptic, e.g. pre-existence in the special apocalyptic sense, are introduced.

In what we have said above it has been assumed that the Similitudes of Enoch are the work of one seer and, further, no attempt has been made to differentiate between things said of the Son of man figure on the basis of the different Ethiopic expressions which are represented by Son of man or Man in the English version of I Enoch. With regard to the first point, even if there are several seers represented in the Similitudes as they now stand, their work is sufficiently homogeneous to be treated as a unity. With regard to the second, the Ethiopic text itself is a translation of a Semitic original, and a division into sources on the basis of linguistic factors would only be justified if the use of different terms corresponded to the occurrence of different conceptions, which is certainly not the case in this instance.

3. The vision of the Man from the sea in IV Ezra 13 also makes use of Dan. 7. This Man has 'as it were the form of a man' and he flies 'with the clouds of heaven' (v. 3). In the interpretation of the vision he is the one whom the Most High is keeping many ages (v. 26), i.e. he is pre-existent in the apocalyptic sense. But, as we noted above, the Man from the sea is not called Son of man, and the description of his activity is largely taken from Ps. Sol. 17.

The vision in IV Ezra 13 is not a vision of the Son of man at all but a vision of the Messiah ('my [i.e. God's] Son', vv. 32, 37, 52). It is reminiscent of Ps. Sol. 17 (which concerns the 'Son of David'), from which it takes much of its language, and, indeed, it might be described as a translation of Ps. Sol. 17 into the more fanciful style of apocalyptic fantasy. In the course of the vision the imagery of Dan. 7.13 is used to describe the manner of the Messiah's appearance ('as it were the form of a man') and the mode of his movement ('this Man flew with the clouds of heaven'). The argument that we have here a transcendent sovereign Son of man conception must turn entirely upon two points, that the Messiah here is 'kept many ages'[1] and that he functions as a redeemer, for these are the only things in common between this figure and the Enochic Son of man.

The latter point cannot be held to be significant. The central concern of apocalyptic is with the coming redemption, and the fact that two figures function as redeemers only unites them into some such

---

[1] R. H. Charles, *Apocrypha and Pseudepigrapha of the Old Testament* II, 616, n. 26, finds this sufficient to identify the figure with the Son of man of I Enoch (G. H. Box).

broad category as 'apocalyptic redeemer figures', of which, incidentally, there is a large number. This is especially the case in this
instance, since the main thrust of the redemptive activity is clearly
derived from different sources in each case. The activity of the Son of
man in Enoch has been derived largely from the concept of his taking
the throne of God, while that of 'my Son' in IV Ezra comes from the
description of the redemptive work of the Son of David in Ps. Sol. 17.
Everything turns, then, upon the fact that pre-existence, in the special
apocalyptic sense, is attributed to both figures. But that pre-existence
is attributed to many things in apocalyptic. If this were not the case
there could be no apocalyptic literature, for, as we pointed out earlier,
what the seer sees is always the things which the Most High is 'keeping many ages' until the time of their appearance at the End. Because
of this, we remain completely unconvinced that this one point will
bear the weight of the whole 'transcendent sovereignty of the Son of
man in Jewish apocalyptic', especially in view of the facts that Son of
man is not used as a title in IV Ezra and that there are no other points
in common between the two figures.

One further point about IV Ezra 13 is that this is the first time in
the use of Dan. 7.13 that the phrase 'with the clouds of heaven' is
understood as referring to the movement of the Son of man figure. In
the original text of Daniel it should be understood as introductory to
the whole scene, the clouds forming the background or frame to the
celestial scene, and not as a description of the approach of the Son of
man figure to the throne.[1]

4. The use of Dan. 7.13 in connection with eschatological expectation
does not end with the apocalyptic literature, but continues into the
talmudic and midrashic tradition, where it is also used in connection
with the Messiah. Here the major use is a development of that found
in IV Ezra 13 in that the 'clouds' phrase is understood as descriptive
of the figure's movement, but it goes a step further in that the figure
now moves from heaven to earth. This is the first time that this happens in the use of the imagery in the Jewish traditions. It can be urged
that I Enoch implies that the Son of man will be revealed as judge
from heaven to earth, but it is nowhere definitely stated that he
'comes', much less that he 'comes with the clouds of heaven'. However, this now happens in b. Sanh. 98a: 'R. Alexander said: "R.
Joshua opposed two verses: it is written, 'and behold, with the clouds

[1] R. B. Y. Scott, 'Behold, he cometh with clouds', *NTS* 5 (1958/9), 127–32.

of heaven one like a Son of man came' (Dan. 7.13); while it is written, 'lowly, and riding upon an ass' (Zech. 9.9). If they are meritorious [the Messiah will come] 'with the clouds of heaven'; if not 'lowly, and riding upon an ass'." ' A similar understanding and use of the text is found in the midrashim: Tanḥuma B 70b; Aggadath Bereshith 14a (Billerbeck, *Kommentar* I, 957); Num. R. 13.14, and also in Gen. R. 13.11, where, however, the reference is to the coming rain clouds, not to the Messiah.

5. Finally, the midrashic tradition also maintains the original meaning of the text in that Dan. 7.13 is used as descriptive of the Messiah's coming to God, not of his coming to earth: Midrash on Ps. 2.9 and 21.5. 2.9 is concerned with the glory of the Messiah, and it quotes Dan. 7.13a, interpreting it in terms of the glory and dominion which the Messiah will be given by God; 21.5 is concerned with the manner in which the Messiah will come into the presence of God, quoting and contrasting Dan. 7.13b and Jer. 30.21, and then reconciling the two.

The above is, we believe, an account of the significant eschatological use of Dan. 7.13 in the ancient Jewish traditions, and it can be seen at once that each use is accounted for, the developments envisaged are reasonable and the hypothetical relationships are smooth. What we have is not the conception of the coming of a transcendent, sovereign figure, the heavenly redeemer, the Son of man. There is no sufficient relationship between the use of Son of man in I Enoch and IV Ezra for us to suppose that they are both reflections of a common conception. What we have is the imagery of Dan. 7.13 being used freely and creatively by subsequent seers and scribes. These uses are independent of one another; the common dependence is upon Dan. 7.13 on the one hand and upon the general world of apocalyptic concepts on the other. Similarly, the scribes of the midrashic traditions in their turn use the imagery of Dan. 7.13 in connection with the Messiah. Although they abandon the general world of apocalyptic concepts, none the less they find Dan. 7.13 every bit as useful in their presentation of the Messiah as did the seer of IV Ezra 13 in his.

It is proposed that some such account as the one we have given be accepted as the background against which to view the apocalyptic Son of man sayings in the synoptic tradition. In particular, attention is called to the free development of the tradition in the Enoch saga, once Enoch is identified as Son of man by reason of the interpretation of his translation in terms of Ezek. 1 and Dan 7. It will be argued below that a similar but completely independent thing happened in the Christian tradition as a result of the interpretation of the resurrection of Jesus in terms of Dan 7.13. Just as Enoch becomes Son of man on the basis of an interpretation of his translation, so Jesus becomes Son of man on the basis of an interpretation of his resurrection.

The apocalyptic Son of man sayings with a claim to authenticity fall naturally into three groups: those clearly reflecting Dan. 7.13: Mark 13.26, 14.62; the judgement sayings: Luke 12.8f. par., Mark 8.38; and the comparison sayings: Luke 17.24 par., 17.26f. par., 11.30.

Sayings reflecting Dan. 7.13: Mark 13.26; 14.62

Mark 13.26. And then they will see the Son of man coming in clouds with great power and glory.

Mark 14.62. And Jesus said, 'I am; and you will see the Son of man sitting at the right hand of Power, and coming with the clouds of heaven.'

We have conducted an intensive investigation of the apocalyptic Son of man sayings in the synoptic tradition on the basis of the hypothesis that the point of origin was the use of Dan. 7.13 in a Christian exegetical tradition connected with the resurrection. As a result of this investigation we believe that we can now satisfactorily explain and interpret the sayings Mark 13.26 and 14.62.[1] It is our contention in particular that the synoptic tradition, and related parts of the remainder of the New Testament, preserve traces of three exegetical traditions using Dan. 7.13.

Most obvious of all is the purely apocalyptic and parousia type usage represented by Mark 13.26. As compared with any version of Dan. 7.13 known to us from outside the New Testament, this saying has changed the order of words to bring the 'clouds' phrase into close connection with the verb 'coming', a change common to every allusion to this text in the New Testament. It is a change obviously made to make unambiguous the fact that the clouds are the medium for the figure's movement and that the movement is one from heaven to earth. Such changes in a text are common in, and indeed a hallmark of, the Qumran *pesharim*, to the methodology of which the

---

[1] On Mark 14.62 see N. Perrin, 'Mark 14.62: End Product of a Christian Pesher Tradition?' *NTS* 12 (1965/6), pp. 150–55.

Christian exegetical traditions are certainly indebted.[1] This double emphasis now occurs for the first time in the use of Dan. 7.13 in apocalyptic literature, Jewish or Christian.[2] As we pointed out above, the linking of the clouds with the movement of the figure first occurs in Jewish apocalyptic in IV Ezra, but there the figure does not come from heaven to earth. The LXX version of Dan. 7.13 must certainly be regarded as understanding the figure as moving on the clouds, because it translates the Aramaic preposition involved by the Greek *epi* ('upon'), whereas the Theodotion version uses the more correct *meta* ('with'). But the scene is still purely a heavenly scene, and the change in the word order characteristic of the Christian tradition is not, of course, found.

Mark 13.26 has neither the LXX 'upon the clouds' nor the Theodotion 'with the clouds' (= Aramaic), but uses the preposition *en* 'in clouds'. This is a second change over against the original text, and again it has the appearance of a characteristic pesher type change in the service of the text's reinterpretation. The phrase 'in clouds' is characteristic of Old Testament epiphanies (Ex. 16.10; 19.9; Lev. 16.2; Num. 11.25), and the use of it here, therefore, emphasizes the fact that the coming of Jesus as Son of man is an epiphany.

We are assuming that Mark 13.26 is a Christian product, and that the reference, Son of man, is to Jesus. The latter point would present no difficulties if the former point is to be granted, but there is a considerable body of opinion that Mark 13 is based upon a piece (or pieces) of Jewish apocalyptic and that v. 26 should be reckoned part of that Jewish *Vorlage*.[3] That Mark 13 has been constructed in large part on the basis of Jewish apocalyptic material we do not doubt, but we would argue that the Markan reworking begins in this instance at v. 26 and not, as Suhl and those whom he follows argue, at v. 28. In the first place, for v. 26 to be a product of Jewish apocalyptic, there would have had to exist in late Judaism the complete and consistent Son of man conception, the existence of which we have denied above. Then, this Jewish conception would have had to produce a

---

[1] B. Lindars, *New Testament Apologetic*, pp. 24ff. N. Perrin, 'Mark 14.62 . . .', *NTS* 12 (1965/6), p. 151.

[2] Assuming for the moment that Mark 13.26 represents the first use in Christian apocalyptic. If, as we shall argue below, this text is not the first use in Christian tradition, then we would substitute another text for Mark 13.26, but the essential point would remain the same: this double emphasis is first known to us from a Christian text.

[3] So, most recently, A. Suhl, *Die Funktion der alttestamentlichen Zitate und Anspielungen in Markusevangelium* (Gütersloh: Gerd Mohn, 1965), p. 18, n. 46.

saying which exhibited those characteristics which are regularly to be found in the Christian sayings, but, apart from this one text, not at all in Judaism: the 'they will see', and the change in word order bringing the cloud phrase next to the verb. Further, the Jewish apocalyptic texts would then have had to lose all trace of this form of the conception, for in no other such text does the Son of man 'come with the clouds', except for this one instance preserved by Christians, and, finally, the Christian tradition would have had to be indebted to this one Jewish saying for the features most characteristic of the specifically Christian expectation. All of these things are possible, but they are so extremely unlikely that we will waste no further time on this text as a product of Jewish apocalyptic and seek, instead, an explanation of its features in terms of Christian traditions.

If this text, and the particular form of Son of man expectation which it embodies, is a product of Christian tradition, then one thing becomes clear: Jesus must first be regarded as having ascended to heaven as Son of man before he can 'come with the clouds' from heaven as that Son of man. This is a very important point so far as our discussion of the apocalyptic Son of man sayings is concerned. If a clearly defined conception of the Son of man 'coming with the clouds' existed in late Judaism and produced such a saying as Mark 13.26, then Jesus could have alluded to it, and the Christian tradition have taken it over, simply identifying Jesus as that Son of man. If such a clearly defined conception of the Son of man 'coming with the clouds' did not, however, exist in late Judaism, and Mark 13.26 is a Christian production, then Jesus could not have alluded to it, and the Christians must have had some factor at work in their traditions to produce it. It is for this reason that we have discussed at some length both the Son of man concept in ancient Judaism and the origin of Mark 13.26, and on these points we now simply rest our case and go on to explain the Christian traditions on the assumption that we may be right. We would, of course, regard our case as being strengthened if we are able to explain satisfactorily the Christian traditions on the basis of our assumption.

We have reached the point in our discussion where we must seek a factor in the Christian tradition which could be the occasion for the development of the conception of Jesus 'coming with the clouds' as Son of man, and we claim that the only factor sufficient for this purpose would be an interpretation of the resurrection as Jesus having ascended to heaven as Son of man. In other words, there must be a moment in the Christian tradition when the resurrection of Jesus is interpreted in terms of Dan. 7.13, just as in the Enoch traditions there is the moment when Enoch's translation is interpreted in this way (I Enoch 70, 71). Of course, we may expect to find only traces of such a moment, because it must have been one of the first things to develop in the early Christian theologizing, since the expectation of the return of Jesus as Son of man is a feature of the very earliest forms of Christianity, and all our documents are comparatively late. But if we are correct in our argument thus far, then it should be there. Is it?

Well, the interpretation of the resurrection of Jesus as an ascension is certainly there; indeed, it is the most prominent feature of the New Testament understanding of the resurrection. Moreover, this understanding is reached by means of an interpretation of the resurrection in terms of an Old Testament text, Ps. 110.1. We called attention in our first chapter to B. Lindars's demonstration of the fact that Luke, in Peter's Pentecost speech, has preserved for us the primitive Christian interpretation of the resurrection in terms of various passages from the Psalms, including Ps. 110.1, and his further demonstration of the way in which this exegesis then underlies traditions widespread in the New Testament.[1] As we pointed out there, Lindars is able to establish the fact that Luke, in Acts 2, is reproducing very early Christian theologizing, and, indeed, that Luke is reproducing an early use of Ps. 110.1 rather than himself pioneering in such a use, no one would doubt. The use of Ps. 110.1 is reflected everywhere in the New Testament and cannot, therefore, have been introduced by Luke.

Luke himself emphasizes the ascension aspect of the resurrection; indeed, it becomes a major part of his theology, and he goes so far as to systematize the ascension as an event separate from the resurrection (Luke 24.51 [RSV margin]; Acts 1.9), whereas elsewhere in the New Testament it is always an aspect of the resurrection itself. But for all this, he is not himself responsible for the understanding of the resurrection as an ascension; this he derives from the primitive Christian interpretation of the resurrection in terms of Ps. 110.1, an interpretation reflected throughout the New Testament.

There are two places in the New Testament where Ps. 110.1 and Dan. 7.13 are used together: Mark 14.62 par. and Acts 7.56. Mark 14.62 as a whole will concern us later; for the moment we note only

[1] See above, p. 23.

the first Old Testament allusion in that verse: '. . . the Son of man sitting at the right hand of Power'. This is an allusion to both Dan. 7.13 and Ps. 110.1, and, taken by itself, is evidence that the resurrection of Jesus has been interpreted in terms of both these texts: in his resurrection Jesus is understood to have ascended to God's right hand (Ps. 110.1) as Son of man (Dan. 7.13). Let it be noted that there is here no parousia reference; were it not for the 'you will see' which comes before, and the explicit parousia reference which comes after, also alluding to Dan. 7.13, there would be no hint of a parousia, only of an ascension, in the '. . . Son of man sitting at the right hand of Power' of Mark 14.62a.

Acts 7.56 is Stephen's account of his vision:

> . . . and he said, 'Behold, I see the heavens opened, and the Son of man standing at the right hand of God.'

This is an extraordinarily interesting verse. In the first place it represents a major aspect of the Lukan theology. Luke himself is not greatly concerned with the parousia; although he echoes it (Luke 21.27 [= Mark 13.26]) as a traditional Christian hope, his own concern is with the ongoing present of Christian experience and Christian work, rather than with the future of the parousia. In the course of the rethinking of primitive Christian eschatology which this entailed, and as a part of his own distinctive eschatology, he develops the conception of the death of a Christian as a kind of individual experience of the parousia,[1] and offers us this understanding here in Stephen's vision. At his death Stephen sees Jesus rising (hence, the 'standing') to come to him as Son of man. In the service of this understanding of an individual parousia, Luke has modified Mark 14.62 (Luke 22.69). He has omitted the 'you will see' addressed to the High Priest, since the individual parousia is to be a Christian experience, and substituted for it, 'from now on'; and he also omits the specific reference to the parousia in Mark 14.62, because he is preparing for Stephen's vision and the individual parousia. As we shall argue below, this 'you will see' comes from Christian 'passion apologetic' addressed primarily to Jews, and Luke, knowing this, must have regarded it as inappropriate here. The very reason which makes it appropriate for

[1] We are here indebted to C. K. Barrett, 'Stephen and the Son of Man', in *Apophoreta. Festschrift für Ernst Haenchen*, ed. W. Eltester (Beihefte zur *ZNW* 30 [Berlin: Alfred Töpelmann, 1964]), pp. 32–38. In what follows we are consciously contrasting our views, in part, with those of H. E. Tödt, *Son of Man*, Excursus II, pp. 303–5, to whom we are also, at some points, indebted.

Mark (and Matthew), i.e this allusion to 'passion apologetic', makes it inappropriate for Luke. This gives us: 'But from now on the Son of man shall be seated at the right hand of the Power of God', which is now a preparation for Stephen's vision and is to be read together with Acts 7.56 to give the particular Lukan understanding of an individualized Christian parousia. That Luke is dependent upon Mark, or the tradition which Mark is using, in Luke 22.69 is, we believe, to be argued from the way in which he maintains the Semitic circumlocution for God, 'Power', while adding 'of God' for the sake of his Gentile readers who may not understand the construction. In Acts 7.56 he has not the same immediate *Vorlage* and, hence, there we find the direct 'right hand of God'.

Acts 7.56, therefore, serves a most definite purpose within the Lukan theology, as does Luke 22.69, but this does not mean that the particular thing which concerns us at the moment, i.e. the combination of allusions to Dan. 7.13 and Ps. 110.1 in the 'Son of man standing at the right hand of God', is a wholly Lukan construction, although the particular verb 'standing' may well be supplied by Luke in the service of his particular understanding. The allusions themselves, indeed. cannot be Lukan; not only does Mark 14.62 have the same combination of allusions, but there is also no indication that Luke ever uses Son of man except in dependence upon a *Vorlage*. His use in his gospel is determined by his *Vorlage* there, largely Mark,[1] and this is the only occurrence in Acts. Moreover, there is an indication that Luke is, at any rate in part, dependent upon a *Vorlage* in Acts 7.55f.; witness the clumsy combination of the singular 'heaven' in v. 55 (the normal Lukan use) and the plural 'the heavens' in v. 56 (the non-Lukan use).[2]

One further point about Acts 7.56 to be taken into account is the reference to 'the right hand of God'. In Luke 22.69 we have 'the right hand of the Power of God' which we argued above was a Lukan explanatory expansion of his Markan *Vorlage*, 'the right hand of Power'. It is a well-known feature of Luke's editorial work that he follows his sources as closely as he can; to restrict himself to the explanatory addition rather than to remove the, to him, unnecessary Semitic circumlocution would be quite typical. The other changes he makes in that verse are forced upon him by the theological point he intends to make by the combination of Luke 22.69 with Acts 7.56.

---

[1] H. Conzelmann, *Theology of St Luke*, p. 171, n. 2.
[2] H. E. Tödt, *Son of Man*, p. 305.

But if Luke is dependent upon a pre-Lukan formulation in Acts 7.56, and we are following Tödt[1] in arguing that he is, then the phrase 'the right hand of God' is not specifically Lukan, despite the fact that it is oriented towards the Gentile world in that it mentions God directly and not by circumlocution. This would be in accordance with Luke's own predilections, but if he were going to introduce the phrase for some other phrase in his source he would have done so in Luke 22.69. Hence, 'the right hand of God' must have stood in the pre-Lukan formulation of Acts 7.56. But this means that the combination of Ps. 110.1 and Dan. 7.13 found in Mark 14.62 and the same combination found in the pre-Lukan formulation of Acts 7.56 cannot be dependent upon one another, since the one, Mark with the circumlocution, reflects a Jewish way of thinking, and the other, Acts with the direct mention of God, reflects a non-Jewish way of thinking. Yet both have exactly the same combination of Old Testament texts.

Our thesis is that these two verses represent the remnant of a Christian exegetical tradition in which the original interpretation of the resurrection in terms of Ps. 110.1 was expanded by the use of Dan. 7.13: the resurrection of Jesus is now interpreted as his ascension to God *as Son of man*. Such a use of Dan. 7.13 in connection with the resurrection-ascension of Jesus would parallel the use of the text in connection with the translation of Enoch in I Enoch 70, 71 to which we called attention earlier. Additional support for this thesis, that a tradition linking ascension and Son of man tradition existed in primitive Christianity, can be claimed from the ascension story in Acts 1.9. As an ascension story it is dependent ultimately upon the Ps. 110.1 tradition, and it also contains an echo of Dan. 7.13, the reference to the 'cloud' which takes Jesus away. This is an allusion to the 'clouds' of Dan. 7.13 just as is the same singular 'cloud' in Luke 21.27 (= Mark 13.26 'clouds'), and is, therefore, additional evidence for the existence of a tradition combining Ps. 110.1 and Dan. 7.13. The original text of Ps. 110.1 has 'my right hand', God being the speaker, but in using the text in an exegetical tradition, where God would no longer be directly identified as the speaker, it would be necessary, and natural, to make the 'my' specific. This could be done either directly or by circumlocution, depending on the susceptibility of the scribe concerned. In this case, the Mark 14.62 reference comes from one form of this tradition and the pre-Lukan formulation of Acts 7.56 from another.

[1] *Ibid.*

An argument in favour of our thesis is that it explains an aspect of Acts 7.56 that other exegetes have found puzzling. In his excellent study of the Son of man sayings in the synoptic tradition, Tödt argues convincingly for the existence of a pre-Lukan formulation in Acts 7.56, but then finds it impossible to relate the resultant synoptic-like Son of man saying to the synoptic tradition because the words are not on the lips of Jesus, and there is no specific parousia reference. 'So we cannot share the view that there is a pre-Lukan tradition underlying both Luke 22.69 and Acts 7.56 which would complement and render comprehensible by the concepts expressed in it the synoptic tradition concerning the Son of man.'[1] The first point is not too significant, because Son of man sayings were certainly formulated in the Church, and it is, therefore, the (admittedly surprising) fact that they are normally only found on the lips of Jesus which requires explanation, not an appearance out of such a context. The second point is what really matters, and here Tödt is quite right: in the pre-Lukan formulation of Acts 7.56 there is no parousia reference (since we are dealing with the pre-Lukan formulation, the specifically Lukan individualized parousia does not come into consideration). But then in Mark 14.62a there is also no parousia reference; only when we read the first Old Testament allusion in Mark 14.62 in the light of the second does it become a parousia reference, for the parousia first comes into Mark 14.62 with the second allusion '. . . coming with the clouds of heaven'. Tödt attempts to relate Acts 7.56 to Luke 22.69 directly, and here we would agree there is nothing to be found relating to the general synoptic concepts of Son of man. But if we relate it to Mark 14.62a, then there is very definitely something to be learned, namely, the existence of a non-parousia, ascension usage of Dan. 7.13 in the synoptic tradition like that in I Enoch 70, 71, and the pre-Lukan formulation in Acts 7.56 takes its place in the total structure of synoptic Son of man traditions.

We have so far argued for the existence of two Christian exegetical traditions using Dan. 7.13, one (represented in Mark 13.26) using Dan. 7.13 in the parousia sense, and the other (represented in Mark 14.62a and Acts 7.56) a development of a tradition interpreting the resurrection in terms of Ps. 110.1 and using Dan. 7.13 in its original Danielic, non-parousia sense. But this cannot be the end of the matter, if only because we have so far found no explanation for significant parts of both Mark 13.26 and 14.62: the 'they will see' of the one, and

[1] H. E. Tödt, *Son of Man*, p. 305.

the 'you will see' of the other. If our basic assumptions are correct, then there must be an explanation of this aspect of these texts also in terms of early Christian exegetical traditions. We may not call it a 'characteristic apocalyptic touch' or the like, because in our view these texts are not the product of a general apocalyptic conception, but of specific Christian exegetical traditions.

The next step in our thesis is to claim that there are to be found in the New Testament remnants of a third exegetical tradition using Dan. 7.13, a tradition whose starting-point is not the resurrection but the crucifixion. It is well known that earliest Christianity used the Old Testament extensively in her attempts to present a crucified Messiah to the Jews,[1] and one such text used was Zech. 12.10ff., or rather a selection from these verses: 'They shall look (*epiblepsontai*) upon him whom they have pierced . . . and they shall mourn (*kopsontai*) over him, all the tribes of the earth.' This is used of the crucifixion in the fourth gospel:

> **John 19.37.** And again another scripture says, 'They shall look upon him whom they have pierced',

where it should be noted that the verb represented by 'they shall look' is not the LXX *epiblepsontai*, but *opsontai*. John 19.37 represents an example of early Christian 'passion apologetic'; all Jewish expectation to the contrary notwithstanding, a crucified Messiah is a possibility. Indeed, God had foretold that crucifixion through the scripture fulfilled in Jesus' crucifixion.

Once the use of Zech. 12.10ff. is established in early Christian passion apologetic, it would be natural to go on to use other aspects of the passage to formulate Christian expectation, a practice we find often enough in the Qumran *pesharim*. This could lead to a development in which the 'they will mourn' part of the passage was introduced to add to the apologetic the note that, just as 'they' have seen him crucified, so 'they' will have occasion to mourn, namely, at his coming as Son of man. This is exactly what we find in the Apocalypse:

> **Rev. 1.7.** Behold, he is coming with the clouds, and every eye will see him, every one who pierced him; and all tribes of the earth will wail on account of him. Even so. Amen.

Like John 19.37, this passage varies from the LXX by having *opsomai* for the LXX *epiblepsomai*. In this text we can see that the apologetic

---

[1] B. Lindars appropriately calls this 'passion apologetic'.

begun by using Zech. 12.10ff. of the crucifixion has been carried, not
one stage further, but two. First, the 'they will mourn' has been used
as the basis for the introduction of the note of the crucified one's
'coming with the clouds', and then, a further step, the weight has
been shifted to this aspect of the interpretation of the text. In doing
this, the original reference in 'they will see', to the crucifixion, has
been lost and the reference of that verb now is to the parousia.

The use of Dan. 7.13 in connection with the idea of the crucified
one's 'coming' would be the occasion for the change in the word
order of that text which is common to all parousia uses of it in the
New Testament. We shall argue below that this is, indeed, the first
parousia use of Dan. 7.13 in the New Testament, that the idea of
Jesus' 'coming with the clouds' as Son of man developed out of this
passion apologetic.

Our argument at this point is that John 19.37 and Rev. 1.7 are
remnants of a Christian exegetical tradition using Zech. 12.10ff. and
Dan. 7.13, the one of an early stage of this tradition and the other of
a later. As evidence of this, we offer for consideration the verb
opsomai, found both in John 19.37 and Rev. 1.7. This is a common
divergence from the LXX of Zech. 12.10, which has, as we pointed
out above, *epiblepsomai*. But it is more than this, for the verb *opsomai*
has two very interesting features: in meaning it is the same as *epiblepsomai*, and in form it differs from the other important verb in the
Christian exegetical use of Zech. 12.10ff., 'to mourn', *kopsomai*, only
in omitting the initial *k*. A marked feature of the Qumran *pesharim*
is the play on words, both with regard to meaning and form, and
similar word-plays must have been a feature of the Christian exegetical traditions, related as they are in methodology to the Qumran
pesharim. We suggest that it is such a word-play in a Christian exegetical tradition which has caused *opsomai*, with its relationship in form
to *kopsomai*, to replace *epiblepsomai* in the Christian use of Zech. 12.10
ff. The fact of this common use of *opsomai*, and also the fact that we
are able to explain the switch from crucifixion to parousia reference
on the basis of our hypothesis, is, of course, the hub of our argument
for a relationship between John 19.37 and Rev. 1.7, a common
relationship to different stages of a Christian exegetical tradition.

If our argument is correct, then the verb *opsomai*, when it is used in
relationship to a reference to Jesus 'coming with the clouds', is by no
means a general apocalyptic touch, but a specific allusion to an
exegetical tradition in which Zech. 12.10ff. and Dan 7.13 have been

used together in Christian passion apologetic, and this is then the case in both Mark 13.26 and 14.62. So far as 13.26 is concerned, we have proof that we are right, for we can show that Matthew has understood it in this way. In his version of Mark 13.26, Matthew adds a reference to Zech. 12.10ff.!

> **Matt. 24.30.** . . . then will appear the sign of the Son of man in heaven, and then all the tribes of the earth will mourn, and they will see the Son of man coming on the clouds of heaven with power and great glory.

That, we would argue, is the Christian exegetical tradition in its fulness, with the word-play *kopsomai/opsomai*, and it is evidence that the 'they will see' of Mark 13.26, and with it the same verb in 14.62, is an allusion to this tradition.

We have argued that there are three Christian exegetical traditions using Dan. 7.13: a parousia tradition (Mark 13.26); an ascension tradition developing from an interpretation of the resurrection in terms of Ps. 110.1 (Mark 14.62a and Acts 7.56); and a passion apologetic tradition using Zech. 12.10ff. (John 19.37; Rev. 1.7; Matt. 24.30). How these are related to one another, and specifically which came first, we cannot know for certain. They are all much earlier than any text we now have in the New Testament; all that we have are remnants and reminiscences of them reflected in the various authors' works. It is for this reason that the comparative dates of the various New Testament works are completely unimportant in this connection; a comparatively late work could include a reminiscence of a comparatively early stage of such a tradition, and *vice versa*. But Lindars is able to show in general terms that the interpretation of the resurrection comes first,[1] as, indeed, we would expect, since without the experience of the resurrection there would have been no Christian theology at all, and this would lead us to assume that the Christian exegetical tradition using Ps. 110.1 and Dan. 7.13 is the first to use Dan 7.13 at all. We can support this by arguing (1) that the use of Ps. 110.1 is so early and so widespread in the New Testament that it would be natural to assume that a tradition using Dan. 7.13 in association with it antedates any other use of that text. Again, (2) the use of Dan. 7.13 in an ascension sense is the most natural one from the text of Dan. 7.13 itself, witness the use in I Enoch where this is the first use (70, 71) and the parousia use never develops at all. Further,

[1] B. Lindars, *New Testament Apologetic*, esp. pp. 32ff.

(3) the full-blooded apocalyptic use in Mark 13.26 embodies the 'you will see', itself dependent upon the tradition using Zech. 12.10ff. and Dan. 7.13, so this cannot be the earliest of the traditions; it must represent a tradition secondary to the one using Zech. 12.10ff. Finally, (4) the parousia tradition in Mark 13.26 shows signs of developing away from the exegetical tradition which gave it birth and moving towards becoming an independent Christian apocalyptic tradition. Specifically, it has 'in clouds', which is moving away from Dan. 7.13 in the interests of defining the coming of Jesus as Son of man as an epiphany. Christologically, this is a more developed conception than that of the passion apologetic of Rev. 1.7.

So we argue that it is reasonable to regard the traditions as having developed in the following order. First, there was the ascension use of Dan. 7.13 in a tradition already using Ps. 110.1. This tradition establishes the concept of Jesus at the right hand of God as Son of man. Second, there came the use of Dan. 7.13 in a passion apologetic tradition already using Zech. 12.10ff., adding to that tradition the idea that the one who has ascended to God as Son of man will return as that Son of man, and 'they' will see him as such and mourn. This would be the first parousia use, and it would be here that the characteristic word order of Dan. 7.13 in the New Testament would be established. Third, there developed the full parousia use, in which the connection with Zech. 12.10ff. and the passion apologetic is gradually lost, although it is still there in Mark 13.26 and 14.62, as emphasis came to be put more and more upon the expectation of Jesus' 'second coming', as Son of man, and as this expectation came to exist in its own right, independently of the exegesis which gave it birth.

The hypothesis that we have advanced accounts satisfactorily for every part of Mark 13.26 (and of its Matthaean version!), but there remains something to be said about Mark 14.62 as a whole; thus far we have discussed only the first part of the text. The problem with the interpretation of Mark 14.62 as a whole has always been that it implies both an ascension reference ('the Son of man sitting . . .') and a parousia reference ('coming with the clouds . . .'). On the basis of the hypothesis of Christian exegetical traditions, both are readily accounted for, because we have an ascension and a parousia tradition, both using Dan. 7.13. The common use of this text would be what brought them together, and the fact that the usage is different in each case has presented no problem to a tradition which does not resent ambiguity. Indeed, some such explanation is demanded by the text itself; there has to be a reason for the ambiguity. On our hypothesis the text of Mark 14.62 is to be accounted for as follows: '*And you will see*' is the characteristic claim of passion apologetic and, like the same verb in Mark 13.26, it is to be regarded as a reminiscence of Zech. 12.10ff., the change of person from 3 pl. to 2 sing. being accounted for by its position in the present narrative as addressed to the high priest. '. . . *the Son of man sitting at the right hand of Power*' is from the tradition using Dan. 7.13 and Ps. 110.1. '. . . *the Son of man coming with the clouds of heaven*' is from the tradition using Dan. 7.13 and Zech. 12.10ff. Note that it agrees with Rev. 1.7, which represents this tradition, in having '*with* the clouds of heaven' against the LXX.

Our final conclusion is, then, that Mark 13.26 and 14.62 are reflections of early Christian exegetical traditions, and, as such, have no basis in the teaching of Jesus. We have spent a lot of time on this point, not only because of the intrinsic importance of these two texts and, hence, of the question of their authenticity, but also because of the importance of Christian exegetical traditions in the New Testament as a whole, of which these traditions using Dan. 7.13 and their significance for the synoptic Son of man traditions are only an example. It is our hope to develop a full-scale study of christological traditions in the New Testament on the basis of the hypothesis of the existence of such early Christian exegetical traditions.

The Judgement Sayings: Luke 12.8f. = Matt. 10.32f.; Mark 8.38

Luke 12.8f. And I tell you, every one who acknowledges me before men, the Son of man also will acknowledge before the angels of God; 9but he who denies me before men will be denied before the angels of God.

Matt. 10.32f. So every one who acknowledges me before men, I will acknowledge before my Father who is in heaven; 33but whoever denies me before men, I also will deny before my Father who is in heaven.

Mark 8.38. For whoever is ashamed of me and of my words in this adulterous and sinful generation, of him will the Son of man also be ashamed, when he comes in the glory of his Father with the holy angels.

These sayings have recently been the subject of an intensive discussion in German by a group of scholars who are all experts in the techniques of form criticism and of enquiry into the history of a tradition in which sayings are set. The fact that the scholars differ from one another in their results has both added to the intensity of the discussion and also indicated the potentials and limitations of the methodologies employed. All in all, it would be fair to say that they have advanced discussion of these sayings by a generation, outdated all previous work on them, and yet failed to solve the problem![1]

This discussion has established certain conclusions. Käsemann's hypothesis of an eschatological judgement pronouncement tradition in the early Church[2] in which these sayings have a *Sitz im Leben* is to be accepted. That such a tradition as Käsemann describes existed in the early Church is clear enough, and that these sayings are at home in it is shown both by their form, the two-part sentence with the same verb in each referring to present action and eschatological judgement respectively, and by the fact that a Christian prophet makes use of one of them in Rev. 3.5b ('I will confess his name before my Father and before his angels'). Mark 8.38 is to be accepted as a revision of Luke 12.8f. par., because the verb used has a more general meaning and is less Semitizing than those in Luke 12.8f., and a decision concerning the proclamation would be a later demand than one concerning the Son of man (Käsemann). Thus far the discussion is convincing and the participants are in agreement, but now the participants go their separate ways, or rather they fall into two separate groups, and that for most interesting reasons. All accept the hypothesis that there existed in ancient Judaism the conception of the Son of man as a pre-existent heavenly being whose coming as judge would be a feature of the eschatological drama, which we discussed and, in this definite form, rejected above. On the basis of this hypothesis, Käsemann and Vielhauer reject the authenticity of Luke 12.8f., largely because they believe that Jesus' message was concerned with the Kingdom and with God drawing near to men in the immediacy of the proclamation of that Kingdom, and that, therefore, Jesus could not also have proclaimed the coming of an eschatological figure other than himself in the future. 'Jesus proclaimed the immediacy of the near God.[3] Whoever does this cannot, in my opinion,

---

[1] The course of the discussion is given in Annotated Bibliography No. 7: Jesus and the Son of Man (*b*).

[2] On this see above, pp. 22f.

[3] German: 'die Unmittelbarkeit des nahen Gottes'. This is one of those pregnant German phrases to which it is impossible to do justice in English. The adjective *nah* means 'near', but also 'approaching', and *Unmittelbarkeit* is literally 'unmediatedness'. So the phrase carries with it the connotation of God having drawn near to man so as to grant him the experience of his direct, unmediated nearness.

have expected to wait for the coming Son of man, the ingathering of the twelve tribes into the messianic kingdom and the associated parousia in order to experience God as the Near.'[1] They also argue, especially Vielhauer, that the concepts Kingdom of God and Son of man are mutually exclusive, never being found together in ancient Judaism, or united in the Jesus tradition.[2] Their opponents are not impressed by these arguments. They feel that Jesus could have referred to a coming judgement by a figure other than himself that would validate his ministry; they claim that the fellowship between Jesus and his disciples is thought by Jesus to play a role in the coming of the Kingdom, and, hence, it would be confirmed by the Son of man.[3] Jüngel goes to some pains to argue that the Kingdom proclamation and these Son of man sayings do belong together in the message of Jesus in that the one is concerned with God in his nearness and the other in his distance, both finding their focal point in the fact that Jesus' proclamation and conduct towards men demands of them a conduct towards himself which will be validated by the conduct of the Son of man towards them. So the future of the Son of man is related to the present of men, that present already being qualified by the nearness of the Kingdom, and the nearness of God remains guaranteed to men.[4]

We begin our own discussion, then, by concentrating attention entirely on Luke 12.8f. par., accepting the fact that Mark 8.38 is secondary to this. Luke 12.8f. par. uses two verbs (*homologein* [confess] and *arneisthai* [deny]) which are regularly used in early Christian literature in the forensic way in which they are used here: John 1.20; I John 2.23 (both verbs); John 9.22; Rom. 10.9; I Tim. 6.12; Heb. 13.15; I John 4.2, 3, 15; II John 7 (all 'confess'): Acts 3.13, 14; 7.35; I Tim. 5.8; II Tim. 2.12; Tit. 1.16; II Peter 2.1 (all 'deny'), etc. But the use of *homologein* in Luke 12.8f. par. is most unusual in that the object of the verb is expressed by means of the preposition *en*: *en emoi* and *en autō*. Now, this is completely un-Greek; II Clement 3.2 avoids this construction while explicitly quoting the saying in its Matthaean

---

[1] E. Käsemann, *ZTK* 57 (1960), 179.

[2] This point had been noted several times in the English language discussion, e.g. H. B. Sharman, *Son of Man and Kingdom of God*, New York: Harper & Bros., 1943; H. A. Guy, *The New Testament Doctrine of the Last Things*, London: Oxford University Press, 1948. Vielhauer remarks that he had no access to the former; he does not mention the latter (*Festschrift für G. Dehn*, p. 51, n. 5).

[3] H. E. Tödt, *Son of Man*, pp. 55–60, esp. 60. F. Hahn, *Christologische Hoheitstitel*, pp. 33–36.

[4] E. Jüngel, *Paulus und Jesus*, pp. 261f.

form, the version in Rev. 3.5 does not have it, and the Greek fathers Heracleon, Clement of Alexandria and Chrysostom all puzzle over what it can mean.[1] It is, in fact, an Aramaism representing the root *ydy* (Syriac *yd'*) which in Aramaic and Syriac regularly takes the preposition *b* with its object. It should be noted that the Hebrew equivalent *ydh* does not do this. Luke 12.8f. par. is the only place in the New Testament where *homologein* has *en* with its object, and it is hard to resist the conclusion that here, therefore, *homologein* is being used in a way different from the normal. In other words, while the second part of this saying, the 'denying', fits smoothly into the liturgical language of the early Church, the first part, the 'acknowledging', does not. On the basis of this observation and our acceptance of the results of the recent German discussion, we propose the following transmission history for the sayings with which we are concerned.

1. The most original form of the saying consisted of only the first half of the present doublet:

Everyone who acknowledges me before men,
(?) the Son of man will acknowledge before the angels of God.

This is suggested by the fact that Luke 12.8 (Matt. 10.32) with its marked Aramaism (*homologein en*) is linguistically distinct from Luke 12.9 (Matt. 10.33) with its regular ecclesiastical use of *arneisthai*. Also, sayings with an element of promise do tend to be 'completed' in the tradition by the addition of an antithesis in the form of a threat, e.g. the Woes added to the Beatitudes in the gospel tradition, and the development of Matt. 6.14f. from the petition concerning forgiveness in the Lord's Prayer. This creates a presupposition in favour of the hypothesis that the present Luke 12.9 (Matt. 10.33) has been supplied in the tradition. Also Semitic poetic and gnomic style has a marked preference for parallelism.

A question mark has been set before the second part of Luke 12.8 (Matt. 10.32) above, because although Luke has the form given, Matthew has: 'I also will acknowledge him before my Father who is in heaven.' The fact that this still has the Aramaism (*homologein en autō*) shows that it is close to the Lukan version, but the variations present problems. The 'my Father who is in heaven' could well have

---

[1] References given by Eb. Nestle, *ZNW* 8 (1907), 241; 9 (1918), 253. See further Arndt and Gingrich, *Lexicon*, p. 571b.

crept in for 'angels of God', probably in two stages: first, and still pre-Matthew, 'my Father', and, second, the addition by Matthew of 'who is in heaven'. That both 'my Father' and 'before the angels of God' are known in the tradition can be seen from Rev. 3.5, which has the two side by side, with the necessary variation of 'his' for 'of God'. The question of the original subject of this clause, however, presents very difficult problems. It can be argued that since Matthew does not normally substitute 'I' for 'Son of man', the Matthaean form is the more original. But we are not necessarily dealing with a Matthaean modification, because the occurrence of the form with 'I' in Rev. 3.5b suggests that this form existed in the tradition independently of Matthew, rather than that it was produced by Matthew directly from the form with 'Son of man' as the subject. Therefore, the normal practice of Matthew has no necessary bearing upon the problem. Another complication is the possibility that Son of man could be used as a circumlocution for 'I' in Aramaic, which could mean that the two forms in Greek are possibly simply translation variants of this Aramaic idiom.[1] Moreover, there is a third possible form: '. . . will also be acknowledged before the angels of God'. This is suggested by the passive now found in Luke 12.9; it would also be an Aramaism (the passive voice as a circumlocution for the divine activity), and it would provide a basis from which the 'I' and 'Son of man' forms could have developed in the tradition, as variant ways of giving Jesus a role in the judgement. Further, if an increasing emphasis upon apocalypticism is a feature of the tradition, and this would be generally accepted, then the progression 'will be acknowledged before the angels of God'—'Son of man will acknowledge'—'Son of man . . . when he comes' is a natural one. We argue, therefore, that the earliest form was the one using the passive. This passive was a circumlocution for the activity of God, as is regularly the case in Aramaic. As the tradition developed, there was an increasing christological emphasis and this led to the ascription to Jesus of the original function of God in the saying. This took place in two ways, with the use of 'I' and with the use of 'Son of man', giving us the double tradition now found in Luke 12.8f. par.

[1] We mention this as a possibility without thereby intending to take sides in the dispute as to whether this idiom did or did not exist in the first-century Aramaic. The matter is not important enough in connection with this saying to warrant a full discussion of the problem; it becomes important in connection with the 'present' sayings which lie outside the scope of our present enquiry. See further, above, p. 120, n. 1.

2. Given the saying:

> Every one who acknowledges me before men, the Son of man will also acknowledge before the angels of God,

the next step would be to complete the antithesis by adding a parallel using 'denying'. This has been done, giving us the form(s) found now in Luke 12.9; Matt. 10.33 (cf. II Tim. 2.12b) and probably also a form:

> Every one who denies me before men, the Son of man also will deny before the angels of God,

now no longer preserved in the tradition. Evidence for the hypothesis that Luke 12.9 par. was created in the tradition was given above: the fact that it uses *arneisthai* ecclesiastically, and the tendency in the tradition to add an antithetical second element to 'promise' sayings and to complete a parallelism.

3. The next step would be to develop the reference to Son of man in the saying, and this would naturally take the form of bringing into the saying elements from the 'coming of the Son of man' tradition discussed in connection with Mark 13.26 and 14.62. So the saying develops into one concerned with the explicit 'coming' of the Son of man as in Mark 8.38. The fact that the characteristic reference to the clouds is missing here would seem to indicate that the reference is taken from a developing Christian exegetical tradition rather than directly from Dan. 7.13. We have already argued that there is no general 'coming of the Son of man' concept in late Judaism, apart from a use of Dan. 7.13, from which the reference could be drawn.

The result of this discussion of the history of this particular branch of tradition is, we believe, to establish the strong possibility that the earliest form of this 'judgement' saying must be one using the passive: 'Everyone who acknowledges me before men, he will be acknowledged before the angels of God.' In this case, the reference would be to a future vindication such as that envisaged in the symbolism of Dan. 7.13. Such a form could go back to Jesus; certainly he could have used the passive in this way; indeed, such a use of the passive must have been a feature of his teaching. It is not possible to prove that such a saying does go back to Jesus, although the arguments for it are fairly strong: the non-ecclesiastical use of *homologein en*, the quite characteristic passive as a circumlocution for the divine activity, and the absence of any specifically 'Christian' expectation. But the point is that, even if it does go back to Jesus, it is evidence only for the teaching of a future vindication by God of the present ministry of Jesus and men's proper response to it. It says nothing whatever about the form of this vindication, and it says nothing about the time element, except that it looks toward the future. Rather than saying anything specific about God and the future, it offers general reassurance to men that, if they have responded to the challenge of Jesus' present, they may have confidence in God's future. As such it coheres with an aspect of the teaching of Jesus we have already noted in the parables.

If our argument with regard to the earliest form of this saying is not granted, and it is insisted that the earliest form was:

> Every one who acknowledges me before men, the Son of man will acknowledge before the angels of God,

then this is still not necessarily a reference to the 'coming' Son of man. It becomes such a reference only if it is read in the light of Mark 8.38, and Mark 8.38 is a Markan reinterpretation of the saying, not evidence for its original reference. If we take the saying by itself, then the reference is only a general one to the imagery of Dan. 7.13, this imagery being used as a symbol for vindication. There is no 'coming' of the Son of man, only vindication before God. Jesus could have made such a general reference to Dan. 7.13, but, if he did, this does not change our thesis one iota. Such a reference would still only be a general assurance of vindication; it would say nothing about the form or time of that vindication.

The Comparison Sayings: Luke 11.30 = Matt. 12.40; Luke 17.23f. = Matt. 24.26f.; Luke 17.26f.

Luke 11.30. For as Jonah became a sign to the men of Nineveh, so will the Son of man be to this generation.

Matt. 12.40. For as Jonah was three days and three nights in the belly of the whale, so will the Son of man be three days and three nights in the heart of the earth.

This saying is itself an explication of the preceding verse: 'This generation is an evil generation; it seeks a sign, but no sign shall be given to it except the sign of Jonah' (Luke 11.29 = Matt. 12.39 [with insignificant variations]). The Matthaean version of this (12.39) is duplicated at Matt. 16.4, and there is a parallel in Mark 8.12 which, however, omits any reference to the sign of Jonah ('Truly, I say to you, no sign shall be given to this generation'). There is another, but completely different, reference to Jonah in v. 32 in Luke, v.41 in Matthew: 'The men of Nineveh will arise at the judgement with this generation and condemn it; for they repented at the preaching of Jonah, and behold, someone greater than Jonah is here' (Luke 11.32 = Matt. 12.41), which itself is firmly linked with a parallel saying about the queen of the South and Solomon: 'The queen of the South will arise at the judgement with (Luke, the men of) this generation and condemn it (Luke, them); for she came from the ends of the earth to hear the wisdom of Solomon, and behold, something greater than Solomon is here' (Matt. 12.42 = Luke 11.31). Thus, we have the following situation:

(a) A saying, 'No sign shall be given to this generation', found only in Mark (8.12).

(b) A saying exactly the same as this, but adding 'except the sign of Jonah' found in Luke 11.29 = Matt. 12.39 and clearly, therefore, from Q. This saying is duplicated in Matt. 16.4, where it is the Matthaean version of Mark 8.12, (a) above.

(c) An interpretation of this reference to the sign of Jonah in terms of the Son of man becoming a sign as did Jonah (Luke 11.30 = Matt. 12.40), whereby Matthew makes the reference to Jonah explicitly a reference to his being swallowed and regurgitated by the sea monster.

(d) A double saying which compares 'this generation' unfavourably with the queen of the South and the men of Nineveh in the matter of repentance. Here the reference to Jonah is an explicit reference to his preaching, not to his being saved from death.

Although the sayings (b), (c) and (d) are now joined together in a single discourse, and this was already the case in Q, this linking is certainly editorial. Originally there must have been two distinct units: the reference to the sign of Jonah, (b) above, and its interpretation, (c) above, on the one hand, and the double saying, (d) above, on the other. The common reference to Jonah will have brought them together in the tradition leading to Q.

Before discussing these two entities further, we must deal with (a), the saying not included in either. It is clearly a variant of (b) and the question is, which of the two is the original? Has the Q tradition added 'except for the sign of Jonah' or has Mark omitted it? The latter seems the more probable in that Mark puts great emphasis upon the mighty deeds of Jesus as the only, but complete, demonstration of his messiahship, and it would be natural for him to omit the reference to some other sign, however that reference was to be understood. Further, the saying in its Q form contains a regular Aramaic idiom, the idiom of relative negation, in which the apparent exception is, in fact, an affirmation. It is to be translated: 'How this generation seeks a sign! Truly, I tell you, no sign will be given to this generation. The sign of Jonah will be given to this generation!'[1] and is, therefore, a complete unit in its Q form. We, therefore, conclude that Mark 8.12 is derived from a version of the saying now in Luke 11.29 = Matt. 12.39, and we will concern ourselves no further with it.

Turning to the two entities in the tradition, (b) and (c), the reference to the sign of Jonah and its interpretation, and (d), the unfavourable comparison of 'this generation' with the queen of the South and the men of Nineveh, we begin by pointing out that their original independence from one another is not only to be supposed on the basis of our knowledge of the tendencies at work in the developing tradition. It is also to be seen in the fact that (d) has no reference to a 'sign' at all; it is not here a question of the sign of Jonah, but of his preaching. Indeed, the two entities have nothing in common whatever except the verbal references to Jonah and the men of Nineveh, references which are, however, completely different in concern and purpose.

The Son of man saying occurs, therefore, as the second part of the first entity; it interprets the reference to the 'sign of Jonah'. It should be noted that, on the basis of the Aramaic idiom pointed out by Colpe, the sign of Jonah saying is complete in itself; the interpretation must have been supplied later. The sign of Jonah saying itself is certainly authentic: exhibiting an Aramaic idiom, it must be early; it stands at the beginning of a stream of tradition the history of which we can trace; it coheres with teaching attested elsewhere (Luke 17.20, 21). The interpretation can have been supplied either by Jesus himself or by the early Christian community, and of these alternatives we prefer the latter. Matt. 12.40 clearly interprets the 'sign of Jonah' in the light of knowledge both of the passion narrative and of the passion predictions, the author regarding the phrases 'on the third day' (Matt. 16.21) and 'after three days' (Matt. 27.63) as

[1] C. Colpe, *TWNT* article, C I 1c. He gives other instances from the New Testament: Matt. 15.24; Mark 2.17; John 1.11; 7.16; Matt. 25.29b = Luke 19.26b.

equivalents, and the Jonah story as prefiguring the burial and resurrection of Jesus. But if we accept the 'sign of Jonah' saying as authentic and Matt. 12.40 as a later ecclesiastical interpretation of it in terms of the burial and resurrection of Jesus, where does Luke 11.30 stand? Surely halfway between the two: it makes the Son of man a sign, as was Jonah, but does not specify in what manner. The implication is certainly that he will become a sign when he comes in judgement, in the manner of Luke 21.27: '. . . and then they will see the Son of man coming in a cloud with power and great glory.' But it is our argument throughout that such a conception is dependent upon the developing Christian exegetical tradition and cannot, therefore, have had a place in the teaching of Jesus. For this reason we reject Luke 11.30 as part of the teaching of Jesus and regard it as a product of the developing Christian tradition, against Tödt,[1] who accepts it because he accepts the hypothesis that such a developed Son of man conception existed in pre-Christian Judaism and argues that Jesus referred to this figure as distinct from himself in sayings such as this one.

The authentic element in this particular branch of tradition is, then, the refusal of a sign and the idiomatic affirmation: 'The sign of Jonah will be given to this generation.' What did this mean in the teaching of Jesus? The answer to this question is simply that we do not know, because we do not know what Jesus and his contemporaries would have understood by the phrase 'the sign of Jonah'. As we saw above, the Christian tradition understood it as a reference to the parousia (Luke), or to the burial and resurrection of Jesus (Matthew), but these interpretations come from the world of ideas to be found in early Christianity and say nothing about ancient Judaism. In the absence of definite information, it is possible to assume that the reference is to some future event which will vindicate the message and ministry of Jesus, and be analogous to the deliverance of Jonah, despite the fact that neither the Old Testament nor the Jewish rabbinical literature exhibits any knowledge of a significance for the Ninevites to be ascribed to the deliverance of Jonah.[2] Another possibility, one which we ourselves would prefer, would be to interpret the 'sign of Jonah' by means of the reference to the 'preaching of Jonah', for although these are completely independent sayings, and the references to Jonah quite different, they are both dominical. In

[1] H. E. Tödt, *Son of Man*, pp. 53ff.
[2] So Colpe, *TWNT* article, C I 1c.

this case we could argue that the significant thing about Jonah, for Jesus, was not his deliverance from the sea monster, but his preaching and its effectiveness. Then the 'sign of Jonah' is his preaching and the reference is to the fact that the preaching of Jesus will be effective to this generation—in ways beyond its imagination. This would come, in effect, to the same thing as the interpretation offered by Colpe; the reference would be to a future in which the message and ministry of Jesus is vindicated, without saying anything specific about the form of that future, or about the time element involved except that it is future.

The second entity in this group of sayings, the parallel references to the queen of the South and the men of Nineveh (Luke 11.31f. = Matt. 12.41f.), is certainly dominical. The double saying has no earlier history in the tradition; the point at issue is the question of repentance in face of a challenge, certainly a major concern of the message of the historical Jesus; the references to the queen of the South and the men of Nineveh are vividly apposite and absolutely in accord with Jesus' use of unlikely good examples in his comparisons (the Good Samaritan); and the element of warning in the saying coheres with a major aspect of the message of the parables. But the reference to the queen of the South and the men of Nineveh arising at the judgement is no more than a conventional way of speaking of a future moment at which Jesus' ministry will be vindicated. It is this, but it is no more than this, and in particular it says nothing about the form of this future moment, nor about the time element involved, beyond the fact that it is future.

Luke 17.23f. And they will say to you, 'Lo, there!' or 'Lo, here!' Do not go, do not follow them. [24]For as the lightning flashes and lights up the sky from one side to the other, so will the Son of man be in his day.

Matt. 24.26f. So, if they say to you, 'Lo, he is in the wilderness', do not go out; if they say, 'Lo, he is in the inner rooms', do not believe it. [27]For as the lightning comes from the east and shines as far as the west, so will be the coming of the Son of man.

The present settings of this saying are editorial; Luke puts it in the esoteric teaching addressed to the disciples following Jesus' reply to the question of the Pharisees (17.20f.), and Matthew in the apocalyptic discourse based upon Mark 13. We will consider it as an independent logion. The striking thing about the saying is that it closely parallels the immediately preceding saying in Luke 17.20f.: 'The

Kingdom of God is not coming with signs to be observed; nor will they say, "Lo, here it is!" or "There!" for behold, the Kingdom of God is in the midst of you.' The differences are (1) the addition of the exhortatory 'do not go, do not follow them'; (2) the reference to the lightning flash, a commonplace of apocalyptic, e.g. Apoc. Bar. 53.9: 'The lightning shone exceedingly, so as to illuminate the whole earth'; and (3) the substitution of 'the Son of man in his day' or 'the coming of the Son of man' for the reference to the Kingdom of God. The first two of these changes are characteristic of a developing tradition in the Church, and since the early Christians spoke of the coming of the Son of man very much as Jesus had spoken of the Kingdom as a future hope, we can readily imagine that they could have taken the original and genuine saying of Jesus, Luke 17.20f., and transformed it in this way to express their expectation. Note that the transformation misunderstands the original; by concentrating on the 'Lo, here!' 'Lo, there!' it has misunderstood the reference to a present experience of the Kingdom by taking it to be one to a sudden and unexpected future experience. The explicit parousia reference in the 'coming of the Son of man' is certainly Matthaean, which makes 'the Son of man in his day' the more original of the two without thereby enhancing its claim to authenticity. 'In that (these, those) day(s)' is a commonplace of apocalyptic, e.g. I Enoch 48.8; 50.1; 51.3; 54.6; 60.5; 62.3, 8, and as soon as the concept of Jesus as Son of man is established, and his return as Son of man expected, the idea of the 'day of the Son of man' as a phrase to express his coming would be natural. We can compare IV Ezra 13.52: '. . . no one . . . (can) see my Son, but in . . . his day.' It is for these reasons that it is out of place on the lips of Jesus. Even if the concept of the coming of the apocalyptic Son of man were firmly and widely established in Judaism, which we do not for one moment believe, a reference to it in this commonplace way would be quite out of keeping with the originality of the teaching of Jesus. Let us remember that when he used Kingdom of God, an apocalyptic concept, he none the less used it in a way most unusual in apocalyptic. Expression of a Christian hope in commonplace apocalyptic terminology is a characteristic of the evangelical tradition, not of Jesus. We, therefore, regard the saying as inauthentic, although it is accepted by Bultmann, Tödt and Colpe.[1] We believe we have offered grounds for the denial of the existence of a Son of man concept

[1] R. Bultmann, *History of the Synoptic Tradition*, p. 122. H. E. Tödt, *Son of Man*, p. 224. C. Colpe, *TWNT* article C I 3a.

in Judaism that could be referred to in this way, and that we have accounted for it in terms of a development going on within the Christian traditions.

Luke 17.26f. As it was in the days of Noah, so will it be in the days of the Son of man. [27]They ate, they drank, they married, they were given in marriagé, until the day when Noah entered the ark, and the flood came and destroyed them all.

The idea of the 'day of the Son of man' having been established in the tradition, it would be natural to expand and develop it by the use of Old Testament imagery, in this instance, the destruction at the time of Noah. Here we have a use of imagery taken from one catastrophe to fill out the picture of a second now to be expected. Matthew characteristically modifies the saying by introducing a specific reference to the parousia (Matt. 24.37–41: 'the coming of the Son of man' [twice]), and then the tradition goes on to expand the imagery further by making use of another Old Testament catastrophe: 'the days of Lot' (Luke 17.28–30). All of these sayings are testimony to the developing tradition in the Church; they are not evidence for the teaching of Jesus.[1]

We have devoted a great deal of space to this discussion of the apocalyptic Son of man sayings because of their intrinsic importance. The problems connected with them are so complex that nothing less than a complete presentation of our proposed solution would do justice to it or to them. If we may now briefly recapitulate the main points of our thesis for the sake of clarity, they are as follows:

1. No 'coming apocalyptic Son of man concept' in the sense of a definite set of expectations associated with a distinct figure, in this instance that of a pre-existent heavenly redeemer, existed in ancient Judaism.

2. What did exist was the imagery of Dan. 7.13, itself derived from an ancient Canaanite myth. This imagery concerns a mysterious figure coming to power, and probably originally concerned the coming to power of a younger god in place of an older one.

---

[1] Against Tödt (*Son of Man*, pp. 224, 50), who accepts the saying as representing a warning by Jesus to 'the present generation, [which] though living before the end, does not watch the signs of the times . . . in the way Noah did' (p. 50,) and Colpe (*TWNT* article, C I 3a), who can find no ground for rejecting the saying in its earliest form. R. Bultmann (*History of the Synoptic Tradition*, p. 152) suggests that the saying could either have come from Jesus or be of Jewish origin, but (p. 126) inclines to the Jewish origin.

3. This imagery is used by the author of Daniel to express the concept of the 'saints of the Most High' (the Maccabean martyrs) being given their reward.

4. The imagery is used by the scribe(s) of the Similitudes of Enoch to interpret the translation of Enoch, and by those of early Christianity to interpret the resurrection of Jesus. These two things are completely independent of each other, as are the resultant Enoch-Son of man and Jesus-Son of man concepts.

5. Both the Enoch saga and the early Christian traditions go on to develop concepts of the present glory and future function of their hero-figures. These are developed quite independently of one another and the features they have in common, e.g. the concept of the function of the Son of man at the Last Judgement, they owe to a common dependence upon general and widespread apocalyptic ideas.

It follows from the above that Jesus could not have spoken of the coming of the Son of man, either in reference to himself or in reference to an eschatological figure other than himself. No such concept of a coming Son of man existed to be referred to in this way. This conclusion, we claim, is supported by the examination of the apocalyptic Son of man sayings in the tradition; they all reveal themselves to be products of the early Church.

The one thing that Jesus could have done is to use the imagery of Dan. 7.13 to express the concept of a future vindication of his ministry and of men's proper response to it. He could also have expressed the same idea by referring to the 'sign of Jonah' that would be given to this generation, as he certainly expressed it by speaking of the men of Nineveh or the queen of the South arising at the judgement to condemn his contemporaries. In all of this we have the concept of a future vindication; but we have nothing of the form it will take, nor of the time element involved, except the fact that it is future. This is so different from Jewish apocalyptic, and from the early Church, that it demands careful attention.

We would like to point out that we are not here arguing in a circle. If we had used our criterion of dissimilarity to deny the authenticity of the apocalyptic Son of man sayings, then it could have been urged that we were using a criterion of dissimilarity to define the teaching of Jesus and then making a big thing of the dissimilarity! But, in fact, the apocalyptic Son of man sayings are to be rejected, not on the basis of the criterion of dissimilarity, but because they do not survive the enquiry into the history of the tradition. So we are entitled to call attention to this radically dissimilar aspect of the teaching of Jesus.

EXEGESIS 4. SAYINGS SETTING A TIME LIMIT TO THE COMING OF THE END: MARK 9.1 PAR.; MARK 13.30 PAR.; MATT. 10.23[1]

Mark 9.1. Truly, I say to you, there are some standing here who will not taste death before they see the kingdom of God come with power.

Mark 13.30. Truly, I say to you, this generation will not pass away before all these things take place.

These two sayings have to be discussed together, since they present parallels of both form and meaning. Each begins with the solemn 'Amen, I say to you . . .'; each has the same form of emphatic negation (double negative and subj.); each has the same overall structure: solemn asseveration—'until'—statement concerning the End. At the same time there are important differences. The asseverations are both equally regular apocalyptic promises, but 13.30 is general and 9.1 specific: 'this generation', 'some of these standing here'. 13.30 uses *mechri* for 'until' (nowhere else in Mark; Matthew and Luke have *heōs*); 9.1 *heōs* (the regular Markan word; so Matthew and Luke).

9.1 has some distinctively Markan characteristics: the concept of 'seeing' the parousia, and the use of 'power' and 'glory' in this connection. This we pointed out above (pp. 16ff.) and there we also argued, following Haenchen, that 9.1 serves a distinct function as the climactic promise bringing to an end the pericope 8.27–9.1. As such it is the promise antithetical to the threat in 8.38: '. . . of him will the Son of man be ashamed when he comes in the glory of his Father . . .' This parallelism of function between 8.38 and 9.1 is matched by a verbal parallelism in their final clauses: '. . . Kingdom come (lit. 'has come') with power' = '. . . Son of man . . . comes in the glory of his Father . . .' Furthermore, the perfect in 9.1 is readily explicable on the basis of the function of 9.1 to express a climactic promise, a promise for a *completion* of experience, whereas it is inexplicable if 9.1 is an original isolated saying.

We suggest the following thesis to explain these phenomena.

[1] See Annotated Bibliography No. 8: 'Imminent Expectation' in the Teaching of Jesus.

1. Mark 13.30 is a product of early Christian apocalyptic. It is entirely characteristic of apocalyptic in general, and the 'these things' clearly refers to the whole sequence of signs, portents and events with which the apocalyptic discourse, Mark 13.5–27, is concerned. Also, it finally answers the question of the disciples which provides the narrative setting for the discourse: 13.3f. Most probably the discourse at one time had a form: Mark 13.3–27, 30, before the addition of further sayings and the insertion of the parable of the Fig Tree. So the saying will have been composed to bring the discourse to a close and it is, therefore, not a saying of Jesus, since the discourse certainly does not come from him.[1] It has been suggested that 13.30 is a genuine saying which originally referred to the destruction of the Temple and the fall of Jerusalem, and which has been adapted to serve its present purpose in the apocalyptic discourse.[2] The difficulties with this suggestion are that we have absolutely no evidence that the saying ever existed in a form different from that in 13.30; that its present form fits its function as ending the discourse so perfectly that it seems likely that it was composed for this purpose; and that there is no single dominical feature about the saying except the solemn introduction, which could be, as it sometimes is, prophetic imitation of a dominical style. In a case such as this, where an early Christian prophet is certainly offering to his church an apocalyptic discourse in the name of the risen Lord, the imitation of the dominical style would be perfectly natural. The saying is not to be regarded as a Markan construction, because Mark never uses *mechri* for 'until', but *heōs*.

2. Mark 9.1 has been constructed by Mark to bring to an end his pericope 8.27–9.1. It is doubly derivative. In form it is built upon 13.30—hence the parallels noted above—and its second part is a deliberate echo of 8.38. In purpose it is linked with 8.38 to bring the pericope to an end. As we noted earlier, the two statements, of the coming of the Son of man and of the coming of the Kingdom in power, clearly refer to different aspects of the eschaton, the one to it as threat and the other to it as promise. Hence, the parallelism of expression is no doubt deliberate, and artistically very effective. In referring to the eschaton as threat Mark has used traditional material,

---

[1] N. Perrin, *Kingdom*, pp. 130–4. R. Bultmann, *History of the Synoptic Tradition*, p. 123, suggests v. 30 originally followed v. 27 and ended the apocalypse.

[2] V. Taylor, *Gospel According to St Mark* (London: Macmillan, and New York: St Martin's Press, 1959 [= 1952]), p. 521.

adapting a saying from the apocalyptic Son of man tradition. In referring to it as promise, he has adapted a saying from the apocalyptic discourse he already knew and was to use later in his gospel.

The actual process of the composition of 9.1 would be (a) the acceptance of the basic form of 13.30: solemn asseveration—'until'—promise. Then (b) the asseveration is varied from that in 13.30 by the use of a stock phrase from apocalyptic '. . . (those) standing here who will not taste death' (cf. IV Ezra 6.25f.) for '. . . this generation will not pass away'. The reason for this change is clear. It is that 9.1 is directed to a specific group, the members of the Church under threat of persecution, whereas 13.30 is addressed to a totality, all who will overhear or read it. At this point we have the solemn introduction (from 13.30), the varied form of the asseveration (but with the same construction as 13.30 [double negative and subj.]) and the 'until' (but with the more regular Markan *heōs* for the unusual *mechri*). The last step is then (c) the construction of the promise. This is modelled on 8.38, varying from that by using 'Kingdom' for the eschaton, a usage from the Jesus tradition with which Mark is fully familiar (1.15!), and by putting the verb 'to come' in the perfect and adding 'in power', both changes stressing the promise as being a promise for an experience of complete fulfilment.

Thus we are able to account for every aspect of the present form and function of Mark 9.1, and for its obviously complex relationships to 13.30, to 8.38 and to the Jesus tradition.

Matt. 10.23b. Truly, I say to you, you will not have gone through all the towns of Israel, before the Son of man comes.

We earlier regarded this as a genuine saying of Jesus, claiming that as an unfulfilled prediction it was not lightly to be brushed aside.[1] 'Lightly', perhaps not, but the arguments against its authenticity are, in fact, by no means light, as we have found on further investigation. Above all, our investigation of the apocalyptic Son of man sayings has convinced us that all sayings which speak of the 'coming of the Son of man' are necessarily products of the early Church, since the conception they embody arose in Christian circles on the basis of an interpretation of the resurrection. Further, a more careful attention to Grässer's argument, especially to his argument that the *situation* envisaged by the saying is that of the early Church and her experience

[1] N. Perrin, *Kingdom*, p. 83.

rather than that of the ministry of Jesus,[1] showed us that our previous opinion had been much too lightly reached.[2] Matt. 10.23 has no claim to authenticity. It is the product of a Christian prophet, with the solemn introduction also to be found in Mark 13.30 and imitated in Mark 9.1, and it is directed to the early days of the Church's mission to the Jews when the imminent expectation was at its height.

One other element from the teaching of Jesus often adduced as evidence for an 'imminent expectation' in the teaching of Jesus[3] is the parable of the Fig Tree.

> **Mark 13.28f.** From the fig tree learn its lesson: as soon as its branch becomes tender and puts forth its leaves, you know that summer is near. [29]So also, when you see these things taking place, you know that he is near, at the very gates.

Verse 29 has clearly been added to make the parable serviceable in terms of early Christian apocalyptic, the 'he is near' referring to the type of expectation found in I Thess. 4.16 and in the prayer *Maranatha* (I Cor. 16.22). The simile in v. 28 may be authentic, but if it is, it by no means necessarily indicates an imminent expectation. Jeremias, who regards it as authentic, includes it in his section 'Now is the Day of Salvation',[4] claiming that it expresses the concept: 'the hour is come, the final fulfilment has begun.' In other words, it is concerned with the Kingdom as present, not as future. In view of this ambiguity of reference, this parable, even if authentic, is not evidence for an 'imminent expectation' in the teaching of Jesus.

THE FUTURE ELEMENT IN THE TEACHING OF JESUS

We have now completed our analysis and exegesis of those elements in the teaching of Jesus which can be claimed to give an indication of his expectation concerning the future. The one thing we have

---

[1] E. Grässer, *Das Problem der Parusieverzögerung in den synoptischen Evangelien und in der Apostelgeschichte* (Beihefte zur *ZNW* 22 [Berlin: Alfred Töpelmann, 1957]), p. 138.

[2] In view of our previously negative reaction to Grässer's work (N. Perrin, *Kingdom*, pp. 145–7), we may perhaps be permitted to add that now we would be much more sympathetic to parts of it, although we still could not accept its total thesis.

[3] Most recently by W. G. Kümmel, 'Die Naherwartung in der Verkündigung Jesu', *Zeit und Geschichte* (1964), p. 35 (= *Heilsgeschehen und Geschichte* [1965], pp. 460f.).

[4] J. Jeremias, *Parables of Jesus* (rev. ed., 1963), pp. 119f.

not done is to repeat our interpretation of the Lord's Prayer from this perspective, because we desire neither to add to, nor to change, our previous work on the prayer.[1] We will simply assume the results of that discussion in what follows.

The results of the investigation we have carried out in this chapter, and that of the Lord's Prayer in our previous work, have been to convince us that there is an element of futurity in the teaching of Jesus. This is not actually a point disputed in the contemporary discussion, so we need waste no time on it. What is at dispute is the nature, form and proper interpretation of this element of futurity, and this is a point we must discuss with some care.

The first result of our investigation to become significant in this connection is the obvious one, namely, that almost all the elements in the tradition which give a definite *form* to the future expectation in the teaching of Jesus fail the test of authenticity. The regular apocalyptic type expectation of Mark 13 and its parallels is from early Christian apocalyptic; the expectation of the 'parousia' is a Matthaean development from the apocalyptic Son of man tradition; and the apocalyptic Son of man tradition has itself developed from an early Christian interpretation of the resurrection and early Christian passion apologetic. The only elements which go back to Jesus here are such general things as the expectation of vindication and judgement implied by the parables, by the possible use of Dan. 7.13, and by the references to the queen of the South, the men of Nineveh and the sign of Jonah. These express confidence in *a* vindication, but they tell us nothing about its form. The difference between this and the general expectation of the first century, both Jewish and Christian, is spectacular. Nor, as we pointed out above, is this difference due to a use of the criterion of dissimilarity to establish it. These elements fail to meet the test of writing a history of the tradition.

Equally spectacular is the way in which sayings which express an imminent expectation fail to stand up to serious investigation. Mark 13.30 is a commonplace bit of apocalyptic, an integral part of the 'little apocalypse' in Mark which can be shown, on literary and linguistic grounds, not to go back to Jesus. Mark 9.1 is a Markan product; Matt. 10.23 speaks of the coming of the Son of man and reflects the conditions of the early Church; and the parable of the Fig Tree is far from an unequivocal expression of an imminent expectation. Again, here, the difference between Jesus and both

[1] N. Perrin, *Kingdom*, pp. 191–9.

ancient Judaism and primitive Christianity is notable, indeed.

The first result of the investigation is, then, to establish major differences between Jesus and his contemporaries in that, although he spoke of the future, he gave neither specific form to his future expectation (beyond the general one of vindication and implied judgement), nor did he express it in terms of a specific time element.

What else can we say of Jesus' expectation as it is revealed in his teaching? Extraordinarily significant, in our view, is the way in which elements of the disciples' experience in the present form an integral part of the teaching concerning the future. The disciples experience the Kingdom of God in their present; they are taught to pray: 'Thy Kingdom come.' They gather together in the table-fellowship of the Kingdom; they are reminded that this is an anticipation of the table-fellowship in the Kingdom. The whole tenor of the teaching of Jesus at this point is that the experience of the present is an anticipation of the future. Further, the experience of the present is a guarantee of the future, as the parables we discussed earlier in this chapter show, in that they challenge men to learn from their experience in the present to have confidence in the future. The disciples' present has become God's present; God's future will be their future!

It is at this point that we must remind ourselves that we are not dealing here with teaching which is couched in terms of a modern western concept of linear time.[1] We are dealing with a concept in which time is thought of not so much as something which passes from future to past, or past to future, but as opportunity or occasion, as something which is given meaning by that which fills it. So the present time of the disciple is filled with the reality of God—that is what gives it its meaning—and the promise is that nothing is to be expected other than a consummation of the experience of this reality in the future. Although the reality is there in the present, filling it and giving it its meaning, it is a reality known in terms of ambiguity, of conflict, of temptation: a reality known in terms of Now, but also of Not Yet. The assurance is that this is not the whole to be expected, but rather the foretaste of an unambiguous future.

In any statement of this theme we must use the words 'present' and 'future', but let us be careful to remind ourselves that the empha-

---

[1] N. Perrin, *Kingdom*, p. 185. Similarly, R. Schnackenburg, *God's Rule and Kingdom*, p. 213; E. Fuchs, *Studies of the Historical Jesus*, p. 123. Further references are given by W. G. Kümmel, *Zeit und Geschichte*, p. 32, n. 6 (= *Heilsgeschehen und Geschichte*, p. 458, n. 6).

sis is not temporal, but experiential. The men confronted by the ministry of Jesus are challenged to recognize that this is the beginning, but not the end. The man responding to the challenge of that ministry is assured that he does not now know or have all that is to be known or had. The ministry of Jesus makes the present of that ministry, and of the people confronted by it, God's present in a new and radical manner. But it also guarantees that, because of this new present, the future is also God's. The future of the ministry, the future of Jesus, the future of the men challenged, all this suddenly becomes God's future, and God's future becomes their future.

There are no ways to express this theme, except to use words such as 'Thy Kingdom come', or to speak of 'sitting at table in the Kingdom', or to contrast a handful of seed sown with the bushels of grain harvested, the small lump of leaven with the mass of leavened dough. The moment a time is set, or the type of expectation categorized, then we have an objective expectation which men may love or fear, for which they may wait in hope or despair, but which has retreated out of the range of their immediate experience as they wait for it as something to be experienced at some future time. The act of objectification loses the dynamic of the tension between present and future so characteristic of the teaching of Jesus[1] and is, therefore, strenuously avoided in that teaching. In the teaching of Jesus the emphasis is not upon a future for which men must prepare, even with the help of God; the emphasis is upon a present which carries with it the guarantee of the future. The present that has become God's present guarantees that all futures will be God's future.

It can be seen that further work and reflection has in no way modified our understanding of this theme in the teaching of Jesus. The conclusion we reached on the basis of an exegesis of the Lord's Prayer has been substantiated by the further investigation of the teaching as a whole. The question remains, of course, the question of *interpreting* this aspect of the teaching. Granted that this teaching is of some relevance to a Christian today (and the question of how far and in what ways this would be the case will occupy us in our next chapter), how are we to express it in categories that would be meaningful today? This is a question that each must answer for himself, but the points to which any answer must remain true are clear. It must resist objectification of the hope. It must, further, do justice to the element

---

[1] On this tension see N. Perrin, *Kingdom*, pp. 190–9, with its detailed exegesis, in particular, of the Lord's Prayer.

of experience in the expectation. It must, lastly, recognize the inadequacies of a linear concept of time. Time, in the teaching of Jesus, is something which God fills and fulfils, and it is something which man experiences, rather than something which moves from past to future.

V

THE SIGNIFICANCE OF KNOWLEDGE OF THE HISTORICAL JESUS AND HIS TEACHING[1]

MOST BOOKS ON THE teaching of Jesus have simply assumed that the results of the historical-critical discussion of that teaching were significant to Christian faith. It is not only that the significance of Jesus in the cultural history of the world guarantees interest in the reconstruction of what he actually taught, as might be the case with, say, Socrates; but a significance over and beyond that is assumed, at any rate for Christians, because of the nature of Christian faith itself. So, for example, T. W. Manson claimed that '. . . if God did in fact speak to us through the life, death and resurrection of Jesus it is vitally important to know as fully and as accurately as possible what sort of life and death and resurrection became the medium of divine revelation',[2] and wrote a series of brilliant books on Jesus, and especially on his teaching. He assumed that the study of the teaching of Jesus '. . . has an independent interest of its own and a definite interest of its own and a definite task of its own, namely, that we use every resource we possess of knowledge, of historical imagination, and of religious insight to the one end of transporting ourselves back into the centre of the greatest crisis in the world's history, to look as it were through the eyes of Jesus and to see God and man, heaven and earth, life and death, as he saw them, and to find, if we may, in that vision

---

[1] See Annotated Bibliography No. 9: the Question of the Historical Jesus. The bibliography has been arranged to follow the text of this chapter, and it also supplements it in various ways. Publication details of all works mentioned in the text will be found there.

[2] T. W. Manson, 'The Life of Jesus: Some Tendencies in Present-day Research', *The Background of the New Testament and its Eschatology*, ed. W. D. Davies and D. Daube (Cambridge: University Press, 1954), p. 221.

something which will satisfy the whole man in mind and heart and will'.[1]

Today both of these things would be questioned: it is no longer self-evident that the historical Jesus is, in fact, the central concern of Christian faith, and it may no longer be assumed that the major aspect of that faith is to follow the dictates, encouragements and challenges of the teaching of that Jesus.

To understand the true nature of our problem, we must set it in its historical perspective and explore the whole discussion of the 'question of the historical Jesus', especially the very vigorous discussion of the last ten or fifteen years, but also something of that which has been going on continually ever since the Enlightenment.

In one respect the question of the historical Jesus is as old as Christian faith itself, for Christian faith is, by definition, faith in Jesus Christ: there our problem begins. Jesus is the name of a historical figure: Jesus bar Joseph from Nazareth, whereas Christ is a transhistorical title: the one appointed by God for the salvation of mankind. Here lies our problem: How are these two things related to one another in the one person? In the ancient world this was already something of a difficult question to answer. The world of Hellenism could think readily enough of 'divine men', of 'heavenly redeemers', but found it hard to think of these as also human. Hence, the rise of Docetism in which Jesus Christ was held to be only apparently human; in which, so to speak, the 'Christ' had swallowed up the 'Jesus'. The world of ancient Judaism, on the other hand, could think of divinely inspired figures, of men anointed by God, but these were always strictly human figures, an influence which made itself felt in early Christianity and produced Ebionitism, a form of the faith in which Jesus Christ was entirely human, in which the Jesus had swallowed up the Christ. But the Christian Church branded both these opinions as heresies and characteristically maintained that Jesus Christ was both . . . and . . .: both human and divine, both historical and transhistorical.

Also characteristic of Christian faith is that unique literary form: the gospel. The gospels, and more particularly the synoptic gospels, are unique in their conscious combination of historical and transhistorical elements, to use our current jargon: in their combination of historical report and kerygmatic Christology. Religious literature in general tends either to be basically *historical* narrative, interwoven

[1] T. W. Manson, *Teaching of Jesus*, pp. 5f.

with elements of interpretation due to later insights, overlaid with legend, but consciously intended to be historical; or to be pure *myth*: a concept clothed in narrative form, and consciously only clothed in that form. The synoptic gospels, however, are both of these things at the same time—we would claim consciously so—and, as such, characteristic of the unique element in Christian faith.

The history of the discussion of the question of the historical Jesus is the history of a series of attempts to do justice to the unique characteristic of Christian faith. The problem comes into focus with the Enlightenment and the rise of the historical sciences, for here we have the establishment of the concept of history in what we may call its 'modern sense', i.e. as 'what actually happened', the *'wie es eigentlich gewesen ist'*. With this, the historical Jesus becomes the man Jesus, 'as he actually was', the Jesus who may be the subject of historical critical research, Jesus as he may be known as the result of that research.

The immediate consequence of this, so far as an understanding of the gospels and of Jesus was concerned, was the controversy between the English Deists and their opponents. The Deists characteristically claimed Jesus as an example of rational humanity and understood the gospels as historical, availing themselves of all kinds of rationalistic explanations of the various phenomena, such as apparent miracle, in them. Their opponents strenuously resisted this, arguing for the reality of the supernatural at the historical level and for the understanding of Jesus as a divine-human figure. This controversy now no longer concerns us in any detail; we must simply note that this is where our problem begins.

More important to us is the work of H. S. Reimarus (1694–1768), a professor of oriental languages at a *Gymnasium* in Hamburg, who, under the influence of the English Deists, wrote a four-thousand-page manuscript *Apologie oder Schutzschrift für die vernünftiger Verehrer Gottes*, a defence of the deistic approach to religion, which he refrained from publishing. G. E. Lessing (1729–81), a leading figure in the German Enlightenment, found the manuscript in the library at Wolfenbüttel, on his appointment there as librarian in 1770, and published parts of it as 'Wolfenbüttel Fragments by an Unnamed Author' between 1774 and 1778. There are seven of these fragments, and the two most important to our purpose are the sixth and seventh: *'Über die Auferstehungsgeschichte'* ('Concerning the Resurrection Story') and *'Vom Zwecke Jesu und seiner Jünger'* ('On the purpose of Jesus and that of his Disciples'). In these Reimarus attempts a rationalistic reconstruction of the history of the beginnings of Christianity, in which Jesus is an unsuccessful political messianic pretender, and the disciples disappointed charlatans who, rather than go back to working for a living after Jesus' failure, invent the whole of early Christian faith and steal the body of Jesus so as to have an empty tomb to support their story of resurrection. In this way, Reimarus seeks to discredit both the historical Jesus, an unsuccessful messianic pretender, and the Christ of the gospels, a product of the disciples' fantasy, and so leave the way clear for a rational worship of God free from the delusion of a revealed religion.

The important thing about Reimarus, however, is not his conscious purpose, nor his reconstruction of earliest Christian history, but the way in which he is able to show, in instance after instance, that the gospel narratives may not be understood as historical accounts of actual events, but must be recognized as the product of conceptions arrived at subsequent to the events which they purport to narrate. True, Reimarus is a hostile historian, thinking in terms of delusion and fantasy, but he is none the less a brilliant historian, and his instinct is surer than his own conscious purpose. So he is able to take the first step on the way to understanding the essential nature of the gospels, by recognizing the determinative character of the influence of early Christian conceptions on the narratives. In one other respect also his instinct is sure: he interprets both the purpose of Jesus and that of his disciples in terms of Jewish messianic conceptions, and in this way puts his finger on eschatology as a key element in both the ministry of Jesus and the life of the early Church. In this he was to be shown to be absolutely correct, some two hundred years later!

Reimarus was a historian, but his work was published by a philosophically minded man of letters, Lessing, who thereafter found himself under attack from the orthodoxy of his day, especially that of *Hauptpastor* Goetze of the city of Hamburg. In the course of the subsequent controversy Lessing developed a viewpoint that later became very influential, namely, that faith cannot be grounded either on a book regarded as inspired or on facts regarded as historical. He himself regarded faith as dependent on reason and propounded his famous dictum: '*Zufällige Geschichtswahrheiten können der Beweis von notwendigen Vernunftswahrheiten nie werden*' (The accidental truths of history can never become the necessary proofs of reason). With

Glaube (faith) substituted for *Vernunft* (reason) this is a viewpoint widely accepted in our current discussion.

After Reimarus and Lessing, the next important figure in the discussion from our perspective is that stormy petrel, David Friedrich Strauss (1808–74). A theologian and philosopher, he arrived in Tübingen in 1832 to take up a post as *Repetent* (instructor) in the theological *Stift* (a hall of residence with instructional and tutorial facilities). As a philosopher he was an ardent Hegelian, and from his arrival he exercised for three semesters the traditional right of a theological *Repetent* to lecture on philosophy, lecturing enthusiastically and successfully as an apostle of Hegel. However, the philosophical faculty was less than enthusiastic about his success and forced him to give up his lectures. Stung by this, he shut himself up in the *Repetentenzimmer* and gave himself to a task he had had in mind since having heard Schleiermacher lecture on the Life of Christ in Berlin in 1831: the writing of a critical life of Christ. He worked in a combative spirit, and with the rapidity of genius, and in 1835 and 1836 published the first and second volumes respectively of his two-volume *Leben Jesu, kritisch bearbeitet*, with a total of 1,476 pages of text.

The book made him famous and for ever closed all academic doors to him, for it was received with exclamations of horror, and there began a process of academic persecution which was to follow him all his life through. His subsequent life and work have been graphically described by Albert Schweitzer in his *Quest of the Historical Jesus* (pp. 68–120) and need not concern us. What must concern us is his contribution to our discussion: the introduction of the concept of myth into the consideration of the gospel narratives.

Strauss's concept of myth has been very influential among New Testament scholars. He uses myth in the sense of a narrative giving expression to religious concepts, whether derived from Judaism or Hellenism, from the Old Testament or Christian experience. His methodology in his book is to discuss the gospel narratives in sequence, thoroughly and carefully, and he is able to show that such myth is a major factor in the narratives. His discussion is such as thoroughly to discredit both the supernaturalistic approach to the gospel narratives, i.e. the understanding of them as historical as they stand, and the rationalistic approach, i.e. the understanding of them as historical after the miraculous element in them has been explained away. Having shown that the gospels are essentially purveyors of a Christ myth, Strauss concludes his work with a last chapter in which he presents Jesus as a religious genius who achieves in himself the unity with the Father which, as unity between God and man, is the goal of the religious development of humanity. Humanity will learn from this example presented in a form it can grasp. This is Hegelian ideal-ism applied to Christology, and its relationship to the critical work on the gospels is that the destructive effect of that criticism clears the ground, so to speak, for the planting of this Hegelian seed. The apostle of Hegel is refusing to be silenced!

The long-term effectiveness of Strauss's work, however, has not been in terms of a growth of a Hegelian-Strauss Christology, but in terms of a growth of understanding of the gospels as myth and saga. Reimarus taught us to see the gospels as products of the conceptions of earliest Christianity; Strauss opened our eyes to the form in which these conceptions are clothed, the form, above all, of myth.

Before continuing to review the discussion as it has been carried on within Protestant theological circles, we may perhaps be permitted a brief excursus into the realm of Roman Catholic biblical scholar-ship, for Strauss's book produced an immediate reaction from a Roman Catholic New Testament professor in which what has come to be, to the best of our knowledge, the standard Roman Catholic viewpoint, was developed. We are referring to J. E. Kuhn, *Das Leben Jesu, wissenschaftlich bearbeitet*, published in 1838.

Kuhn argues that the Enlightenment view of history is inadequate, and inappropriate to the gospels, but whereas Strauss turned to the concept of myth to explain the phenomena of the gospels, Kuhn argues that there are two kinds of history: history and sacred history. History is concerned with cause and effect; its characteristic question is: 'Whence?' Sacred history, on the other hand, is concerned with end and purpose; its characteristic question is: 'Whither?' So we have, we may say, an anthropocentric view of history on the one hand and a theocentric view on the other. The gospels represent the second view of history. They are not concerned with the ordinary history of Jesus bar Joseph from Nazareth, but with the sacred history of Jesus the Messiah of God, and to this end they select and present material from the tradition available to them. So the transhistorical elements in their stories are not to be understood as myth, but as the means whereby the sacred-historical aspects of the story are revealed within the history itself. Kuhn reaches the point of recognizing the gospels as kerygma, i.e. as proclamations of Jesus the Messiah in his significance for faith; but whereas the later Protestant view was that the kerygmatic element was in the service of a post-Easter view of Jesus as risen Lord, read back into the narratives by the later community, Kuhn's view is that this element was present in the tradition from the very beginning, part of the gospel before the gospels, part of the message of the apostles from the very first days, part of the very fabric of the ministry of Jesus itself.

A hundred years ahead of its time in many ways, Kuhn's book represents a view that has maintained itself in Roman Catholic circles. So, for example, the Roman Catholic reaction to form criticism has always been extremely cautious, emphasizing the limits that must be set to this kind of enquiry, and the authority and reliability of the apostles as 'eyewitnesses and ministers of the word'.[1] Even when recognizing the fact that the Church has modified the tradition of the ministry of Jesus, the tendency is always to insist that the tradition is basically historical, and the modification and reinterpretation was made necessary by the changing circumstances (for example, to apply the teaching on marriage and divorce in Mark 10 to Roman marital conditions), and that it does not do violence to the original. We would have two criticisms of this view: (1) form criticism is bursting the bounds here set to it, and is showing that gospel narratives and sayings can be purely and entirely products of the early Church; and (2) the view involves an unnecessary capitulation to the very view of history it sets out to controvert, since it seems to agree that there must be a 'something actually happened' quality to the gospel myths for them to be 'true'. But there are signs that we may be approaching a meeting of minds here, because the recently published Roman Catholic *Lexikon für Theologie und Kirche* has articles on 'Jesus Christus' and 'Leben-Jesu-Forschung' which come very near to what might have been written by a contemporary Protestant scholar such as Conzelmann or Bornkamm.

After this brief excursus, let us return to the discussion on Protestant theology. As was to be expected, the work of Reimarus and Strauss produced extensive reactions, including the next major development to concern us: the rise of the liberal Life of Christ research (*Leben-Jesu-Forschung*). Liberal critical scholarship, coming into full flower at the time of Strauss and thereafter, was not prepared to accept a rendering of the gospel texts into a Christ myth and then the dissolution of that myth into a speculative Christology. Rather, it

[1] On this see above, pp. 25ff., where we quote and discuss this Roman Catholic and conservative Protestant viewpoint.

sought a kernel of history in the narratives, which would stand the test of criticism and could become the basis for faith. Quite typically, H. Weinel regarded Strauss as having two fundamental weaknesses. Although he accepted the synoptic account of Jesus' teaching as largely authentic, he made no attempt to construct a picture of Jesus from that teaching, and, although he quite properly criticized the element of myth in the gospels, he then went on to replace that dogmatic mythology of the Church with a conceptual mythology of his own. 'We should not concern ourselves with conceptions and allegories, when we have the opportunity to find a historical person, the one who has had the greatest influence in the world. And since the one to whom we are drawing near was a religious genius, we should learn to understand and experience religion from him.'[1] This epitomizes the concern of liberal scholarship, namely, to establish by historical-critical methodology the authentic teaching of Jesus and the historical core of the gospel narratives concerning his life, to recapture the person mirrored in that teaching and revealed in that life, to accept that person and that teaching as the concern and object of faith, and to seek to imitate him and to learn from him. It was knowledge of the historical Jesus, the reassurance of this human historical personality within the gospel story, which constrained men to say 'Jesus is Lord.'[2] Liberal scholarship, therefore, accepted the full burden of historical critical scholarship without hesitation and without reserve, believing that the historical core of the gospel narratives, when reached, would reveal Jesus as he actually was, and that he would then be revealed as worthy of all honour, respect and imitation, revealed as the founder of a faith which consisted in following him and his teaching closely and purposefully.

This liberal position on the question of our knowledge of the historical Jesus and the relationship of that knowledge to Christian faith is too well known to need further elaboration, so let us turn at once to the combination of theological and critical considerations and external historical circumstances which led to its downfall in Germany. As we consider this, however, we must be conscious that a downfall in Germany does not necessarily mean a collapse elsewhere, and that, as a matter of fact, the position was maintained in Britain

---

[1] H. Weinel, *Jesus im neunzehnten Jahrhundert* (Tübingen: J. C. B. Mohr [Paul Siebeck], 1904), p. 44.

[2] So D. M. Baillie, a contemporary representative of the liberal position, *God Was in Christ* (London: Faber and Faber, and New York: Scribner's, 1948), p. 52.

and America for another fifty years, and still is so maintained, although now only to a very limited extent. So our concern is not only with the history of its fall in Germany, but also with the factors revealed in that history which, we would claim, are also valid factors in the British or American situations.

The first thing to be mentioned in this connection is always Albert Schweitzer's brilliant and excitingly written *Von Reimarus zu Wrede* (ET *The Quest of the Historical Jesus*), a history of the liberal Life of Christ research which is now generally recognized as having been also its funeral oration (Bornkamm). The core of Schweitzer's argument is that the liberal quest of the historical Jesus was not historical enough. Instead of following through with their historical research to the end, the liberal scholars always stopped at a point at which they were able to present a Jesus who was, in fact, an image of the scholar himself, or of the scholar's ideals. To use a British image: a Cromwell without warts! If the research is carried through to the end, however, we find a Jesus who was an apocalyptic fanaticist. Disappointed in his expectation of the irruption of God into the world's history to bring that history to an end in the very year he began his ministry, this Jesus was deluded enough to attempt to force the hand of God by his own sufferings, which he conceived to be the 'messianic woes' which would prove to be the beginning of the End. This historical Jesus is necessarily a stranger and a foreigner to us and to our time, and the recognition of this fact sets us free to follow the dictates in our own consciences of the spirit of Christ released into the world by the death of the historical Jesus.

The significance of Schweitzer's work as a long-term contribution to the discussion is that he succeeded in his demonstration of the fact that the liberals had failed to reach the historical Jesus, that they had, indeed, tended to read their ideals into this figure, and that they had spectacularly missed the eschatology. Subsequent attempts to carry on the 'quest' in the sense of reaching a historical Jesus who would be the concern of faith have had to make strenuous attempts to guard themselves against the weaknesses which Schweitzer had inexorably exposed.[1] But it is questionable whether it is, in fact, possible to avoid the ultimate weakness: the tendency to find a Christ of a liberal or personal faith when in theory one is seeking the historical Jesus. Even

[1] The most important example of this is J. Jeremias, *The Problem of the Historical Jesus* (ET by N. Perrin of *Das Problem des historischen Jesus*. Philadelphia: Fortress Press, 1964), pp. 15–20.

if steps are taken to avoid psychologizing, to give due emphasis to the eschatology, etc., the fundamental weakness remains the fact that the deliberate elevation of a historically reconstructed figure to the central concern of faith must inevitably lead to the confusion of two quite separate functions: the reconstruction of a historical figure and what we shall call the construction of a faith-image. A theological tradition which 'believes in Jesus' encourages the believer to construct the faith-image of this Jesus, an image made up as a result of many different influences: the preaching and teaching of the Church, the reading of the gospels and of devotional literature, the lives and ideals of influential individuals, and so on. Significant in this process can be also the results of historical critical research, mediated through the books of influential liberal scholars. In itself this is a wholly natural, and, indeed, wholly admirable process, and the liberal faith-image is altogether excellent, *as a faith-image*. The difficulty was that the liberal critical scholar was engaged at one and the same time in constructing a faith-image and reconstructing the historical image, the one as a believer and the other as a scholar, and this led to the confusion between these two tasks to which Schweitzer, in effect, pointed, and which was, indeed, unavoidable. In the very nature of the case, the liberal Jesus of history became the Christ of a liberal kerygma, and *vice versa*.

The second critic of the liberal quest who must concern us is Martin Kähler, whose work *Der sogennante historische Jesus und der geschichtliche, biblische Christus* (ET *The So-called Historical Jesus and the Historic, Biblical Christ*) was practically ignored at the time of its publication in 1892, but has since been recognized as a major contribution to the discussion. In 1892 the liberal movement was at its height, Schweitzer's work was still fourteen years in the future, and the discussion was between, on the one hand, an orthodoxy still claiming the gospels as historical documents and the Christ of the Church's faith as a historical figure, and, on the other hand, a liberalism claiming the gospels as non-historical in their present form, but as capable of being used as historical sources, sources for the reconstruction of a historical Jesus to be distinguished from the Christ of the gospels. Both sides had capitulated completely to the post-Enlightenment view of history, and they had accepted the conclusion that the object of Christian faith must be historical in this sense. To the one the historical Jesus must be found directly in the gospels, to the other he must be reconstructed from them; but to both he is the object of

Christian faith. Kähler, however, now challenged this basic assumption. He regarded himself as arguing for orthodoxy against liberalism and he claimed, (1) that the gospels are not and cannot be sources for the life of Jesus, and (2) that the Christ of the gospels is the only concern of Christian faith, not the historical Jesus. He distinguished between the historical Jesus, the Jesus known as a result of historical research, and the historic Christ, the Christ of the gospels in his significance for the faith of later generations, and in so doing established the distinction between *der historische Jesus* and *der geschichtliche Christus* which has come to play such a role in the contemporary theological discussion. Although written on behalf of orthodoxy, the ultimate effect of Kähler's work was radical both as over against orthodoxy and as over against liberalism. In effect, his insights lead to a challenge to orthodoxy to give up the myth of claiming that the Christ of the gospels was a historical figure and to content itself instead with recognizing that he is a historic figure, admittedly known to us only from Christian preaching but in any case the only legitimate concern of Christian faith. At the same time they challenged liberalism to give up the myth that it was possible to reconstruct a recognizable figure from the gospels used as historical sources. They are products of early Christian preaching and do not contain the necessary material; for example, they have no account of Jesus' personal development, and attempts to supply this material by analogy from other historical figures are inappropriate to the subject. In any case, again, the historical Jesus is not the concern of faith.

At the time of its publication, Kähler's challenge fell upon deaf ears. One suspects that the reason for this was that in 1892 neither orthodoxy nor liberalism was prepared to abandon *Historie* for *Geschichte*. But Kähler had pointed the way forward, because it is, in fact, true that the historical Jesus is not directly the concern of faith. Once the modern concept of history was established, and with it the concept of the historical Jesus as the man Jesus 'as he actually was', then it became inevitable that it should first be argued that this was the direct and immediate concern of faith, and then recognized that, after all, it was not. Faith is concerned with the risen Lord in his fulfilment and in his significance for later generations, with the historic Christ, and it is to Kähler's immense credit that he recognized this and was prepared to distinguish between *Geschichte* and *Historie* in this connection. Of course, the recognition of the validity of this distinction, and of faith's concern with *Geschichte* rather than *Historie*, means the end of both liberalism and orthodoxy in their nineteenth-century forms, which is why Kähler is so immensely important today. It also means the raising of the question of the relationship between *Geschichte* and *Historie*: granted that faith's immediate concern is with the *geschichtliche* Christ, what is then the relationship between this figure and the *historische* Jesus? This is a question with which we are concerned in our current discussion, but before it could be asked a number of other factors had to play their part in the discussion, including the first world war and its aftermath, the rise of form criticism and the coming of Rudolf Bultmann.

The events of 1914–18 effectively ended the reign of liberalism in German theology, because historically speaking liberalism arose in the context of *Kulturoptimismus*: the sense of progress, the optimism about the social, political and moral possibilities of reform and development in the world, in society, among individuals, which was such a feature of the second half of the nineteenth century. But so far as Germany was concerned, all this came to an end, suddenly and drastically, in the summer of 1914, and the liberal theology related to it could not survive without it. The new times called forth a different understanding of the nature of the Christian faith, epitomized by the rise of Karl Barth, and the liberal concern for the historical Jesus as the object of Christian faith died, because the liberal theologians had no successors in the Germany of the 1920s. The Anglo-Saxon tradition did not have the same drastic experience; in it liberalism was able to live on for another half-century. But the continuing experience of the first half of the twentieth century was not such as to encourage *Kulturoptimismus* even in Britain and America; in this tradition also liberalism has been, or is being, abandoned in a search for more satisfactory expressions of faith. The relationship between theological liberalism and cultural optimism is, however, by now an old, old story, so let us leave the external historical circumstances and return to more purely academic and theological considerations, of which the next to concern us is the rise of form criticism in the 1920s.

At the academic level form criticism is the single most important development in the history of the discussion of our problem, for it provides what must be regarded as the only satisfactory understanding of the nature of the synoptic gospel material—satisfactory, that is, from the viewpoint of being able to explain the phenomena demonstrably present in the texts themselves. We use the term 'form criticism', as always in our work, widely and loosely to describe the approach to the gospels which considers them as products of a process of oral transmission of tradition, that is, to describe the oral process of transmission of a tradition which has been given its present form in response to the needs of the early Church and to express her theological viewpoints, a tradition which was to a large extent created to meet those needs and to express those viewpoints. At this point we do not propose to repeat the arguments for accepting this view of the synoptic tradition which we adduced in our first chapter, but only to repeat our claim that this is the only justifiable view of the nature of that tradition. It must be recognized that the narratives in the synoptic gospels were created to express the theology of the early Church, that they are through and through mythical in Strauss's sense of the word. It must be recognized, indeed, that there are comparatively few narratives which correspond in any way to events in the ministry of Jesus, and that where such correspondence is to be found, as for example in the baptism or crucifixion narratives, the gospel account has been so influenced by the theological conceptions and understanding of the Church that we can derive little, if any, historical knowledge of that event from those narratives. Even the fact that the baptism or crucifixion are historical events is not to be derived with any certainty from the gospel narratives; it has to be argued on other grounds. With form criticism the original insights of Reimarus and Strauss come into their own, and the possibility of writing a Life of Christ vanishes for ever.

The effect of the demise of liberalism, with its concern for the historical Jesus, and the rise of form criticism, with its confirmation that the gospels can never be sources for a Life of Christ, was to clear the way for an acceptance of the challenge of Martin Kähler. With the effectual disappearance of the *historische Jesus* from the scene, it was natural to follow Kähler and to concentrate attention on the *geschichtliche Christus*. So we reach Rudolf Bultmann, whose views are the basis for our current debate.[1]

Perhaps the best way to detail Bultmann's position is in terms of its relationship to that of Martin Kähler, without thereby intending to claim that this relationship is as conscious as our explication will tend to make it appear. There are three particular points at which Bult-

[1] R. Bultmann, *Jesus and the Word* (1958); *Theology of the New Testament* I (1951); *Primitive Christianity* (1956); 'New Testament and Mythology' and 'A Reply to the Theses of J. Schniewind' in H. W. Bartsch (ed.), *Kerygma and Myth* (1953); 'The Primitive Christian Kerygma and the Historical Jesus', in *The Historical Jesus and the Kerygmatic Christ*, ed. C. E. Braaten and R. A. Harrisville (1964).

mann seems to be developing insights to be found in Kähler's work.

1. There is a distinction between historical Jesus and historic Christ. It is the distinction between the one who proclaimed the Kingdom of God as the imminently expected eschatological act of God and the one who is proclaimed as eschatological act of God. This is Bultmann's famous distinction between the Proclaimer and the Proclaimed and it should be noted that it includes three elements, all of which are very important to Bultmann.

(a) The distinction between historical Jesus and historic Christ, which is ultimately derived from Martin Kähler.

(b) The introduction of a reference to the eschatological act of God, proclaimed by Jesus in terms of the Kingdom of God and by the early Church in terms of the cross and resurrection of Christ.

(c) The emphasis upon the fact that in the message of Jesus this eschatological act of God is still future, albeit imminent and even now beginning to break in, whereas in the kerygma of the early Church it is already past, although available ever anew as God manifests himself as eschatological event in the kerygma. So Bultmann always maintains that salvation is only a promise in the message of Jesus, but a present reality through the kerygma of the Church.

2. The object of Christian faith is the historic Christ, the Christ of the kerygma, and not the historical Jesus. The Christ present in the kerygma is necessarily distinct from the historical Jesus, above all in what we may call his effectiveness. The historical Jesus did not demand faith in himself, but at the most in his word, especially in his word of proclamation of the imminence of the Kingdom of God, and he did not offer salvation, but only promised it for the future. The kerygma does, however, demand faith in the Christ present in it, and offers salvation now to those who believe in him. Again, the historical Jesus proclaimed the future eschatological event, whereas the kerygmatic Christ is the eschatological event as he confronts the man addressed by the kerygma. The historical Jesus proclaimed a message that was the last word of God before the End; the kerygmatic Christ is the word of God and the End.

At this point we should pause for a moment to note that there is one concept which is decisive for an understanding of Bultmann's approach to the question of the historical Jesus, and, indeed, of his whole approach to the interpretation of the New Testament: the concept of 'paradoxical identity'. There is a paradoxical identity of proclamation and saving event as the saving event becomes the saving event *for me* in the proclamation. There is the paradoxical identity of eschatology and history in the cross, which is at one and the same time historical and eschatological event. This is an absolutely essential paradox. The cross is historical and also necessarily eschatological (so far as Christian faith is concerned). The saving event necessarily combines the 'thatness' of Jesus and his cross and the presence of Christ as eschatological event *for me* in the proclamation.

Lastly on this point we come to the reformation principle 'by faith alone' as restated by Kähler, maintained by Bultmann, and generally acceptable in the Germany in which liberal theology was dead and reformation theology in revival: faith as such is necessarily independent of historical facts, even historical facts about Jesus. In practice, today's assured historical facts tend to become tomorrow's abandoned historian's hypotheses, and, in principle, a faith built upon historical fact would not be faith at all but a work. Further, faith is faith in the eschatological act of God in Jesus Christ, but that God has acted in Jesus Christ is not a fact of past history open to historical verification, and this is shown by the way in which the New Testament describes the figure and work of Christ in mythological—not historical—terms.

3. The gospels are not and cannot be sources for a Life of Jesus; they are products and embodiments of the preaching of the early Church. Bultmann's critical studies convinced him that the gospels as such are necessarily concerned with only one historical fact: the 'thatness' of Jesus and his cross. That there was a Jesus and that he was crucified is the necessary historical presupposition for the kerygma, the proclamation of the Church. But beyond this the synoptic gospels themselves are uninterested in the historical element as such, since they freely overlay the historical with the mythical, they present much of their material as a historicization of myth, and they make absolutely no attempt to distinguish the historical as such from the mythical. They are a unique combination of historical report and kerygmatic Christology, the purpose of which, however, is proclamation, not historical reporting. This is even more clearly true of Paul and John, both of whom require no more of history than the 'that' of the life of Jesus and his crucifixion for their proclamation. So the nature and purpose of the gospels as this is revealed by critical scholarship support Bultmann's understanding of the significance of the historical Jesus for Christian faith.

In addition to the three things related to Kähler's work, there is
one further element in Bultmann's thinking that needs to be considered at this point: the significance of the historical Jesus for an
individual's self-understanding, or understanding of existence. Bultmann espouses an existentialist understanding of historiography,
whereby the individual enters into dialogue with the past, and is
challenged by an understanding of existence (self-understanding)
from the past which becomes significant to him in the historicity of
his own existence. So in the case of the historical Jesus there is an
understanding of existence (self-understanding, not self-consciousness)
revealed in his teaching which challenges us in terms of our understanding of our own existence. Hence, Bultmann writes a Jesus book,
Jesus and the Word, from this perspective.

Three things, however, must be said at this point:

(*a*) As the subject of this existentialist historiography Jesus is not
unique. A similar study, with similar consequences in terms of a
possible challenge to our understanding of existence, could be carried
out in connection with any figure from the past for whom we had
sources: Socrates the philosopher, or even Attila the Hun, as well as
Jesus the Christ.

(*b*) This historiographical challenge to our self-understanding is
not for Bultmann the challenge to faith, not even though the challenge
to faith could be, and is, expressed by him in similar existentialistic
terminology. He himself stresses the facts that the Jesus of history is
not kerygmatic and that his book *Jesus and the Word* is not kerygma,
because the essential aspect of the kerygma is that Christ is present in
it as eschatological event, and Christ is not so present in existentialist
historiographical studies of the historical Jesus. If he were, then they
would cease to be existentialist historiographical studies and become
kerygma.

(*c*) This type of study of Jesus is to be sharply distinguished from
the liberal Quest. In the liberal Quest attempts were made to reach,
and to understand, the psychology and personality of Jesus (i.e. his
self-consciousness) which was an endeavour both impossible (no
sources) and illegitimate (use of analogy), whereas in the Bultmann
study the concern is with the understanding of existence (self-understanding) revealed in the teaching of Jesus.

We should perhaps attempt to clarify this distinction between self-
understanding and self-consciousness which Bultmann makes. It is

difficult to grasp, and it becomes important in the post-Bultmannian debate. By self-understanding Bultmann means the understanding to which the self comes concerning the nature of its historical existence. In his *History and Eschatology*, originally written in English, he often uses the expression in close connection with the untranslatable German word *Weltanschauung*, and it is to be understood as referring to a person considering the existence which is his and reaching an understanding of it in all its historicity. The actual word in German is *Existenzverständnis*, and James M. Robinson has properly urged that the English 'understanding of existence' should be used to express it.[1] The difficulty lies in grasping the fact that it means the understanding of the self's own existence, but, at the same time, it does not mean the process of experience, reflection, decision, and so on, by means of which that understanding is reached; that would be self-consciousness. Similarly, it refers to the understanding of existence which an individual comes to have, but it does not refer to the conscious decisions to which this understanding leads and in which it may be expressed; this, again, would be self-consciousness. The self-understanding of Jesus is a legitimate concern for the historian, because it can be deduced from his teaching. The self-consciousness of Jesus, however, is not a legitimate concern, because we have no sources for such knowledge, and when we supply the deficiency by analogy from other historical individuals, we are psychologizing about Jesus.

This position of Bultmann's on the question of the historical Jesus and his significance for faith has been attacked from three standpoints, one might say: from right, left, and centre.

The attack from the right has been motivated by the conviction that the historical nature of Christian faith or the meaning of the Incarnation necessitates more emphasis upon the actual historical events *circa* AD 30 than Bultmann will allow. In this camp we find all kinds of strange comrades in arms united in their conviction that the historical events of the ministry of Jesus, in addition to the cross, are necessary to Christian faith. We can find the whole gamut of possibilities from the extreme conservative insisting on the factual historicity of everything from the Virgin Birth to the Resurrection to the old-fashioned liberal to whom only the Jesus reconstructed by historical study can be of significance to faith. Of all the possible names here we will mention only that of our own teacher, the

[1] J. M. Robinson, 'The New Hermeneutic at Work', *Interpretation* 18 (1964), 347–59, esp. 358.

moderately conservative Joachim Jeremias, who deserves to be heard on this point, if only because he has done more than any other single scholar to add to our knowledge of the historical Jesus. He has published a booklet on the question, *The Problem of the Historical Jesus*. In this he argues that the proclamation is not revelation, but leads to revelation, so that the historical Jesus is the necessary and only presupposition of the kerygma (a play on Bultmann's famous opening sentence of his *Theology of the New Testament*), since only the Son of man and his word, by which Jeremias means the historical Jesus and his teaching, can give authority to the proclamation. This is a major issue in the contemporary debate: does Bultmann's view do less than justice to the historical nature of Christian faith or violence to the Incarnation? Is the historical Jesus as such the necessary ultimate concern to whom the kerygma points?[1]

The attack from the left has taken the opposite position, namely that Bultmann is inconsistent in his views in that he properly sees Christian faith as a transition from inauthentic to authentic existence, and then illogically maintains a necessary link with the historical Jesus in this process. Surely he should recognize the fact that all he is really saying is that there are those for whom this is true. But there are those for whom the transition can be made in other ways, and there is in particular the existentialist philosopher Karl Jaspers, who debated this issue with Bultmann,[2] maintaining that the link with the historical Jesus introduces an objective factor into an existential moment where it has no place. Jaspers's views are actually in one respect reminiscent of liberalism of the Harnack type in that he sees Jesus as an example, an example of the kind of existential relationship to the transcendent which the philosopher seeks for himself. It must be admitted that Jaspers appears to have the better of his immediate argument with Bultmann, Bultmann's final reply being a three-sentence letter refusing to commit himself further at that time. But he returned to the discussion later, in a quite different context, and then it became obvious that he regarded himself as committed by the New Testament itself to a necessary link with the historical Jesus, for he could only reiterate his major point, that Christian faith as such is committed to the paradoxical assertion that a historical event

[1] For further discussion of this position see our review of some more recent works representing it, *JR* 46(1966), 396–9.

[2] K. Jaspers and R. Bultmann, *Myth and Christianity* (1958). R. Bultmann, 'Das Befremdliche des christlichen Glaubens', *ZTK* 55 (1958), 185–200.

within time, Jesus and his cross, is the eschatological event, and support it by exegesis of New Testament texts, especially Paul and John. Thus, we come to the unbridgeable gap between the New Testament theologian and the theistic existentialist, and we find that it is an old issue returning in a new form: is the historical Jesus necessarily anything more than an example we seek to imitate in his worship of the Father (Harnack) or in his breakthrough to true existential self-understanding (Jaspers)?

A similar point becomes evident in the interchange between Bultmann and another of his critics from the left, Schubert Ogden.[1] Here it turns upon Bultmann's existentialistic understanding of Christian faith as authentic existence. Bultmann had always contended that authentic existence was a 'possibility in principle' (*ontological* possibility) for man outside of Christian faith, but a 'possibility in fact' (*ontic* possibility) only within that faith. Ogden criticized this as inconsistent, arguing that the possibility in principle is always a possibility in fact because of the primordial love of God, 'which is, indeed, decisively revealed in Jesus the Christ, but is by no means simply to be identified with him'.[2] The point is that this love is manifest to men in every aspect of life, not only in the Christ-event.

> To be sure, the church stands by the claim that the decisive manifestation of this divine word is none other than the human word of Jesus of Nazareth and thence of its own authentic proclamation. But the point of this claim is not that the Christ is manifest only in Jesus and nowhere else, but that the word addressed to men *everywhere*, in all the events of their lives, is none other than the word spoken in Jesus and in the preaching and sacraments of the church (*ibid.*, p. 156).

Bultmann replied to this further attempt to abandon the particularity of Christian faith as follows:[3]

> Christian faith contends that the gift of radical freedom is the gift of God's grace. And Christian faith speaks about the grace of God not as an idea but as an act of God: an act which reveals itself as grace in Jesus Christ, that is, in a historical event. This assertion cannot be proved by philosophy; indeed, it is a stumbling block, a *scandalon* for rational thinking. And therefore I must ask Ogden whether what he calls the inconsistency of my proposal is not rather *the legitimate and necessary character of what the New Testament calls the stumbling block*? [Italics ours.]

---

[1] Schubert M. Ogden, *Christ without Myth* (New York: Harper & Bros., 1961).
[2] *Ibid.*, p. 143.
[3] In a review of Ogden's book, *JR* 42 (1962), 225–7. Quotation from p. 226.

The next major development in the discussion came, so to speak, from the centre, from a pupil of Bultmann's, Ernst Käsemann, who, in 1953 raised the question as to whether or not Bultmann was, in fact, doing justice to the New Testament. In his essay, 'Das Problem des historischen Jesus',[1] he sounded a warning about the danger of a position in which there was not a real and material continuity between the historical Jesus and the kerygmatic Christ: the danger of falling into Docetism, or of having faith degenerate into a mere mysticism or moralism. But the important thing about the essay is not his warning in itself, but the fact that Käsemann was able to support it by observing that the synoptic gospels are more concerned with the pastness of Jesus and his ministry than Bultmann's position, built largely on an exposition of John and Paul, would allow. Not that the gospels are uniform in their understanding of the relationship of the past ministry and present life in faith, far from it. They agree that the 'once' of Jesus' ministry has become the 'once for all' of revelation (we may put it: the *chronos* of Jesus has become the *kairos* of faith), but the relationship between the 'now' and the 'then' is a problem for them, and a problem for which they find their several different solutions.

The really important thing about Käsemann's essay is this challenge to a consideration of the synoptic tradition, for the problem of the historical Jesus is ultimately a problem for us because of the material in the synoptic gospels and the Acts of the Apostles. If our New Testament consisted of the gospel of John, the epistles and the apocalypse we would have no problem, for we would have nothing in any way relevant to what we would call the historical Jesus. If it were not for the synoptic gospels and Acts, Bultmann's position would be unassailable; the remainder of the New Testament certainly has no interest in what we would call the historical Jesus, apart from the 'thatness' of this Jesus and his cross. So the discussion ought to have turned to an intensive consideration of the synoptic tradition, especially since we now had form criticism to guide us as to the true nature of that tradition, but unfortunately it did this only in part. The issues which were taken up most immediately and most vigorously in the subsequent discussion were, rather, those of the question of continuity between the Christ of the kerygma and the historical

---

[1] Originally published in *ZTK* 51 (1954), 125–53, and then reprinted in Käsemann's collected essays, *Exegetische Versuche und Besinnungen* I (1960), 187–214. ET in E. Käsemann, *Essays on New Testament Themes* (1964), pp. 15–47.

Jesus, and of the significance of an existentialist view of history in connection with the 'problem of the historical Jesus'.

The final point in Käsemann's essay is, in effect, an exploration of our actual (i.e. post-form-critical) knowledge of the historical Jesus, in order to show that we are able to say that the messianic claims of Jesus explicit in the kerygma are already implicit in the teaching of Jesus. So the continuity between the historical Jesus and the kerygmatic Christ is already more than merely chronological; it is material in that it is a continuity between implicit and explicit messiahship. Actually, Bultmann himself had used the term 'implicit Christology' in connection with the message of the historical Jesus, so it might be said that Käsemann was only bringing out an element already present in Bultmann's position. But the subsequent discussion showed that Bultmann was concerned to minimize this element of continuity for the following reasons: (1) he was fearful that historical research might come to be used to legitimate the kerygma, which would be a denial of its nature as kerygma; and (2) he insisted that there can be no real material continuity, because the kerygma lays major emphasis upon a particular understanding of the death of Jesus, whereas we can never know how the historical Jesus understood his own death, and must always face the possibility that he simply broke down before it.[1]

This question of the continuity between historical Jesus and kerygmatic Christ became a major aspect of the discussion, other Bultmann *Schüler* adding their particular contributions, until eventually it resulted in the development of a wholly new position: the 'new hermeneutic' of Ernst Fuchs and Gerhard Ebeling.[2]

To understand the 'new hermeneutic' it helps to recognize that it grew out of the exploration of the continuity between the historical Jesus and the kerygmatic Christ, which, of course, in view of form criticism, is necessarily a question of the continuity between the message of Jesus, to the limited extent that we know it, and the kerygma proclaiming the Christ. Fuchs and Ebeling brought to this exploration the conception of a 'word-event' (*Wortgeschehen* or *Sprachereignis*), i.e. a reality which is manifest in language itself (with obvious dependence

[1] R. Bultmann, 'The Primitive Christian Kerygma and the Historical Jesus', *The Historical Jesus and the Kerygmatic Christ*, pp. 15–42.

[2] *The New Hermeneutic*, ed. J. Cobb and James M. Robinson (1964). G. Ebeling, *The Nature of Faith* (1961); *Word and Faith* (1963); *Theologie und Verkündigung* (1962). E. Fuchs, *Studies of the Historical Jesus* (1964). E. Jüngel, *Paulus und Jesus* ([2]1964). James M. Robinson, 'Neo-Liberalism', *Interpretation* 15 (1961), 484–91; 'The New Hermeneutic at Work', *ibid.* 18 (1964), 347–59.

on Heidegger's 'language is the house of being'), and in particular the conception of faith as 'word-event'. In the message of Jesus, faith is manifest as such a word-event because Jesus himself, by virtue of a decision he himself had made over against the reality of God and the possibility of his own fate, is the witness of faith. Since he is the witness to faith, faith comes to word, i.e. it is manifest as word-event, in him, and particularly in his message. The continuity with the kerygmatic Christ is that faith is also manifest as word-event in the kerygma, and this continuity is particularly strong in that the believer, in responding to the kerygma, actually echoes the original decision which Jesus had made. So the witness of faith becomes the ground of faith, and faith, as word-event, is the element of continuity between the message of Jesus and the kerygma of the early Church.

For Fuchs and Ebeling, we may say, faith comes to word or language in Jesus for those who heard his message and for subsequent generations in the Church's message about him. This is the continuity of proclamation and the continuity of faith coming to word or language in proclamation for the believer. So far as we are concerned, the primary source in which we hear the word being proclaimed is the New Testament; thus, the New Testament is to be interpreted in such a manner as to facilitate the coming of faith to word or language for us through its words. A true existentialist interpretation of the New Testament is one through which faith comes to be word- or language-event for us, and the hermeneutic by means of which this is to be achieved is the 'new hermeneutic'.

In this new and interesting development, hermeneutic has, in effect, taken the place of kerygma and a concern for an existentialist interpretation of the kerygma has been modified by a concern for the historical Jesus until it has become a concern for an existentialist interpretation of the New Testament—now seen not as a source book for knowledge of the historical Jesus, as in the older liberalism, but as a means whereby that faith which came to word or language in Jesus may come to be word- or language-event for us. James M. Robinson appropriately suggests that this position be designated 'Neo-liberalism'.

This bald summary is only a caricature of this most recent development, but we hope it is sufficient to show that we do, indeed, have here a new theological position. By pushing a Lutheran emphasis upon faith to an extreme, Fuchs and Ebeling have arrived at a point at which faith is practically personified. By taking a Lutheran emphasis upon the Word to a similar extreme, they have achieved a concept of faith coming into being or being manifested in 'word' or 'language', and so have made a new use of the parallel between the message of Jesus and the message about Jesus. By being prepared to think of decisions which Jesus himself made and in which the believer imitates him, they have reached a point at which they are restating a position which Schleiermacher and Harnack would surely have recognized, despite the difference in conceptualization.

Bultmann has reacted very sharply against this development, which he accuses of psychologizing about Jesus in the manner of an already discredited liberalism.[1] In the light of Bultmann's criticism Ebeling carefully restated his position,[2] making the following points:

1. It is not a case of psychologizing about Jesus but of recognizing that a person is necessarily involved in his word, that the message necessarily involves the messenger, that a message challenging to faith necessarily involves a witnessing to faith on the part of the messenger.

2. Bultmann himself speaks of the Proclaimer becoming the Proclaimed. In the new terminology Ebeling is using, this is expressed as the witness to faith becoming the ground of faith.

3. The kerygma as such is kerygma by act of God, but it needs historical knowledge for its proper interpretation. Since it identifies kerygmatic Christ and historical Jesus, knowledge of the historical Jesus may properly be used to interpret the kerygma.

It is clear that we are only at the beginning of what promises to be a most lively discussion.

The second of the issues raised in the discussion sparked by the publication of Käsemann's essay was that of the significance of an existentialist historiography in connection with our problem. This arose in connection with the concern for parallels between the message of Jesus and the message about him, parallels between the proclamation of Jesus and the kerygma of the early Church. Käsemann had pointed to the parallel between the implicit Christology of the message of Jesus and the explicit Christology of the kerygma, and the subsequent exploration of such parallels became a major feature of what came to be called the 'new quest of the historical Jesus'. We might mention particularly the work of Herbert Braun, who argued

---

[1] In his essay 'The Primitive Christian Kerygma and the Historical Jesus', *The Historical Jesus and the Kerygmatic Christ*, esp. p. 33.

[2] In his *Theologie und Verkündigung*, pp. 19–82; 119–25.

that throughout the New Testament, from the message of Jesus to the developed kerygma of the Hellenistic church, there is a constant and a variable. The constant is the self-understanding of a man before God, the anthropology; the variable is the expression of the significance attached to Jesus, the Christology (implicit and explicit).[1] In 1959 James M. Robinson published his *New Quest of the Historical Jesus* in which he gave this new movement both its title and its definitive form. He explored the parallels already pointed out between the message of and about Jesus, and he added to them some of his own derived from a study of the Kingdom sayings. Then, in addition, he took the post-Diltheyan, modern, existentialist historiography which seeks to mediate an encounter with the past at the level of self-understanding, and approached the historical Jesus and his message in this way. Now we have two sets of parallels: between the historical Jesus and the kerygmatic Christ at the level of meaning of the message of and about the one and the other, and between the encounters mediated by modern historiography with the one and by kerygmatic proclamation with the other. 'It is because modern historiography mediates an existential encounter with Jesus, an encounter also mediated by the kerygma, that modern historiography is of great importance to Christian faith.' In the encounter with Jesus, one is confronted '. . . with the *skandalon* of recognizing in this all-too-human Jewish eschatological message the eternal word of God', which means that in the encounter with Jesus, 'one is confronted by the same existential decision as that posed by the kerygma'. So 'one has proved all that can be proved by a new quest of the historical Jesus: not that the kerygma is true, but rather that the existential decision with regard to the kerygma is an existential decision with regard to Jesus'.[2]

The immediate retort to this, made by R. H. Fuller and echoed with approval by Bultmann, was that '. . . the effort to demonstrate the continuity between Jesus and the kerygma may so blur the difference between them as to make the kerygma unnecessary'.[3] In

---

[1] H. Braun, 'Der Sinn der neutestamentlichen Christologie', *ZTK* 54 (1957)' 341–77 (= H. Braun, *Gesammelte Studien zum Neuen Testament und seiner Umwelt* [Tübingen: J. C. B. Mohr (Paul Siebeck), 1962], 243–82). See also his essay 'The Significance of Qumran for the Problem of the Historical Jesus', *The Historical Jesus and the Kerygmatic Christ*, pp. 69–78.

[2] James M. Robinson, *A New Quest of the Historical Jesus*, pp. 90, 92.

[3] R. H. Fuller, *ATR* 41 (1959), p. 234. R. Bultmann, 'The Primitive Kerygma . . .', *Historical Jesus and Kerygmatic Christ*, ed. Braaten and Harrisville (1964), p. 39.

reply to this criticism, and to others made by Bultmann himself, Robinson reformulated his position in an essay 'The Recent Debate on the New Quest'.[1] In this essay a good deal of the emphasis upon the encounter with the historical Jesus by means of an existentialist historiography was quietly dropped, and attention was more sharply focused on the basic parallel between the message of Jesus and the kerygma of the early Church, and on the significance of scholarly study of the message of Jesus for the Church.

The responsibility of Christians today is to proclaim the kerygma in our situation, but '. . . we must nevertheless implement the kerygma's claim to be proclaiming a Lord who is at one with Jesus, and we must do this by critical participation in the discussion of the Jesus-tradition of our day'.[2] So it is, to use our own words, the Church's identification of the risen Lord with the earthly Jesus that poses for us the problem of the relationship between the two figures, and demands an answer to the question of the significance of historical knowledge of the latter. That identification by the early Church requires at least that the Christ proclaimed by the kerygma be consistent with what we come to know of the historical Jesus. For Robinson, the particular function of the 'new quest' is to investigate, not the self-consciousness of Jesus, for which we have no sources, 'but the understanding of existence which emerged in history from his words and deeds',[3] i.e. is implicit in his teaching and in the fact that he accepted the cross. '. . . it is the implicitness of the kerygma in Jesus' understanding of existence that is required by the kerygma, if that reference is in fact a fitting one.'[4]

The last point in Robinson's essay, and a shrewd one, is, in effect, an argument that the kerygma has a content, for 'kerygma' means both the act of proclamation and the content of proclamation. Since the kerygma has a content, historical study of a past form of the kerygma, e.g. the pre-Pauline Hellenistic kerygma or the Palestinian kerygma, can serve '. . . not to replace the (contemporary) minister's preaching but to improve it'.[5] But, in regard to historical study, there is no difference between historical-critical study of a past form of the kerygma and that study of the teaching of Jesus. So '. . . in our situation the historical study of Jesus is not of the *esse* of preaching, but it belongs to its *bene esse*'.[6]

---

[1] *JBR* 30 (1962), 198–208.
[2] James M. Robinson, *ibid.*, p. 204.
[3] *Ibid.*, p. 200.   [4] *Ibid.*, p. 202.   [5] *Ibid.*, p. 207.   [6] *Ibid.*

It seems to us that there are a number of promising points in this statement of the 'new quest' position, and when we develop our own position below it will be seen that we are indebted to it at several places. However, there are three things we would like to say at this stage about the 'new quest' position as a whole, as Robinson has defined it.

In the first place, the quiet but drastic step taken by Robinson between the publication of his book and his essay, of abandoning the concept of an existential encounter with Jesus mediated by a modern historiography in favour of something much less dramatic, is an absolutely essential step to take. No modern historiography can mediate '. . . an existential encounter with Jesus', if only because we do not have the materials necessary to reconstruct the complete figure we would need for such an encounter. In this respect, form criticism is as lethal to this kind of 'modern historiography' as it was to the liberal life of Christ research, and the imagination of an existentialist 'new quester' would have to be every bit as active as was that of any liberal 'old quester'.

Then, secondly, it must be recognized that the 'new quest' is not, in fact, all that new. True, it tends to ask rather different questions, such as those concerning the understanding of existence implicit in Jesus' teaching, but its work is still based on exactly the same kind of historical-critical methodology as that used by Bultmann or Jeremias. It has to begin by asking the questions that have always been asked: What did Jesus mean by 'Kingdom of God'? Did he assert the coming of the 'Son of man'? How was his work related to that of the Baptist? And so on. Only when it has established a core of authentic sayings, etc., can it go on to ask about an understanding of existence which emerges into history from them. When Robinson, after recognizing this, goes on to observe '. . . that material regarded as wholly "unauthentic" in terms of a positivistic historiography may not seem nearly so "unauthentic" in terms of modern historiography',[1] then he is either talking about a rather special form of our 'criterion of coherence', or he is talking nonsense. One may certainly accept sayings which reflect the same 'understanding of existence' as that found in indubitably genuine sayings, but to go beyond that is to run the risk, again, of doing in terms of the new existentialism what was done in terms of the old liberalism. Unless we exercise all possible care, it is just as easy for 'Jesus' understanding of existence' to become 'my

[1] James M. Robinson, *A New Quest of the Historical Jesus*, p. 99, n. 2.

understanding of existence' as it was for 'Jesus' moral principles' to become the liberal scholar's ideals.

Then, finally, a weakness in the 'new quest' position is that it simply assumes the identity of historical Jesus and kerygmatic Christ, arguing that the kerygma and modern historiography provide us with two avenues of access to the same Jesus, or at any rate, have reference, on the one hand, to Jesus, and, on the other, to the Lord who is at one with Jesus. This is a bold assumption indeed! In the first place, it ignores the variety of kerygmata in the New Testament itself, the existence, in fact, of a multiplicity of Christs of different kerygmata; and in the second place, it ignores equally the possibility of tension between the results of historical-critical research and the kerygmata of the New Testament. Are we, for example, to assume that the implicit Christology of the ministry of Jesus corresponds to each of the explicit New Testament Christologies: proto-gnostic heavenly redeemer, fiercely apocalyptic Son of man, Hellenistically oriented Lord, Judaistic Son of God, etc.? And are we further to assume that our historical research will always point to parallels between the message of Jesus and a form of the kerygma, and never to differences? Surely, both of these assumptions are unjustified. The Christologies of the various forms of the kerygmata known to us from the New Testament and Christian history are not necessarily coherent with one another, still less necessarily consistent with the teaching of the historical Jesus, and historical research may well raise problems for a form of the kerygma, as, for example, research into the eschatology of Jesus raised problems for the older liberalism.

Before turning to our own considerations of these matters, there is one last contribution to the discussion to be noted: Ernst Käsemann's recently published essay, 'Sackgassen im Streit um den historischen Jesus'.[1] In this he enters into vigorous debate with two viewpoints expressed during the discussion, those of Jeremias and Braun, and with Bultmann's rejoinder to his own pupils and definitive statement of his own position in light of the discussion: 'The Primitive Christian Kerygma and the Historical Jesus'. From the perspective of our present purpose, however, this aspect of the essay is not what matters most. More important to us is the fact that he seeks to further the discussion by focusing attention sharply upon the phenomena present in the synoptic tradition and the contrast between this and the

---

[1] Published in his second volume of collected essays, *Exegetische Versuche und Besinnungen* II (1964), 31–68. See our review of this volume, *JBL* 85 (1965), 462f.

remainder of the New Testament. Beginning with the New Testament apart from the synoptic gospels, he points out that it is absolutely remarkable how small a role the earthly Jesus plays in the tradition. Apart from a few sayings and reflections on the history of Jesus, only the cross has theological relevance, and not only the history in general, but also the cross in particular has been so overlaid with mythological interpretation and parenetic application that the historical phenomena are more hidden than revealed. In the synoptic tradition, on the other hand, although the same mythological overlay and parenetic application is there, the fact remains that we, do have what we would call historical material and historicizing tendencies in a way we do not have elsewhere in the New Testament. Käsemann's way of formulating this is to say that while the dimension of the past of the gospel and of Christology in Paul and John can be overshadowed by the present and future, in the case of the synoptic gospels this past dimension is dominant in the proclamation, even though it is being made to serve the kerygmatic and parenetic purposes of the present. In this phenomenon our theological problem is revealed and we must explore it and its significance to solve the problem.

On this point we are absolutely in agreement. One must investigate the theological significance of the very fact of the existence of the synoptic tradition, and the significance of its essential nature, in order to throw light on the problem of the historical Jesus. Indeed, we would go further than Käsemann, who against Bultmann still wants to explore the question of continuity between historical Jesus and kerygmatic Christ, for we would limit the question of continuity to the question of whether the Christ proclaimed in a form of the kerygma is consistent with the historical Jesus.

In order to clarify the points at issue in the current discussion, we may say that it is a discussion involving three different kinds of knowledge. First, there is the essentially descriptive historical knowledge of Jesus of Nazareth with which we have been concerned all through this book. Then, secondly, there are those aspects of this knowledge which, like aspects of historical knowledge of any figure from the past, can become significant to us in our present in various ways. Thirdly, there is knowledge of Jesus of Nazareth which is significant only in the context of specifically Christian faith, i.e. knowledge of him of a kind dependent upon the acknowledgement of him as Lord and Christ.

Let us say something about each of these kinds of knowledge. The first, the descriptive historical knowledge, is the post-Enlightenment historical knowledge. It is difficult to achieve for the reasons discussed at the end of our first chapter, but it is our claim that it can be achieved by the appropriate hermeneutical methodology. When it is achieved, its very existence raises the question of its significance, apart, of course, from the significance it has as a series of more or less interesting facts from the past. This knowledge is 'hard' knowledge, by which we mean that it exists independently of any specific interest in it or usefulness to be ascribed to it, or, indeed, independently of any lack of interest in it or even danger found to be inherent in it.

The second kind of knowledge with which we are concerned is essentially a selection from the collection of 'hard' historical knowledge. Some of this knowledge will be found to be directly significant, in various ways, to a man of today. But such significance will depend upon the establishment of some point of contact between that knowledge from the past and the situation of the man in the present. So, for example, the existentialist analysis of the nature of human existence, with its emphasis upon 'self-understanding', or 'understanding of existence', establishes a point of contact between the figure from the past and the man in the present. Since the man in the past is, so to speak, also existential man, it may be possible to discern the self-understanding implied in what we know of that man and so establish our contact with him at the level of self-understanding. Other kinds of contact are also possible. For example, modern artists have found themselves challenged by primitive man at the common level of the use of symbols; a modern humanist could be influenced by, say, the historical Socrates, because of a common devotion to a certain understanding of the meaning and significance of truth; and so on. Historical knowledge from the past becomes directly significant, i.e. it becomes historic knowledge, to us in our present in so far as it 'speaks to our condition', 'has a direct point of contact with us', or the like.

The third kind of knowledge becomes significant to us at the level of religious faith, belief or commitment. It is distinct from the second in that it is particular, i.e. for the individual concerned it has a value beyond that to be ascribed to any other historical knowledge, or to knowledge of any other historical individual. Also, it is particular in the sense that it has this value only to certain individuals or groups, those who share the particular faith, belief or commitment. It is also distinct from both the first and the second in that it is not necessarily historical knowledge. Historical knowledge can come to have this significance, but then so can myth, legend, saga—and any combination of these!

Perhaps we can make our point about these three kinds of knowledge clearer by means of some examples. Let us call the first kind of knowledge 'historical knowledge', the second 'historic knowledge' and the third 'faith-knowledge'.

'Historical knowledge' of Jesus of Nazareth might be held to include the fact that he accepted his death as the necessary consequence of his proclamation of the Kingdom, and of his 'table-fellowship of the Kingdom' with 'tax collectors and sinners', and that he went to the cross with a sure confidence that it would ultimately serve, and not hinder, the purpose of God.[1] Similarly, it might be held to be a fact that Socrates accepted his death as the necessary consequence of his own innermost convictions, and drank the hemlock with a serenity arising out of the courage of those convictions. Finally, to give a more recent example, it has been held that, in early March, 1912, Captain Oates, 'who was too ill to travel further, walked out into a blizzard, hoping, by his sacrifice, to save his companions (of the Scott Antarctica expedition)'.[2] These are three examples of historical knowledge and, as such, they are subject to correction and change on the basis of further research or discovery. So it is theoretically possible, however practically doubtful, that we may one day have to concede that Jesus was carried to the cross, railing against God and his fate; that Socrates had to have his jaws forced open to drink the hemlock; or that Oates's companions drove him out of the tent into the blizzard. If this were to happen, we would simply be exchanging one historical fact, now discredited, for another, and the exchange would make no specific difference beyond this, at the level of historical fact or historical knowledge.

Historical knowledge can, however, under certain circumstances become 'historic knowledge', i.e. it can assume a direct significance for the present. So, to stay with our examples, the historical knowledge of Jesus' acceptance of the cross can become historic knowledge as it influences a future time which finds itself touched or moved by it in some way. So, also, can Socrates' acceptance of the hemlock, or Oates's sacrifice on behalf of his friends. We move from the historical

[1] We are using this as an example without necessarily claiming that this is 'hard' historical knowledge, although, in fact, it could be very strongly argued.

[2] *Encyclopaedia Britannica* 20 (1964), 179.

to the historic as the event from the past assumes a direct significance for a future time. We are thinking of a significance other than that which the event has as part of the chain of causation which has produced the later time. Historic knowledge has a direct, even personal or existential, significance for a later time and its people, or, at any rate, for some of them. Historic knowledge can be affected by the vicissitudes of historical factuality. A Jesus railing against God and his fate, a Socrates being forced to drink the hemlock or an Oates being driven out into the blizzard would have historic significance of a kind very different from that ascribed to these men immediately above.

'Faith-knowledge' depends upon special worth being attributed to the person concerned, so that knowledge of that person assumes a significance beyond the historic. Historic significance can be attributed to almost any number of people from the past, certainly to all three of our examples, but 'faith-knowledge' could be attributed only to the one figure who comes to be of special significance in terms of revelation, religious experience, religious belief. Also, the use of these categories necessarily introduces a reference to a transhistorical reality—strictly speaking, a non-historical reality—in that it introduces the idea of God and his activity. So, for the Christian, it is possible to say: 'Christ died for my sins in accordance with the scriptures.' This, however, is a statement of faith, not of history in the normal sense. It is faith-knowledge, not historical knowledge. It depends upon recognition of Jesus as the 'Christ, the Son of the living God'; it necessitates a recognition of his death as having significance in terms of the religious concept 'my sins'; and it requires that the cross be recognized as being in accordance with the 'definite plan and foreknowledge of God' as this is said to be revealed in the sacred writings of the Jews. None of this is history in the post-Enlightenment sense of that word; nor is it dependent upon the manner or mode of the death of Jesus, only on the fact that it happened. The value here ascribed to that death is not ascribed to it because of what Jesus did, but because of what God is regarded as having done. The death of Jesus is not efficacious for 'my sins' because he died nobly, or because he showed confidence in God, but because the cross is believed to have fulfilled the purpose of God. That Jesus died nobly or showed confidence in God are historical statements, subject to the vicissitudes of historical research, but that his death fulfilled the purpose of God in regard to 'my sins' is certainly not such a statement, and it lies beyond the power of the historian even to consider it, even though, as a Christian, he might believe it.

We should make it clear that the 'historic Christ' of which Kähler speaks is, according to our definition of the terms, not the 'historic Jesus'. Kähler speaks of the Christ of the gospels in all the fulfilment of his significance for faith; he is, therefore, making faith statements and speaking of the Christ of faith, not of the historic Jesus about whom one could make statements of the kind one could make about the historic Socrates or the historic Oates. What we are doing, in effect, is attempting further to refine the terminology in light of the the distinctions introduced into the discussion since Kähler wrote.

These distinctions we have made are important to the contemporary discussion, for the discussion really turns upon a recognition of these three different kinds of knowledge of Jesus of Nazareth. The historical sciences have given us historical knowledge of Jesus, as they have given us such knowledge of other figures from the past. Then, especially in the last few decades, we have become aware of historic knowledge of Jesus, as of such knowledge of other figures. Finally, we have come to distinguish faith and faith-knowledge from history and historical knowledge, largely under the influence of Bultmann.

Let us now briefly reconsider some aspects of the discussion we have portrayed, making use of the distinctions we have suggested.

Bultmann's position becomes immediately clear. He grants that we have historical knowledge of Jesus, although limited in extent and not including any knowledge of how he understood his own death.[1] So also we have historic knowledge of him; we can encounter him as historical phenomenon at the level of historic significance.[2] Finally, and quite distinct from this latter, we have 'faith-knowledge' of him; we encounter him as the eschatological phenomenon in the proclamation. True, this Jesus of the kerygma, this Jesus of faith-knowledge, encounters us in our historic situation, but he is not the historic Jesus, he is the Christ, the eschatological Jesus. Our encounter with him is not like an encounter with the historic Socrates, or with any other historic figure, but it is an eschatological encounter: it changes everything for us and brings our old history to a close, opening up for us a new history and a new future as no other encounter with a figure from the past could do. Even this figure from the past can only do so

[1] R. Bultmann, 'The Primitive Kerygma . . .', *The Historical Jesus and the Kerygmatic Christ*, pp. 22ff.

[2] R. Bultmann, 'Reply to the Theses of J. Schniewind', *Kerygma and Myth*, p. 117.

because, as the eschatological figure, he becomes present for us in the proclamation, and present for us as eschatological act of God.

The attack upon Bultmann's position from the right seeks to establish closer links than Bultmann will allow between historical knowledge and faith-knowledge, between the first and third of our categories. The attack upon Bultmann from the left attempts to make the third category only a variant of the second, so that Jesus becomes not the eschatological, but only a (or, the) supreme historic figure. So, from the right, Jeremias can argue that historical knowledge is directly related to faith-knowledge. The incarnate Word is revelation, not the preaching of the Church. The proclamation is witness *to* the revelation, not itself the revelation. 'To put it bluntly, revelation does not take place from eleven to twelve o'clock on Sunday morning.'[1] From the opposite viewpoint, from the left, Jaspers and Ogden can argue, in effect that faith-knowledge is only a special kind of historic knowledge. Jesus, as an example of existential relationship to the transcendent which the philosopher seeks to emulate, is a historic figure, not a faith image. So also is the Jesus who reveals the primordial love of God which can also be known elsewhere than in him. In these viewpoints, even if it can be claimed that we have a kind of residual reference to the transhistorical reality, God, we certainly do not have an unrepeatable uniqueness ascribed to Jesus. The faith-knowledge has become historic knowledge.

At this point we are at a parting of the ways, so far as the discussion of the 'question of the historical Jesus' is concerned, for here we have fundamental presuppositions as to the nature of faith and the significance of history. On the right we have the presupposition that the Incarnation—or the biblical concept of God active in history, or the traditional view of Christianity as related to certain revelational events in history, or the like—that this demands a real and close relationship between historical knowledge and faith-knowledge, and that justice must be done to this in our discussion of the question of the historical Jesus. On the left we have the conviction that, even if we may speak meaningfully of God or the transcendent, none the less the essential relativity of all historical events means that we cannot think in terms of a knowledge of Jesus that is different *in kind* from knowledge we may have of other historical persons. So, either Jesus becomes an example of an existential relationship with the transcendent, supreme but capable of being imitated (Jaspers), or he becomes

[1] J. Jeremias, *The Problem of the Historical Jesus*, p. 23.

the 'decisive' manifestation of that which may also be known else-where (Ogden). No doubt other variations on this theme could be found, but they would all be variations on the one theme, that faith-knowledge is historic knowledge. What we know in Jesus may be 'decisive', but it is not different in kind from what may be known elsewhere. Finally, in the centre, we have Bultmann, whose position may be expressed, in our terms, as maintaining that the three kinds of knowledge are separate and must be kept separate.[1]

Meaningful debate between representatives of these three positions is difficult, for sooner or later that debate will run aground on the hard rock of the very different fundamental presuppositions. We saw that happening above, in the case of Jeremias over against Bultmann, and in that of Bultmann over against both Jaspers and Ogden. Examples could readily be multiplied from the history of the dis-cussion.[2] When this happens, the debate may become a sympathetic agreement to differ, or it may degenerate into strident disagreement, but it has no future as debate. So at this point the scholar or student finds himself in one of three different groups, according to his basic presuppositions, and from this point on he will be involved in one of three quite different discussions. The question of the historical Jesus has to be faced and discussed, in accordance with one's basic pre-suppositions, in light of the challenge issuing from the other groups and the developments and changes going on in one's own.

Our own presuppositions are such that we find ourselves in what we regard as the centre, with Bultmann, for we find ourselves 'feeling' that the three kinds of knowledge we have described do exist, are different, and should be kept separate. Empirical historical know-ledge is a special kind of knowledge and the question of its existence, factuality or truth should always be kept separate from that of its significance. 'Historic' or significant knowledge from the past should always be subject to the tests of demonstrating that it is, indeed, historical knowledge and that the avenue, channel or point of contact between it and the man from whom it becomes significant in the

[1] This, we would claim, is true for Bultmann even though, in his concern for 'demythologizing', he is prepared to describe almost all of the faith-knowledge in terms of historic knowledge.

[2] Because of their representative nature, the following would be of special interest: E. Ellwein, E. Kinder and W. Künneth in *Kerygma and History*, ed. C. E. Braaten and R. A. Harrisville (New York: Abingdon, 1962), pp. 25–119 (represent-ing an orthodox Lutheranism against Bultmann), and R. E. Brown, 'After Bult-mann, What?—An Introduction to the Post-Bultmannians', *CBQ* 26 (1964), 1–30 (representing Roman Catholicism).

present can be defined. Religious or 'faith' knowledge, on the other hand, should be subject to quite different tests: the understanding of ultimate reality it mediates, the kind of religious experience it inspires, the quality of personal and communal life it makes possible, and so on. It may also be subjected to the test of determining whether or not the knowledge is also factual or true in an empirical historical sense, so far as any such test is possible in connection with it, but it must always be recognized that although historical knowledge can have this kind of significance, this kind of significance is not limited to knowledge that is also historical.

If we consider the 'new hermeneutic' in the light of our distinction between these three kinds of knowledge, a Bultmannian distinction which was the starting-point for the work of Fuchs and Ebeling, then we see that the movement does, in practice, tend to abandon it. This is most clearly to be seen in the work of E. Jüngel, Fuchs's pupil, for he reviews the academic historical investigation of the parables of Jesus in recent times and climaxes this review with the following statement: 'The Kingdom comes to word in parable as parable. The parables of Jesus bring the Kingdom to word as parable.'[1] Now whatever this may mean, it is clearly a faith statement rather than a historical statement (which would have to be limited to: 'Jesus intended to bring the Kingdom to word . . .' or 'Jesus' hearers believed that he brought the Kingdom . . .' or the like). Occurring as it does in the context of a review of one of the most spectacularly successful empirical historical investigations in the whole field of life of Christ research, it is clear evidence of a tendency of the 'new hermeneutic' to blur the distinction between statements possible on the basis of academic historical research and statements possible only on the basis of faith.

The same tendency is very much to be found in the work of Ernst Fuchs himself. One can open his book of *Studies of the Historical Jesus* almost at random and find evidence of it. Take, for example, the following:

> The starting point of Jesus' proclamation in the Synoptics is Jesus' full authority to gather a people for God under the banner of the rule of God (cf. Matt. 9.8). This authority . . . answers the questions: What do you pray for? or, For whom do you pray? Jesus' faith leads him to prayer for the heavy laden, for the poor and for the disciples (cf. by contrast the unmerciful servant, Matt. 18.23–35). In the future

[1] E. Jüngel, *Paulus und Jesus*, p. 135. The statement is italicized by Jüngel.

faith in Jesus will continue this prayer, even though Paul is undecided whether or not he should at once pray for the day of the Lord (Rom. 8.26). For faith it is sufficient that God has listened to Jesus (Heb. 5.7; John 17.10).[1]

This begins with a historical statement, namely (to use our words), that the starting-point of the message of Jesus in the synoptic gospels is the authority of Jesus to proclaim the Kingdom and to gather together Jew and 'Jew who had made himself as Gentile' into the table-fellowship of that Kingdom. Then it ends with the faith statement: 'For faith it is sufficient that God had listened to Jesus.' It is clear that Fuchs is able to move from the one to the other because of his concept of faith as a 'language event'. The faith that comes to word in Jesus is the root of the authority he had; thence, the faith come to word in in Jesus becomes Jesus' faith, and leads to the thought of Jesus' prayer life; from there we move to faith come to word in the future for men of the future, and their prayer practice; and, finally, we arrive at the climactic faith statement. All this may be in accordance with the 'new hermeneutic', but it is a clear abandoning of hard-won distinctions and of the gains from hard-fought battles.[2] For a hundred and fifty years we have been struggling to clarify issues and gain understanding. Are we to throw all this away in an attempt to make the historical Jesus relevant to faith by abandoning legitimate and—we would claim—necessary distinctions? This, it seems to us, is what the 'new hermeneutic' is in danger of doing.

The 'new quest' position also can be approached from the standpoint of this distinction between the three different kinds of knowledge. As represented by Robinson's *New Quest of the Historical Jesus* it formally abandons the distinction between faith-knowledge and historic knowledge. His later position, however, seems to restore this distinction and to claim, rather, that historic knowledge of Jesus (and, by implication, historical knowledge also) may be used 'to improve' the faith-knowledge, i.e. to serve as corrective, where necessary, and as supplement to that knowledge. Our own position approximates to this, so we will now discuss the issues as we ourselves see them.

We start from the premise that the three different kinds of knowledge we have described actually exist, and that the distinctions we

---

[1] E. Fuchs, *Studies of the Historical Jesus*, p. 63.

[2] We might also add that it is an overloading and overworking of the concept 'faith', which is being used in a variety of ways. One of our challenges to the 'new hermeneutic' must be that it should define and clarify its use of 'faith'.

have made can and must be made when we consider our knowledge of Jesus of Nazareth. This does not answer the 'question of the historical Jesus', but rather raises it in what we regard as its proper form, namely: What is the relationship between the three kinds of knowledge of Jesus of Nazareth that we may be said to possess?

Let us consider, first, our faith-knowledge of Jesus. This arises in response to the challenge of the proclamation of the Church; the recent discussion and our own experience have convinced us of this. There are, of course, many different forms of proclamation, including historical narrative, myth and legend. But the claim of faith must be that there is a distinguishing characteristic of each and all of these many possible forms of proclamation: the ability to mediate the encounter of faith with the Christ present to faith in them. In this respect we wholeheartedly accept the contention of Kähler and Bultmann.

Let us spend a moment to distinguish between kerygmatic Christ and historical Jesus as we would see the matter. As a product of an Anglo-Saxon liberal Baptist tradition we have been taught to 'believe in Jesus', and all the various forms of proclamation to which we have been subject have served to produce for us what we would call a 'faith-image' of this Jesus. Part of this faith-image is certainly made up of traits of the liberal historical Jesus, but then the writings of the liberal 'questers' were in their own way kerygmatic; the mistake is to claim them as historical. Again, part of the faith-image could be the result of the existential impact of knowledge of Jesus mediated by a modern historiography, historic knowledge, for to a believer brought up in this tradition almost anything that talks about Jesus can become kerygma, that is, it can contribute to the faith-image. This faith-image is, so far as the individual believer is concerned, the kerygmatic Christ, since it is an image mediated to him by the multiple forms of Christian proclamation, and it has to be distinguished from the historical Jesus, even though historical knowledge of Jesus may have been a constituent factor in its creation. It has to be distinguished from the historical Jesus because its ultimate origin is not historical research, but Christian proclamation, even if it may have been historical research which has unwittingly become proclamation, as in the case of much liberal life of Christ research. It also has to be distinguished from the historical Jesus because the results of historical research are not a *determining* factor in the constituence of this figure; like the Christ of the gospels, the Jesus of one's faith-image is a mixture of historical reminiscence, at a somewhat distant remove, and myth, legend and idealism. What gives this faith-image validity is the fact that it grows out of religious experience and is capable of mediating religious experience; that it develops in the context of the complex mixture of needs, etc., which originally created, and continues to create, an openness towards the kerygma; and that it can continue to develop to meet those needs.

Historical knowledge of Jesus, then, is significant to faith in that it can contribute to the formation of the faith-image. In a tradition which 'believes in Jesus', historical knowledge can be a source for the necessary content of faith. After all, in the Christian use, faith is necessarily faith *in* something, a believer believes *in* something, and in so far as that 'something' is 'Jesus', historical knowledge can help to provide the content, without thereby becoming the main source of that content. The main source will always be the proclamation of the Church, a proclamation arising out of a Christian experience of the risen Lord.

Now there arises immediately the obvious question: If there are so many different forms of proclamation, and, in effect, as many faith-images as there are believers, how do we distinguish true from false? This is a question of peculiar force in America, where the tradition is to 'believe in Jesus' and where there are a multitude of conflicting and competing kerygmata; where everything from radical right racism to revolutionary Christian humanism is proclaimed as kerygma, and as Christian. It is also a question of peculiar force to us, because we must fully admit the highly individualistic character of a believer's faith-image, and yet, at the same time, face the question of which, if any, are to be called 'Christian', and so face the necessity of distinguishing true from false. In this situation we introduce the second aspect of our own position: We believe we have the right to appeal to our limited, but real, historical knowledge of Jesus. The true kerygmatic Christ, the justifiable faith-image, is that consistent with the historical Jesus. The significance of the historical Jesus for Christian faith is that knowledge of this Jesus may be used as a means of testing the claims of the Christs presented in the competing kerygmata to be Jesus Christ. To this limited extent our historical knowledge of Jesus validates the Christian kerygma; it does not validate it as *kerygma*, but it validates it as *Christian*.

This procedure seems to us to be justified by the facts of life with regard to the synoptic tradition, and the differences between this tradition and the remainder of the New Testament. The theological truth revealed by these facts is that of the complete and absolute identification, by the early Christians, of the earthly Jesus of Nazareth and the risen Lord of Christian experience. To early Christianity the Jesus who had spoken in Galilee and Judea was the Christ who was speaking through prophets and in Christian experience. It is for this reason that we have the remarkable phenomenon of sayings of Jesus being treated as simply part of general Christian instruction in the epistles (e.g. Rom. 14.13, 14, 20). For this reason Paul can speak of words from the Lord and mean words possibly originating from Jesus but heavily reinterpreted in the Church and overlaid with liturgical instructions (I Cor. 11.23–25), because he is completely indifferent as to whether all, some *or none* had, in fact, been spoken by the earthly Jesus. For this reason the synoptic evangelists can take words originally spoken by Christian prophets (e.g. the apocalyptic Son of man sayings) and ascribe them to Jesus, and can also freely modify and reinterpret sayings in the tradition to make them express their own theological viewpoint (e.g. Mark 9.1 par.) and still ascribe them to Jesus. The tradition outside the synoptic gospels evinces little interest in the earthly Jesus, because Paul, John and the Hellenistic church generally concentrate attention on the risen Christ aspect of the equation earthly Jesus = risen Lord. But the synoptic gospels are produced in those same Hellenistic communities, and they concentrate on the earthly Jesus aspect of the equation. But the equation is always there, witness the fact that the epistles can include sayings both of the earthly Jesus and of the risen Lord in their tradition, equally without feeling the need to identify them in any special way. The absolute identification of the earthly Jesus of Nazareth with the risen Lord of Christian experience is the key, and the only key, to understanding the phenomena present in the New Testament tradition. With the rise of modern historical knowledge of Jesus, a phenomenon necessarily absent from the New Testament, this early Christian equation justifies us in using that historical knowledge to test the validity of claims made in the name of *Jesus* Christ and the authenticity of a kerygma claiming to present Jesus *Christ*: to be valid and authentic these must be consistent with such knowledge as we have of the historical Jesus.

At this point it may be helpful to refer, by way of an example, to one instance of the kind of thing we have in mind. In the preparation for our previous book, *The Kingdom of God in the Teaching of Jesus*, we had occasion to study the impact of Albert Schweitzer's *konsequente Eschatologie* upon English liberal theology. This study has come to illustrate for us the point we are trying to make, for the fact of the matter is that the historical truth that eschatology played a central role in the teaching of Jesus has played a large part in rendering un-satisfactory the kind of Christ we find presented in the work of men like William Sanday, C. W. Emmett or E. F. Scott.[1] The Jesus of the older liberal faith-image has to be transformed precisely because he was, in some fundamental respects, inconsistent with the historical Jesus revealed to us as a result of the work set in motion by *konsequente Eschatologie*.

Knowledge of the historical Jesus is, then, important in that it can contribute positively to the formation of the faith-image, i.e. it can help to provide faith with its necessary *content*, and in that it can act negatively as a check on false or inappropriate faith-images, or aspects of a faith-image. Can we go beyond this? Yes, we believe we can, and we reach, therefore, the third aspect of our own position: the fact that historical knowledge of Jesus can be directly relevant to faith, apart from aiding in the formation of the faith-image. We reach this by calling attention to the nature of the narratives in the synoptic gospels; like the sayings, they reflect the equation earthly Jesus = risen Lord. So, for example, the confession at Caesarea Philippi and the subse-quent instruction to the disciples (Mark 8.27–9.1 par.) may or may not vaguely correspond to some incident in the ministry of Jesus, but in its present form it is an ideal scene in which Jesus = risen Lord, Peter = typical Christian disciple, and the instruction to the disciples = the risen Lord's instruction to his Church in face of the possibility of persecution (so Mark), or in face of the necessity of settling down to an everyday witness over a long period of time (so Luke). In Mat-thew the whole thing has become a paradigm of the risen Lord's relationship with his Church and the consequent authority of that Church. Now this kind of narrative is possible only because of the equation earthly Jesus = risen Lord and the consequent and subse-quent equation: situation in earthly ministry of Jesus = situation in early Church's experience, which equation is necessarily implied by the methodology of the synoptic evangelists. Incidentally, we have recently had some striking historical evidence for the validity of this equation in that the intensive discussion of the eschatology of Jesus and of earliest Christianity in recent New Testament scholarship has

[1] See N. Perrin, *Kingdom*, pp. 37–57.

shown that there are remarkable parallels between these eschatologies: both challenge men to a new relationship with God in face of a decisive act of God in human experience (Jesus: Kingdom of God; early Church: Christ as eschatological event), and in both the believer stands in a situation theologically the same, for all the difference of terminology involved. But the claim of the equation earthly ministry of Jesus = situation in early Church's experience does not depend on the results of recent research in earliest Christian eschatology; it is involved in the very nature of the synoptic gospel narratives. Again here, historical knowledge of Jesus, which normally means historical knowledge of his teaching, brings a new factor into the situation. If the believer in response to the kerygma stands in a relationship with God parallel to that in which a Galilean disciple stood in response to Jesus' proclamation of the Kingdom of God, which the synoptic gospels necessarily claim, then teaching addressed to that latter situation is applicable to the former. In this way historical knowledge of the teaching of Jesus becomes directly applicable to the believer in any age. It is precisely for this reason, of course, that some actual teaching of the earthly Jesus was taken up into the synoptic tradition, and that the very concept of a Jesus tradition came into being.

In what we have said immediately above we have made no attempt to discuss historic knowledge of Jesus, as distinct from historical knowledge. The reason for this is that we regard it simply as an aspect of historical knowledge. As historic knowledge it can influence us individually, as can similar knowledge of any figure from the past. As an aspect of historical knowledge, it can function in the way that historical knowledge, in our view, can function.

To summarize our own position as to the significance of knowledge of the historical Jesus for Christian faith, we are prepared to maintain (1) that the New Testament as a whole implies that Christian faith is necessarily faith in the Christ of the Church's proclamation, in which proclamation today historical knowledge may play a part, but as proclamation, not historical knowledge. As proclamation it helps to build the faith-image, to provide the content for a faith which 'believes in Jesus'. Then (2) in face of the varieties of Christian proclamation and in view of the claim inherent in the nature of the synoptic gospel material (earthly Jesus = risen Lord), we may and we must use such historical knowledge of Jesus as we possess to test the validity of the claim of any given form of the Church's proclamation to be

Christian proclamation. Then (3) in view of the further claim inherent in the nature of the synoptic gospel material (situation in earthly ministry of Jesus = situation in early Church's experience) we may apply historical knowledge of the teaching of Jesus directly to the situation of the believer in any age, always providing, of course, that we can solve the practical problems involved in crossing the barrier of two millennia and radically different *Weltanschauungen* necessary to do this.

APPENDIX

ANNOTATED BIBLIOGRAPHIES

1. GENERAL WORKS ON THE (LIFE AND) TEACHING OF JESUS

We concern ourselves here only with general treatments of the subject; monographs on specific topics will be found in other bibliographies.

R. Bultmann. *Jesus and the Word.* ET by L. P. Smith and E. H. Lantero of *Jesus* (1926). New York: Scribner's, 1934, 1958, London: Nicholson and Watson, 1935.

When it was first published in German this book was regarded as extremely radical, and many scholars rejected it. However, in the time that has passed since then the book has moved, so to speak, from the extreme left wing to the centre of the stage, and today any treatment of the subject that is to be meaningful has to start with it. It should be read with careful attention to the author's methodology and, particularly, to the relationship between this book and his *History of the Synoptic Tradition.* On this, see our remarks in chapter I above.

T. W. Manson. *The Sayings of Jesus.* London: SCM Press, 1949. The work was originally published as Part II of *The Mission and Message of Jesus* by H. D. A. Major, T. W. Manson and C. E. Wright. London: Nicholson & Watson and New York: E. P. Dutton & Co., 1937 [American edition still in print, 1965].

This is, in effect, a commentary on the material generally ascribed to Q. By today's standards the author accepts material as authentic far too readily, and he conspicuously fails to take notice of form criticism, but this is nonetheless a great book. Manson was absolutely unequalled as an exegete of the teaching of Jesus. His profound knowledge of ancient Judaism, his deep insight into the subject matter, above all, perhaps, his gift of self-expression—all this combines to make the careful reading of this work an unforgettable experience. For all that one has to be more sceptical than was its author on the question of the authenticity of sayings.

G. Bornkamm. *Jesus of Nazareth.* ET by Irene and Fraser McLuskey with James M. Robinson of *Jesus von Nazareth* ([3]1959). London: Hodder & Stoughton and New York: Harper & Bros., 1960.

Easily the best 'Jesus book' of our time, this has to be read with the consciousness that its author was writing for the general public rather than specifically for theologians or theological students. A great deal of the technical material and discussion is, therefore, assumed rather than specifically dealt with. Also the book is a product of the 'post-Bultmannian' movement (see chapter V above), and it therefore represents a specific viewpoint on the 'question of the historical Jesus'. But none of this changes the fact that this is the best treatment of the subject to appear in the last twenty-five years.

H. Conzelmann. 'Jesus Christus', *Religion in Geschichte und Gegenwart*[3] (Tübingen: J. C. B. Mohr [Paul Siebeck]), III (1959), 619–653.
Conzelmann set out to provide a review of the current position in Life of Christ research, and he succeeded admirably. This is a masterly summary and presentation.

J. J. Pelikan. 'Jesus Christ', *Encyclopedia Britannica*, XIII (1964), 13–26.
Although broader in scope and perspective than the other works we are mentioning here (the author is a historical theologian) and therefore not giving so much detail on the teaching of Jesus, this is probably the best encyclopedia article on the subject in English. It provides a valuable introduction, especially to the long history of Life of Christ research.

A. Vögtle. 'Jesus Christus', *Lexikon für Theologie und Kirche* (Freiburg: Herder), V. (1960), 922–932.
Censored before its publication, this article nonetheless retains a great deal of the force and vigour of its author. As is always the case with the best Roman Catholic work (one thinks particularly of Vögtle and R. Schnackenburg), there is a profound knowledge of both Protestant and Roman Catholic research that few Protestant scholars could match.

N. A. Dahl. 'The Problem of the Historical Jesus', *Kerygma and History*, ed. C. E. Braaten and R. A. Harrisville (New York: Abingdon Press, 1962), pp. 138–171.
First appearing in Norwegian in 1953 and then in German in 1955, this article offers a good discussion of the problems of current Life of Christ research in general. The author is confessedly conservative in his approach, but he achieves a real balance, both of perspective and in presentation.

H. K. McArthur. 'A Survey of Recent Gospel Research', *Interpretation* 18 (1964), 39–55 (=*New Theology No. 2*, ed. M. E. Marty and D. G. Peerman [New York and London: Macmillan, 1965], pp. 201–221). Particularly interesting here is the author's discussion of the criteria of authenticity for the teaching of Jesus. He distinguishes four possible criteria: (1) multiple attestation; (2) discounting the tendencies of the developing tradition; (3) attestation by multiple forms; (4) elimination of all material which may be derived either from Judaism or from primitive Christianity.

The first and third of these we put together under the heading of the first in our discussion in chapter I above. This is justifiable since, as McArthur himself points out, the third is simply a special form of the first. The second we regard as valid, but as included in the writing of a history of the tradition which we claimed was always the essential first step in any consideration of the question of authenticity. In writing that history one becomes aware of these tendencies and necessarily discounts them in the reconstruction of an earliest form which could possibly go back to Jesus himself. The fourth is our criterion of dissimilarity.

E. Käsemann. 'The Problem of the Historical Jesus', *Essays on New Testament Themes* (1964 [see further below, Annotated Bibliography No. 9]), pp. 15–47.

James M. Robinson. *A New Quest of the Historical Jesus* (1959 [see further below, Annotated Bibliography No. 9]).

Although having their proper place in the discussion of the 'question of the historical Jesus', these works are also important contributions to the questions and problems of Life of Christ research in general.

2. THEOLOGY OF THE SYNOPTIC EVANGELISTS AND THEIR TRADITION

R. Bultmann. *History of the Synoptic Tradition.* ET by J. Marsh of *Die Geschichte der synoptischen Tradition* ([1]1921, [3]1958 [the edition translated]). Oxford: Basil Blackwell and New York: Harper & Row, 1963.

In this pioneer form-critical work the first attempt was made to write a history of the synoptic tradition and to isolate the influences at work in and on that tradition as it changed and developed. The final section of the book focuses attention on the activity of the evangelists in editing their material and composing their gospels. All this is basic to contemporary work on the theology of the synoptic evangelists and their tradition; indeed, this contemporary work is consciously built upon the foundations laid by Bultmann in this most important book. The book has become a classic. It has also, most unfortunately, been very badly translated, so much so that it is advisable never to quote the ET as giving Bultmann's opinion on a matter without first checking the German to see that Bult- did, in fact, say whatever it is the ET says he said.

The influence of form criticism was mediated to the English language academic world by R. H. Lightfoot, and it is in his works that we have the first attempts in English to move in the direction to which Bultmann had pointed. On this, see the memoir by D. E. Nineham in *Studies in the Gospels. Essays in Memory of R. H. Lightfoot*, ed. D. E. Nineham (Oxford: Basil Blackwell, 1955), pp. vi–xvi.

R. H. Lightfoot. *History and Interpretation in the Gospels.* (The Bampton Lectures, 1934) London: Hodder & Stoughton and New York: Harper & Bros., 1935. *Locality and Doctrine in the Gospels.* London: Hodder & Stoughton, and New York: Harper & Bros., 1938. *The Gospel Message of St Mark.* Oxford: Clarendon Press, 1950 (and Oxford Paperbacks, 41, 1962).

After the second world war German New Testament scholars took up this type of work with spectacular results.[1]

W. Marxsen. *Der Evangelist Markus.* (FRLANT 67.) Göttingen: Vandenhoeck & Ruprecht, [1]1956, [2]1959. Contains important methodological reflections (pp. 7–16) and proposes the term *Redaktionsgeschichte* to describe this approach to the work of the evangelists.

H. Conzelmann. *The Theology of St Luke.* ET by G. Buswell of *Die Mitte der Zeit* ([1]1954, [2]1957, [3]1960). London: Faber & Faber, and New York: Harper & Bros., 1960. The ET is of the second German edition. The third German edition is the final revision Conzelmann intends to make and so is the definitive edition of this work, the classic in its field.

G. Bornkamm. 'Enderwartung und Kirche im Matthäusevangelium', *Studies in Honour of C. H. Dodd*, ed. W. D. Davies and D. Daube (Cambridge: University Press, 1954), pp. 222–60.

E. Haenchen. 'Die Komposition von Mk. 8.27–9.1 und Par.', *Novum Testamentum* 6 (1963), 81–109.

G. Bornkamm has had a number of pupils in Heidelberg who have worked along these lines.

G. Bornkamm, G. Barth, H. J. Held. *Tradition and Interpretation in Matthew.* ET by P. Scott of *Überlieferung und Auslegung im Matthäusevangelium* (1960). London: SCM Press, and Philadelphia: Westminster Press, 1963. Contains a revised version of Bornkamm's essay noted immediately above, and two dissertations by pupils of his.

H. E. Tödt. *The Son of Man in the Synoptic Tradition.* ET by D. M. Barton of *Der Menschensohn in der synoptischen Überlieferung* ([2]1963). London: SCM Press, and Philadelphia: Westminster Press, 1965. Not only is this book the major contribution to its particular subject in recent time [see Annotated Bibliography No. 7, below], but it is also a very considerable contribution to the study of the theology of the synoptic tradition, especially that of Q.

Ferdinand Hahn. *Christologische Hoheitstitel. Ihre Geschichte im frühen Christentum.* (FRLANT 83.) Göttingen: Vandenhoeck & Ruprecht, [1]1963,

---

[1] On this movement see further our review article, 'The Wredestrasse becomes the Hauptstrasse', *JR* 46 (1966), 296–300.

[2]1964. Applies the methodology to christological traditions, with most notable results.

English-speaking scholars have responded to the impetus of this recent German work, e.g.,

James M. Robinson. *The Problem of History in Mark.* (Studies in Biblical Theology 21.) London: SCM Press, 1957.

E. Best. *The Temptation and the Passion: the Markan Soteriology.* (Society for New Testament Studies Monograph Series, 2.) Cambridge: University Press, 1965.

J. Marsh. 'The Theology of the New Testament', *Peake's Commentary on the Bible* (revised edition; ed. by M. Black and H. H. Rowley [London and New York: Thos. Nelson & Sons, 1962], pp. 756–768.

William C. Robinson, Jr. *Der Weg des Herrn. Studien zur Geschichte und Eschatologie im Lukasevangelium.* (Theologische Forschung 36.) Hamburg: Herbert Reich, 1964 [no English publication is planned]. 'The Theological Context for Interpreting Luke's Travel Narrative (9.51ff.)', *JBL* 79 (1960), 20–31.

H. H. Oliver. 'The Lucan Birth Stories', *NTS* 10 (1963–4), 202–26.

3. Thomas and the Synoptic Gospels

We give here a brief selection from the literature available on this subject. The scholars mentioned have been chosen because of the representative nature of their positions.

(a) Regarding Thomas as dependent on the canonical tradition

Robert M. Grant. *The Secret Sayings of Jesus: The Gnostic Gospel of Thomas.* With D. N. Freedman, and with an ET of the Gospel of Thomas by W. R. Schoedel. (Dolphin Books) New York: Doubleday and (Fontana Books) London: Collins, 1960. 'Notes on the Gospel of Thomas', *VC* 13 (1959), 170–90. 'Two Gnostic Gospels', *JBL* 79 (1960), 1–11.

E. Haenchen. *Die Botschaft des Thomasevangeliums.* (Theologische Bibliothek Töpelmann 6.) Berlin: Töpelmann, 1961. 'Literatur zum Thomasevangelium', *TR* 27 (1961), 147–78, 306–38.

H. K. McArthur. 'The Gospel According to Thomas', *New Testament Sidelights* (Essays in Honour of A. C. Purdy), ed. H. K. McArthur (Hartford: Hartford Seminary Foundation Press, 1960), pp. 43–77. 'The Dependence of the Gospel of Thomas on the Synoptics', *ExpT* 71 (1960), 286–7.

(b) Regarding Thomas as essentially independent of the canonical tradition

O. Cullmann. 'The Gospel of Thomas', *Theologischer Digest* 9 (1961), 175–81. 'The Gospel According to St Thomas and its significance for Research into the Canonical Gospels', *HJ* 60 (1962), 116–24. 'The Gospel of Thomas and the Problem of the Age of the Tradition Contained Therein', *Interpretation* 16 (1962), 418–38.

C.-H. Hunzinger. 'Unbekannte Gleichnisse Jesu aus dem Thomas-Evangelium', *Judentum, Urchristentum, Kirche* (Festschrift für Joachim Jeremias), ed. W. Eltester (Beihefte zur *ZNW* 26 [Berlin: Töpelmann, 1960]), pp. 209–20. 'Aussersynoptisches Traditionsgut im Thomas-Evangelium', *TLZ* 85 (1960), 843–6. [The article, 'Pre-Synoptic Material in the Coptic Gospel of Thomas', which he cites here as to appear in *JBL* 79 (1960), seems not to have appeared.]

H. Montefiore. 'A Comparison of the Parables of the Gospel According to Thomas and of the Synoptic Gospels', *NTS* 7 (1960–1), 220–48 (= H. E. W. Turner and H. Montefiore, *Thomas and the Evangelists* [Studies in Biblical Theology 35 (London: SCM Press, 1962)], pp. 40–78). [Montefiore's opinion is based on his work on the parables. The parables in Thomas are the strongest indication of independence and scholars who have worked on them do tend to favour this opinion, most notably J. Jeremias, *Parables of Jesus* (revised edition, 1963), p. 24.]

G. Quispel. 'The Gospel of Thomas and the New Testament', *VC* 11 (1957), 189–207. 'Some Remarks on the Gospel of Thomas', *NTS* 5 (1958–9), 87–117.

R. McL. Wilson. *Studies in the Gospel of Thomas.* London: A. R. Mowbray, 1960. 'The Coptic "Gospel of Thomas" ', *NTS* 5 (1958–9), 273–6. 'The Gospel of Thomas', *ExpT* 70 (1958–9), 324–5. 'Thomas and the Synoptic Gospels', *ibid.* 72 (1960–1), 36–39. ' "Thomas" and the Growth of the Gospels', *HTR* 53 (1960), 231–50. 'The Gospel of Thomas', *Studia Evangelica* III, ed. F. L. Cross (Texte und Untersuchungen 88 [Berlin: Akademie Verlag, 1964]), 447–59.

(c) Regarding Thomas as in part dependent on, and in part independent of, the canonical tradition

B. Gärtner. *The Theology of the Gospel According to Thomas.* ET by Eric J. Sharpe. New York: Harper and Row, and London: Collins, 1961.

Wolfgang Schrage. *Das Verhältnis des Thomas-Evangeliums zur synoptischen Tradition und zu den Koptischen Evangelienübersetzungen.* (Beihefte zur *ZNW* 29.) Berlin: Töpelmann, 1964.

H. E. W. Turner. 'The Gospel of Thomas: its History, Transmission and Sources', and 'The Theology of the Gospel of Thomas', H. E. W. Turner and H. Montefiore, *Thomas and the Evangelists* (Studies in Biblical Theology 35 [London: SCM Press, 1962]), pp. 11–39, 79–118.

4. RECENT WORK ON THE KINGDOM OF GOD

G. Lundström. *The Kingdom of God in the Teaching of Jesus.* ET by J. Bulman of *Guds Riki i Jesu Förkunnelse* (1947) brought up to date by a brief postscript. Edinburgh: Oliver & Boyd, and Richmond: John Knox Press, 1963 [representing the perspective of Scandinavian scholarship].

R. Schnackenburg. *God's Rule and Kingdom.* ET by J. Murray of *Gottes Herrschaft und Reich* (1959). New York: Herder & Herder, 1963 [Roman Catholic].

H. Ridderbos. *The Coming of the Kingdom.* ET by H. de Jongste of *De komst van het koninkrijk.* Philadelphia: Presbyterian and Reformed Publishing Co., 1962.

G. E. Ladd. *Jesus and the Kingdom.* New York. Harper & Row, 1964. [Both this and the previous work represent extremely conservative Protestant scholarship.]

O. E. Evans. 'Kingdom of God, of Heaven', *Interpreter's Dictionary of the Bible* (New York: Abingdon Press, 1962) III, 17–26.

H. K. Luce. 'Kingdom of God (or Heaven)', *Hastings Dictionary of the Bible* (revised edition; New York: Scribner's, and Edinburgh: T. & T. Clark, 1963), pp. 552–4.

Very interesting are two works from the standpoint of the 'new quest' and the 'new hermeneutic' respectively [on the terms see chapter V, above].

James M. Robinson. 'The Formal Structure of Jesus' Message', *Current Issues in New Testament Interpretation*, ed. W. Klassen and G. F. Snyder (New York: Harper & Bros., and London: SCM Press, 1962), pp. 91–110.

E. Jüngel. *Paulus und Jesus* (Hermeneutische Untersuchungen zur Theologie 2 [Tübingen: J. C. B. Mohr (Paul Siebeck), ²1964]), pp. 72–214.

5. LITERATURE ON LUKE 17.20f.

B. Noack. *Das Gottesreich bei Lukas: eine Studie zu Luk. 17.20–24.* (Symbolae Biblicae Upsalienses 10.) Uppsala, 1948. Gives a history of the interpretation of the text.

R. J. Sneed. *The Kingdom's Coming: Luke 17.20–21.* (Studies in Sacred Theology 133.) Washington, D.C., 1962. [A dissertation accepted by the Catholic University of America and now available from University Microfilms, Inc., Ann Arbor, Michigan.]

This is the most thorough recent study. It gives a history of the interpretation of the text which is both later and more extensive than Noack's
and hence supersedes it. On the basis of a thorough investigation of the
linguistic problem, Sneed decides that '. . . the phrase *entos hymōn* in
Luke 17.21b may mean "within you" or "within your power" or "in your
midst".' He then goes on to a form-critical analysis of the text, differentiat-
ing between three *Sitze im Leben*: the *Sitz im Leben Jesu* ('setting in life' in
the ministry of Jesus), the *Sitze im Leben Ecclesiae* ('settings in life' in the
Church [in our own work above we always referred to this in the singular
and as the *Sitz im Leben der alten Kirche*—we regarded the singular as inclu-
sive and we preferred to keep the whole phrase in German rather than to
mix German and Latin]), the *Sitz im Evangelium* ('setting' in the gospel
[i.e. in the purpose of the evangelist]). These distinctions are important
and should certainly be observed, even if not necessarily described by these
phrases. So far as the *Sitz im Leben Jesu* is concerned, Sneed eventually
decides for the essential historicity of the incident as recorded by Luke and
for the traditional interpretation, i.e. 'that the Reign of God was to be
something interior'. But his main concern is with the second and third of
the *Sitze*, and here his work is both more original and more interesting.
Sneed published a summary of his work, 'The Kingdom of God is within
you', *CBQ* 24 (1962), 363–82.

A. Strobel. 'Die Passa-Erwartung als urchristliches Problem in Luc.
17.20f', *ZNW* 49 (1958), 157–83; 'In dieser Nacht (Lk. 17.34)', *ZTK* 58
(1961); 'Zu Lk 17.20f.," *BZ* 7 (1963), 111–13.

F. Mussner. 'Wann kommt das Reich Gottes?' *BZ* 6 (1962), 107–11.

All discussions of the teaching of Jesus, of the Kingdom of God or of
New Testament eschatology include an interpretation of this saying.
Particularly significant are:

W. G. Kümmel. *Promise and Fulfilment*. ET by D. M. Barton of *Verheissung und Erfüllung* ([3]1956). (Studies in Biblical Theology, 23.) London:
SCM Press, 1957 [with extensive bibliographical notes].

H. Conzelmann. 'Gegenwart und Zukunft in der synoptischen Tradition', *ZTK* 54 (1957), 277–96; *Theology of St Luke*. ET by G. Buswell of
Die Mitte der Zeit ([2]1957). London: Faber & Faber, and New York:
Harper & Bros., 1960 [from the perspective of its setting in the Lukan
theology].

E. Jüngel. *Paulus und Jesus* (Hermeneutische Untersuchungen zur
Theologie 2 [Tübingen: J. C. B. Mohr (Paul Siebeck), [2]1964]), pp.
193–6.

6. MODERN RESEARCH ON THE PARABLES

A. Jülicher. *Die Gleichnisreden Jesu.* 2 vols. Tübingen: J. C. B. Mohr (Paul Siebeck), I ([1]1888, [2]1899), II (1899).

Jülicher establishes the distinction between *parable* (simile, fable, exemplary story) and *allegory*. Parable is 'authentic' speech, i.e. it means what it says, using pictures to express its meaning. Allegory, on the other hand, is 'inauthentic' speech, i.e. it does not mean what it says, but hides its meaning in symbol. The parables of Jesus were parables and not allegories, and they were designed to be readily understood and to express one single truth, a truth of the widest possible general application.

Subsequent research has validated all of Jülicher's conclusions except the last one, the nature of the one truth expressed in a parable. In particular the distinction between parable and allegory, and the claim that the parables of Jesus were parables and not allegories, has been shown to be justified. It can be supported by the following arguments: (1) the parables of ancient Judaism, to which Jesus is indebted for his method and form, are parables and not allegories. (2) The allegorizing touches in the parables, and the allegorizing explanations added to some of them in the gospels, have been shown to be later additions to the stories and to the tradition respectively (especially by Jeremias). (3) The parable and the allegory represent fundamentally different approaches to the nature of the reality to be revealed (pictorial and direct against symbolic and hidden), as also to the concept of teaching involved (direct to all who can be challenged against esoteric to a limited group who possess the key). The tradition that Jesus taught in one way to the crowd and in another way to the disciples is a literary device of the evangelists. The two methods are, in fact, quite incompatible with one another.

A. T. Cadoux. *The Parables of Jesus, Their Art and Use.* London: James Clarke & Co., 1931. Cadoux took the next step (to that of Jülicher) by arguing that the parables must be placed in their setting in the ministry of Jesus. Unfortunately, he did not develop the insight adequately in his own work.

B. T. D. Smith. *The Parables of the Synoptic Gospels.* Cambridge: University Press, 1937. Smith follows Cadoux's suggestion cautiously, limiting himself to the details of the stories, which he illuminates very well, rather than concerning himself with their message. To a limited extent he also dealt with the history of the transmission of the parables in the tradition.

C. H. Dodd. *The Parables of the Kingdom.* London: Nisbet, and New York: Scribner's, [1]1935, [2]1936, [3]1961. This is the decisive 'breakthrough' in the modern research. Dodd established the fact that the 'setting in life' of the parables is the eschatological proclamation of Jesus, and he achieved a presentation of the message of the parables. The limitation of the work is the unduly one-sided understanding of the eschatology of Jesus as 'realized eschatology'.

J. Jeremias. *The Parables of Jesus.* German editions: [1]1947, [6]1962. English editions (translation by S. H. Hooke): [1]1954 (from German [3]1954), [2]1963 (from German [6]1963). London: SCM Press, and New York: Scribner's. The epoch-making work in this field, and, at one and the same time, both the major contribution and greatest impetus to contemporary research into the teaching of Jesus.

E. Linnemann. *Parables of Jesus: Introduction and Exposition.* ET by John Sturdy of *Gleichnisse Jesu. Einführung und Auslegung* (1961). London: SPCK, and New York: Harper and Row, 1966. Bringing to the results of the work of Jeremias insights derived from her own teacher, E. Fuchs, Miss Linnemann both interprets the parables historically and also applies the results of this interpretation to proclamation and instruction today. A most important and useful book.

E. Jüngel. *Paulus und Jesus.* (Hermeneutische Untersuchungen zur Theologie 2.) Tübingen: J. C. B. Mohr (Paul Siebeck), [2]1964. Has an extensive and critical review of modern work on the parables (pp. 87–135) designed to lead up to an approach to them in terms of the 'new hermeneutic' of Jüngel's teacher, E. Fuchs. The key to this is: 'The kingdom comes to word in parable as parable. The parables of Jesus bring the Kingdom to word as parable' (p. 135). On this see our comments in chapter V above.

G. V. Jones. *The Art and Truth of the Parables. A Study in Their Literary Form and Modern Interpretation.* London: SPCK, 1964. Contains a useful review of the history of the modern interpretation of the parables (pp. 3–54).

Amos N. Wilder. *The Language of the Gospel.* New York: Harper & Row, and (as *Early Christian Rhetoric*) London: SCM Press, 1964. Wilder is unique among contemporary New Testament scholars because of his profound combination of the techniques of New Testament scholarship with those of general literary criticism. Chapter V of this book (pp. 79–86) is a study of the parables of Jesus from this perspective.

Ian T. Ramsey. *Christian Discourse. Some Logical Explorations* (London and New York: Oxford University Press, 1965), pp. 6–13. This is an important discussion of the essential difference between parable and allegory. The purpose of parable is to lead to a 'disclosure point', that of allegory to correlate 'two areas of discourse'.

7. JESUS AND THE COMING SON OF MAN

(a) Reviews of the discussion

A. J. B. Higgins. 'Son of Man-*Forschung* since *The Teaching of Jesus*', *New Testament Essays. Studies in Memory of T. W. Manson, 1893–1958*, ed. A. J. B. Higgins (Manchester: University Press, 1959), pp. 119–35.

M. Black. 'The Son of Man Problem in Recent Research', *BJRL* 45 (1962–3), 305—18.

N. Perrin. *The Kingdom of God in the Teaching of Jesus* (London: SCM Press, and Philadelphia: Westminster Press, 1963), pp. 90–111.

(b) The apocalyptic Son of man sayings in recent German discussion

H. E. Tödt. *The Son of Man in the Synoptic Tradition.* ET by D. M. Barton of *Der Menschensohn in der synoptischen Überlieferung* (²1963). London: SCM Press and Philadelphia: Westminster Press, 1965.

This is the most important book on the whole subject of Son of man in the teaching of Jesus to be published in recent times. Its importance is that it establishes the methodology of enquiring into the history of the use of Son of man in the tradition, and by so doing immediately renders out of date any work not using this methodology.

Tödt regards certain of the 'judgement sayings' as authentic: Matt. 24.27 par.; Luke 17.30; Luke 11.30; Matt. 24.44 par.; Luke 12.8f. par. In this he is supported, with minor variations, by Hahn and Jüngel: F. Hahn, *Christologische Hoheitstitel.* (FRLANT 83.) Göttingen: Vandenhoeck & Ruprecht, ¹1962, ²1964. E. Jüngel, *Paulus und Jesus.* Tübingen: J. C. B. Mohr (Paul Siebeck), ¹1962, ²1964.

Opposed to this view, and in successive publications entering into vigorous debate with Tödt, Hahn and Jüngel (who themselves replied in the successive editions of their books) is Philipp Vielhauer, who argues that no Son of man sayings are authentic.

Ph. Vielhauer. 'Gottesreich und Menschensohn', *Festschrift für Günther Dehn*, ed. W. Schneemelcher (Neukirchen: Verlag der Buchhandlung des Erziehungsvereins Neukirchen, 1957), pp. 51–79. 'Jesus und der Menschensohn', *ZTK* 60 (1963), 133–77. 'Ein Weg der neutestamentlichen Theologie? Prüfung der Thesen Ferdinand Hahns', *EvT* 25 (1965), 24–72.

In general support of Vielhauer's position are: E. Käsemann, 'Sätze heiligen Rechtes im Neuen Testament', *NTS* 1 (1954–5), 248–60; 'Die Anfänge christlicher Theologie', *ZTK* 57 (1960), 162–85; 'Zum Thema urchristlichen Apokalyptik', *ZTK* 59 (1962), 257–84; and H. Conzelmann, 'Jesus Christus', *RGG*³ III (1959), 619–55, especially 630f.

The authenticity of the apocalyptic Son of man sayings is also denied by Eduard Schweizer, who, however, finds an authentic element in the sayings with a present reference.

E. Schweizer. 'Der Menschensohn', *ZNW* 50 (1959), 185–209; 'Son of Man', *JBL* 79 (1960), 119–29; 'The Son of Man Again', *NTS* 9 (1963), 256–61. The first and last of these are also to be found in his collected essays, *Neotestamentica* (Zürich: Zwingli Verlag, 1963), pp. 56–84 and 85–92.

(c) Other recent work on the subject

C. Colpe. *Huios tou anthrōpou*, to be published in *Theologisches Wörterbuch zum Neuen Testament* (founded G. Kittel, ed. G. Friedrich).

We are grateful to Professor Colpe for the privilege of working through his manuscript at Göttingen in the summer semester of 1965, and we have referred to it as C. Colpe, *TWNT* article, in our own work above. It is a fine article, destined to become a classic when published. In view of the importance we attached to our discussion of the Son of man concept in ancient Jewish apocalyptic, above, we would like to point out that Colpe accepts the German contention that such a concept is to be found, but finds that the existing sources (Daniel, I Enoch, IV Ezra 13) are inadequate to present it to us. So he posits the existence of a fourth Jewish source, now lost to us except in so far as it is preserved in the most primitive strata of the New Testament traditions. We remained unconvinced by this argument!

A. J. B. Higgins. *Jesus and the Son of Man.* London: Lutterworth Press, and Philadelphia: Fortress Press, 1965.

Comes very near to the position of Tödt, so far as the authenticity of sayings is concerned, but argues that Jesus thought of himself as Son of God and used the Son of man idea to denote himself 'reinstalled in his heavenly seat . . . exercising his intercessory or judicial functions'. A feature of the book is a discussion of the Son of man Christology of the gospel of John and of the early Church in general.

H. Teeple. 'The Origin of the Son of Man Christology', *JBL* 84 (1965), 213–50.

Teeple accepts the concept of the Son of man as a heavenly, supernatural Messiah in ancient Judaism and argues that the Son of man Christology did not begin with any sayings of Jesus, or even in the original Jerusalem church of Jesus' disciples, but in Hellenistic-Jewish Christianity.

8. 'IMMINENT EXPECTATION' IN THE TEACHING OF JESUS

(a) View that Jesus did expect the End in the very near future, and was mistaken

T. W. Manson. *The Teaching of Jesus* (Cambridge: University Press,

1935 [many subsequent unrevised reprints]), pp. 244–84. A classical statement of this theme, easily its best expression in English.

W. G. Kümmel. *Promise and Fulfilment.* ET by D. M. Barton of *Verheissung und Erfüllung* (³1956). (Studies in Biblical Theology 23 [London: SCM Press, 1957]), especially pp. 54–87. 'Die Naherwartung in der Verkündigung Jesu', *Zeit und Geschichte. Dankesgabe an Rudolf Bultmann zum 80. Geburtstag,* ed. E. Dinkler (Tübingen: J. C. B. Mohr [Paul Siebeck], 1964), pp. 31–46 (= W. G. Kümmel, *Heilsgeschehen und Geschichte* [Marburg: N. H. Elwert, 1965], pp. 457–70). Kümmel offers very complete reviews of the contemporary discussion and, therefore, the best introductions to the literature on the subject.

(b) *Attempts to maintain that Jesus did expect an imminent End, but that this expectation can be interpreted to show that he was not mistaken*

For a review of the Fathers in this connection see T. W. Manson, *loc. cit.*
C. E. B. Cranfield. *The Gospel According to St Mark* (Cambridge Greek Testament [Cambridge: University Press, 1959]), p. 408.
R. Schnackenburg. *God's Rule and Kingdom* (ET by J. Murray of *Gottes Herrschaft und Reich* [1959]. New York: Herder & Herder, 1963), pp. 195–214.

(c) *The view that Jesus set no time limit on the coming of the End*

A. Vögtle. 'Exegetische Erwägungen über das Wissen und Selbstbewusstsein Jesu', *Gott in Welt. Festgabe für Karl Rahner,* ed. J. B. Metz *et al.* (Freiburg: Herder, 1964) I, 608–67.
A brilliant essay by one who must have high claim to being considered the leading Roman Catholic New Testament scholar of the day. Vögtle's knowledge of the relevant literature, Catholic and Protestant, is phenomenal. His argument on the point that concerns us is that Mark 13.32 must be held to be the all-important text; Mark 9.1 has been formed in the tradition from Mark 13.30, which itself originally referred to the Fall of Jerusalem and Destruction of the Temple; and Matt. 10.23 has been formed in the tradition from Matt. 10.14 par. and the promise of the coming of the Son of man.

(d) *The view that there is no parousia element, imminent or distant, in the teaching of Jesus*

T. F. Glasson. *The Second Advent.* London: Epworth Press, ³1963.
J. A. T. Robinson. *Jesus and His Coming.* London: SCM Press, 1957.

(e) *The view that the expectation of Jesus should be interpreted in more or less existentialistic terms*

The proponents of this view were presented and discussed in N. Perrin, *The Kingdom of God in the Teaching of Jesus* (1963), pp. 112–17 (R. Bultmann); 121–4 (G. Bornkamm, E. Käsemann, H. Conzelmann, E. Fuchs, James M. Robinson). Another contribution along these lines published more recently is E. Jüngel, *Paulus und Jesus* (Hermeneutische Untersuchungen zur Theologie 2 [Tübingen: J. C. B. Mohr (Paul Siebeck), ²1964]), where the existentialism is modified by the use of the 'word-event' concept of the 'new hermeneutic', and the present (Kingdom of God) and future (Son of man) elements in the teaching of Jesus are interpreted in terms of the nearness and distance of God to history.

The present writer's own views were presented in N. Perrin, *op. cit.*, pp. 185–201, largely on the basis of an exegesis of the Lord's Prayer.

9. THE QUESTION OF THE HISTORICAL JESUS

(a) Reimarus and Strauss

H. S. Reimarus. *Fragmente des Wolfenbüttelschen Ungenannten.* Herausgegeben von G. E. Lessing. Berlin, ⁴1835. The first edition of the most important fragment, 'Von dem Zwecke Jesu und seine Jünger', was published in 1778.

D. F. Strauss. *Das Leben Jesu, kritisch bearbeitet.* 2 vols. Tübingen: C. F. Osiander, 1835, 1836. ET, *The Life of Jesus, critically examined.* 3 vols. London: Chapman Bros., 1846.

(b) Roman Catholic reply to Strauss

J. Kuhn. *Das Leben Jesu, wissenschaftlich bearbeitet.* Mainz: Florian Kupferberg, 1838. [This is Vol. I, but no second volume was published.]

(c) More recent Roman Catholic discussions

J. R. Geiselmann. *Jesus der Christus. Erster Teil: Die Frage nach dem historischen Jesus.* München: Kösel Verlag, 1965.

Franz Mussner. 'Der "historische" Jesus', *Der historische Jesus und der Christus unseres Glaubens,* ed. K. Schubert (Wien: Herder, 1962), pp. 103–28; 'Leben-Jesu-Forschung', *Lexikon für Theologie und Kirche,* ed. J. Höfner and K. Rahner (Freiburg: Herder) VI (1961), 859–64.

A. Vögtle. 'Jesus Christus', *Lexikon für Theologie und Kirche* V (1960), 922–32.

R. E. Brown. 'After Bultmann, What?—An Introduction to the Post-Bultmannians', *CBQ* 26 (1964), 1–30.

P. J. Cahill. 'Rudolf Bultmann and Post-Bultmann Tendencies', *ibid.*, 153–78.

(d) Martin Kähler

M. Kähler. *The So-called Historical Jesus and the Historic Biblical Christ.* Translated, edited and with an Introduction by Carl E. Braaten, from the German *Der sogennante historische Jesus und der geschichtliche, biblische Christus* (1896). Philadelphia: Fortress Press, 1964. Also, Carl E. Braaten, 'Martin Kähler on the Historic, Biblical Christ', *The Historical Jesus and the Kerygmatic Christ*, ed. C. E. Braaten and R. A. Harrisville (New York: Abingdon Press, 1964), pp. 79–105.

(e) Rudolf Bultmann

R. Bultmann. *Jesus and the Word.* New York: Scribner's, 1958. *Theology of the New Testament* I (New York: Scribner's, and London: SCM Press, 1951). *Primitive Christianity in Its Contemporary Setting.* London: Thames and Hudson, and (as *Primitive Christianity*) New York: Meridian Books, 1956. 'New Testament and Mythology', 'A Reply to the Theses of J. Schniewind', *Kerygma and Myth*, ed. H. W. Bartsch (rev. ed., New York: Harper Torchbooks, 1961), pp. 1–16, 102–23. 'The Primitive Christian Kerygma and the Historical Jesus', *The Historical Jesus and the Kerygmatic Christ*, ed. C. E. Braaten and R. A. Harrisville, pp. 15–42 [Bultmann's reply to the 'post-Bultmannians' and the definitive statement of his own position].

(f) Critics of Bultmann from the 'right'

J. Jeremias. *The Problem of the Historical Jesus.* ET by N. Perrin of *Das Problem des historischen Jesus* (1960). Philadelphia: Fortress Press, 1964. An earlier version appeared in *The Expository Times*, 69 (1958), 333–9, under the title, 'The Present Position in the Controversy concerning the Problem of the Historical Jesus'.

Karl Barth. 'Rudolf Bultmann—An Attempt to Understand Him', *Kerygma and Myth*, ed. H. W. Bartch, II (London: SPCK, 1962), 83–132.

E. Ellwein. 'Rudolf Bultmann's Interpretation of the Kerygma', *Kerygma and History*, ed. C. E. Braaten and R. A. Harrisville (New York: Abingdon Press, 1962), pp. 25–54; E. Kinder, 'Historical Criticism and Demythologizing, *ibid.*, pp. 55–85; W. Künneth, 'Bultmann's Philosophy and the Reality of Salvation', *ibid.*, pp. 86–119 [all representing orthodox Lutheranism].

P. Althaus. *Faith and Fact in the Kerygma of Today.* ET by D. Cairns of *Das sogenannte Kerygma und der historische Jesus* (1958). Philadelphia: Muhlenberg Press and (as *The So-called Kerygma and the Historical Jesus*), and Edinburgh: Oliver & Boyd, 1959.

H. Diem. 'The Earthly Jesus and the Christ of Faith', *Kerygma and History*, ed. C. E. Braaten and R. A. Harrisville, pp. 197–211.

(g) Critics of Bultmann from the 'left'

K. Jaspers and R. Bultmann. *Myth and Christianity.* ET by N. Gutermann of *Die Frage der Entmythologisierung.* New York: Noonday Press, 1958. R. Bultmann, 'Das Befremdliche des christlichen Glaubens', *ZTK* 55 (1958), 185–200 [Bultmann's final reply to Jaspers].
S. M. Ogden. *Christ without Myth.* New York: Harper & Bros., and London: Collins, 1961. (Cited from the American edition.) Bultmann reviewed Ogden's book in *JR* 42 (1962), 225–7. Ogden went on to comment on the 'new quest': 'Bultmann and the "New Quest" ', *JBR* 30 (1962), 209–18; and (with Van A. Harvey) 'How New is the "New Quest of the Historical Jesus?"?', *The Historical Jesus and the Kerygmatic Christ*, ed. C. E. Braaten and R. A. Harrisville, pp. 197–242 [an important essay]. Van A. Harvey further developed a criticism of the 'new quest' and a position to the left of Bultmann, 'The Historical Jesus, the Kerygma, and Christian Faith', *Religion in Life*, 33 (1964), 430–50.

(h) The post-Bultmannian debate

E. Käsemann. 'The Problem of the Historical Jesus' (ET by W. J. Montague of 'Das Problem des historischen Jesus', *ZTK* 51 [1954], 125–53 [= E. Käsemann, *Exegetische Versuche und Besinnungen* I (1960), 187–214]), *Essays on New Testament Themes.* (Studies in Biblical Theology 41 [London: SCM Press, 1964]), pp. 15–47.
G. Bornkamm. *Jesus of Nazareth.* ET by Irene and Fraser McLuskey with James M. Robinson of *Jesus von Nazareth* (³1959). New York: Harper & Bros., and London: Hodder & Stoughton, 1960. 'Glaube und Geschichte in den Evangelien', *Der historische Jesus und der kerygmatische Christus*, ed. H. Ristow and K. Matthiae (Berlin: Evangelische Verlagsanstalt, 1961), pp. 281–8. 'Die Bedeutung des historischen Jesus für den Glauben', *Die Frage nach dem historischen Jesus*, ed. P. Rieger (Göttingen: Vandenhoeck & Ruprecht, 1962), pp. 57–71. 'The Problem of the Historical Jesus and the Kerygmatic Christ', *Studia Evangelica* III (Texte und Untersuchungen 88 [Berlin: Akademie Verlag, 1964]), 33–44.
H. Braun. 'Der Sinn der neutestamentlichen Christologie', *ZTK* 54 (1957), 341–77 = H. Braun, *Gesammelte Studien zum Neuen Testament und seiner Umwelt* (Tübingen: J. C. B. Mohr [Paul Siebeck], 1962), pp. 243–82. 'The Significance of Qumran for the Problem of the Historical Jesus', *The Historical Jesus and the Kerygmatic Christ*, ed. C. E. Braaten and R. A. Harrisville, pp. 69–78.

H. Conzelmann. 'Jesus Christus', RGG³ III (1959), 619–53, especially 648–51. 'The Method of the Life-of-Jesus Research', *The Historical Jesus and the Kerygmatic Christ*, ed. C. E. Braaten and R. A. Harrisville, 54–68. 'Jesus von Nazareth und der Glaube an den Auferstandenen', *Der historische Jesus und der kerygmatische Christus*, ed. H. Ristow and K. Matthiae (Berlin: Evangelische Verlag, 1961), pp. 188–99. At this point Conzelmann moved to the University of Göttingen and there, in his inaugural lecture, announced that he found himself in complete agreement with the position of Bultmann as stated in the essay 'The Primitive Christian Kerygma and the Historical Jesus' and would therefore take no further part in the discussion.

James M. Robinson. *A New Quest of the Historical Jesus.* (Studies in Biblical Theology 25.) London: SCM Press, 1959. 'The Formal Structure of Jesus' Message', *Current Issues in New Testament Interpretation*, ed. W. Klassen and G. F. Snyder (New York: Harper & Bros., and London: SCM Press, 1962), pp. 91–110. [A revised version of the book, incorporating the material in the essay, was published in German as *Kerygma und historischer Jesus* (Zürich: Zwingli Verlag, 1960). A further revision of the German edition is in preparation.] 'The Recent Debate on the "New Quest"', *JBR* 30 (1962), 198–208.

Although the work of Robinson is closely related to that of the Germans, there is a difference between them. They are discussing the *question* of the historical Jesus; he is engaged in the *new quest* of the historical Jesus. This is, however, only true of his book and of the position he there advocates. In his essay, 'The Recent Debate . . .', he abandons the really distinctive element in his own position and takes up one much nearer to theirs.

(j) The 'New Hermeneutic'

G. Ebeling. *The Nature of Faith.* ET by R. G. Smith of *Das Wesen des christlichen Glaubens* (1959). London: Collins, and Philadelphia: Fortress Press, 1961. *Word and Faith.* ET by J. W. Leitch of *Wort und Glaube*, 1960. London: SCM Press, and Philadelphia: Fortress Press, 1963. *Theologie und Verkündigung.* (Hermeneutische Untersuchungen zur Theologie 1.) Tübingen: J. C. B. Mohr (Paul Siebeck), ²1962. 'Hermeneutik', *RGG³* III (1959), 242–62.

James M. Robinson. 'Neo-Liberalism', *Interpretation* 15 (1961), 484–91. [A review of Ebeling's *Das Wesen des christlichen Glaubens*.])

E. Fuchs. *Studies of the Historical Jesus.* ET by A. Scobie of *Zur Frage nach dem historischen Jesus* (Gesammelte Aufsätze II [1960]). (Studies in Biblical Theology 42.) London: SCM Press, 1964.

The New Hermeneutic, ed. James M. Robinson and John B. Cobb. (New Frontiers in Theology 2.) New York: Harper & Row, 1964. [Particular attention should be paid to the introductory essay by Robinson, 'Hermeneutic since Barth', a brilliant report of the discussion.]

E. Jüngel. *Paulus und Jesus.* (Hermeneutische Untersuchungen zur Theologie 2.) Tübingen: J. C. B. Mohr (Paul Siebeck), 1962, ²1964.

James M. Robinson. 'The New Hermeneutic at Work', *Interpretation* 18 (1964), 347–59. [A review of Jüngel's book.]

BIBLIOGRAPHICAL SOURCES

Further bibliographical information can be obtained from the standard bibliographical sources. These are as follows:

(*a*) *Sources giving an abstract of the material*

Internationale Zeitschriftenschau für Bibelwissenschaft und Grenzgebiete. Düsseldorf: Patmos-Verlag, 1952–
New Testament Abstracts. Weston College, Weston, Massachusetts, 1956–
Religious and Theological Abstracts. 301 South College Street, Myerstown, Pennsylvania, 1957–

(*b*) *Sources simply listing the material*

Ephemerides Theologicae Lovanienses. Elenchus Bibliographicus. Louvain University, 1924–
Biblica. Elenchus Bibliographicus Biblica. Pontifical Biblical Institute, Rome, 1920–
Index to Religious Periodical Literature. American Theological Library Association, 1949–
Scripta Recenter Edita. Nijmegen, Netherlands: Bestel Centrale V.S.K.B., 1959–

In addition, a number of journals feature bibliographical information. The two most important are:
Theologische Literaturzeitung, 1876–
Zeitschrift für die neutestamentliche Wissenschaft, 1900–

INDEX OF NAMES

INDEX OF REFERENCES

OLD TESTAMENT

OLD TESTAMENT APOCRYPHA AND PSEUDEPIGRAPHA

NEW TESTAMENT APOCRYPHA